Library of
Davidson College

WITNESSING: The Seventies

SIDNEY BERNARD

WITNESSING:
The Seventies

INTRODUCTION BY HARRY SMITH

HORIZON PRESS   NEW YORK

Copyright © 1969, 1970, 1971, 1972, 1973, 1974, 1975, 1976, 1977 by Sidney Bernard.

No part of this book may be reproduced in any form whatsoever without permission in writing from the publishers, except by a reviewer who wishes to quote brief passages in a review written for inclusion in a magazine or newspaper or broadcasts.

The majority of the articles, essays and reviews published in this volume have appeared (some in slightly different form) in periodicals, to whose editors I make grateful acknowledgement, as follows: *Crawdaddy*, *Defiance*, *Genesis*, *The Herald*, *The Nada Review*, *NewsArt*, *The Newsletter on the state of the culture*, *The New York Times Book Review*, *The Smith*, *The Unspeakable Visions of the Individual*, and *The Village Voice*.

Library of Congress Catalog Number: 77-74623
ISBN: 0-8180-1172-6
Manufactured in the United States of America

Thanks to various Manhattan restaurants; the Roundhouse Cafe and Bloomsbury tea shop in London; and other "breather" stops—from Madison (Wisconsin) to New Orleans to the California coast; where I spent passing hours, during my travels, and, with coffee or tea boosters, sketched in the openers of many of these essays.

INTRODUCTION / Harry Smith   xi

1969
THE CRY OF THE CITY GULL / Spirit of the sixties   1

1970
THE POLITICS OF SELF-DESTRUCT / Vietnam protest   3
PUTTING SOME RED AND BLUE INTO MAY DAY / Radical Chic   5
THE WHO AT THE WHAT? / Rock invades the Met   8
THE NEW PLASTIQUE / "Revolutionary" film   12
VAMPING ON THE OLD HOME BOX / Warhol and friends   14
DAY OF STAR SAPPHIRES & CANDLES / Moratorium   17
BELLA VICTORIA / Abzug goes to Washington   19

1971
TALES OF HOFFMAN / Abbie pursued   21
NORMAN & DAVID & GERMAINE & JILL & . . . / Women's Lib vs. Norman Mailer   22
WE ARE ALL PART OF ATTICA / "Law and order"   25
THE AMERICAN TUNING FORK / Leopold Stokowski   32
THE MINOTAUR COMPLEX / Charles Henri Ford   34
THE UMPTEENTH RALLY / Out of Vietnam now   38

COLOR IT RASPBERRY / Fillmore East *40*
WOMEN'S LIBERATION: ANOTHER VIEWPOINT / Non-sexist revolution *42*
SCENARIO FOR A BADASS NIGHT / The muggeries *44*

1972

WHERE HAVE ALL THE HOUSES GONE? / Demolition job *47*
"LITERARY TIMES" DOES A LAZARUS / Second city lit *50*
"SLEEPER" *MESSIAH* / Handel and superstar *52*
VOZNESENSKY / YEVTUSHENKO / Town Hall and Felt Forum *56*
MIRACLE ON 53d STREET, THRU EYEDROPS / Pablo Picasso *59*
WHAT ARE THE VIBES OUT THERE? / Vermeer quartet *62*
NAME OF THE GAME IS "ROOTS" / Barrymore and black Hamlet *66*
THE WEEK OF 100-PROOF NIXON & KISSINGER / Mining Haiphong *68*
THE SHORT HAPPY LIFE OF THE LITTLES / Cosmep Inc. *75*
A NON-WATERGATED FOURTH OF JULY, ALMOST / My land, your land *81*
LEGGING IT LENGTHILY IN LONDON / Londinium way *84*
TWO NEW YORK ELECTION WAKES / The McGovern blues *99*

1973

THE SNOWING OF 1972 / Nixon triumphant *101*
DID NBA KNOW WHAT IT WAS DOING? / Corso & Ginsberg *103*
TO NOLA WITH LOVE AND DISTRESS / New Orleans *108*
OUR MR. HARDHAT MEETS JOE HILL / Labor Day songfest *117*

A DAY IN THE LIFE OF A NOBEL LAUREATE / Heinrich
   Böll   *119*
MAN HERE SAYS HE'S BEEN TO CALIFORN' / California
   first   *122*
FLASHBACK FLASHFORWARD / Five Beekman Street   *135*

1974

BOOKS & BERETS & OTHER WINDFALLS / Walter
   Lowenfels   *143*
GETTING BACK ON THE MOVIE VAN / Lindsay Anderson   *144*
JESTER'S DAY AT LINCOLN CENTER / Off Off Broadway   *149*
HEY, POET, WADDAYU READING! / Four radical poets   *151*
MY WEEK ON A BED OF NAILS / Protest rounds   *153*
HOW TO GET TO GEM'S SPA . . . / Cosmep Baedeker   *157*
THE PUSH-AND-SHOVE BOOK FAIR / First New York Book
   Fair   *161*
THE FREEBIE ARTS / Puppets, dancers and baseball   *164*
RETRIPPING / London   *166*
THE VID CROUPIERS COUNT THE VOTE / Independent
   Democrats   *173*

1975

THE 24-HOUR FLOATING PARTY GAME / SoHo   *177*
"EASY RIDER" REVISITED / At the Elgin   *181*
OF BOOK AWARDS & MEDIA TALKATHONS / Books and
   journalism   *184*
WALK ON THE WHITMAN SIDE / Walt Whitman's New
   York   *188*
BOOKING IN AT CUSTOMS / 2nd New York Book Fair   *191*
TOPOL FIDDLES WITH UNIVERSE / Galileo on screen   *194*
CALIFORNIA TAKE TWO / West coast syndrome   *196*

OPEN LETTER TO AN ARIZONA CONGRESSMAN / New York City "bailout"   *210*

1976

THE PARTY-GO-ROUNDS / Literary society   *215*
MORE PARTY-GO-ROUNDS / Jonathan Williams and James T. Farrell   *219*
THE PRESIDENTIAL TIDINGS / End & beginning   *221*
THE BRONX KID'S MEDICAL DETENTE / Park Avenue Specialist   *223*
ULTIMATE FRISBEE / New game on Sheep Meadow   *225*
CRAZY TO LIVE IN NEW YORK / Block Fairs, Inc.   *226*

1977

CELEBRATIONS / Ginsberg, Lowell & Anaïs Nin   *229*
BE-IN OR NOT BE-IN / Ten years after   *231*

Introduction

WHO IS THIS MAN? "Who is this man?" Harold Hayes, then editor in chief of *Esquire*, asked while scrutinizing a photograph of Sidney Bernard, who looked much like an Old Testament prophet, with a finger raised in warning, in the foreground of a demonstration later known as "The Grand Central Bust" where Abbie Hoffman emerged as the crown jester of the Yippie movement.

"I see him everywhere," Hayes remarked wonderingly: "at Carnegie Hall, in the Village . . . I saw him last week—where? Oh, I remember, at the New Yorker bookstore. What is the word? *Ubiquitous.*"

"Who *is* Sid, really?" asked poet Ed Sanders, when proprietor of the Peace Eye bookstore in the sixties, after the roving witness had already chronicled Sanders' earlier career as a Fug and editor of the famous under-the-counter literary magazine *Fuck You*. "I've talked to him many times, seen him many places, yet I don't know anything about *him.*"

Sanders and the rover have since become close friends, but for thousands of people Sidney Bernard is familiar yet mysterious—often observed observing, conversing, disputing, appreciating, unpredictably materializing—where next?—seemingly at any important artistic, political or neighborhood occasion in New York, not that you might not find him in London or San Francisco or New Orleans.

I first met Sid at the Museum of Modern Art in 1964 when he was New York editor of the Literary Times. He was taking notes for an essay on the landmark exhibition of Bonnard, and he soon became roving editor of my publication, *The Smith*, quickly acclimating himself to the realm of the little magazine, becoming a chronicler of the small press movement.

I have never stopped marveling at his almost uncanny ability to be at the right place at the right time in an unprogrammed and receptive way. For instance, one of his early contributions was an account of the student uprising at Columbia, reported from the *inside*, with the students behind the barricades, sharing their experience yet sympathetically detached from their political involvement.

Looking at this book on The Seventies, I see much that similarly amazes me, beginning at the beginning, with his Christmas Day, 1969, essay, which conveys the spirit of that time, provides perspective on the great social movements of the sixties and anticipates important issues of the seventies. The first full year of this chronicle, 1970, finds the reporter bearing witness to the peace movement's "politics of self-destruct" and degeneration into Radical Chic, the politics fitting together with other pieces on the culture, from essence of Warhol to the significance of Abzug's triumph. In 1971, Sid gives us a last look at Hoffman before his flight from the public stage and at the Fillmore East just before its fall that signaled the fadeout of the East Village, along with events as personal and symptomatic as a mugging (his own) on the West Side. Sometimes he is the ultimate appreciator. Sometimes he moves like an Isaiah through our years.

Always he is unique. He shows us the rise of SoHo, the destruction of Old New York; he gives us the ambience of literary scenes in London; he guides us through the artscapes of California and the underground of New Orleans. The serendipity of coverage leads to discovery—of interrelationships among movements and to a clear sight of the transitions we have made. And to many surprises. For Sid is a professional journalist who became an *amateur*, in the best sense of the word. He has for many years refused, despite many offers, to write "on assignment." Thus he is a lover in his approach to his subjects, knowledgeable yet lustily naive, unawed yet on terms of easy intimacy with the likes of Norman Mailer and Allen Ginsberg, while equally conversant with avant-garde outsiders in all the arts, a finder wherever he wanders, free to relive the walks of Whitman or to become a sports reporter for Ultimate Frisbee in Central Park.

As I write this appreciation and introduction, I am interrupted by a telephone call from David McReynolds, longtime field marshal of the War Resisters League who has just come back to town and is looking for Sid, hoping for a Phebe's tête-à-tête, the Off-Off Broadway bar, where Sid would drink light coffee and McReynolds iced ginger ale. Earlier a call came from Maurice, the famous Greenwich Village character, erstwhile *Village Voice* pusher, who at his Lion's Head headquarters was trying to tip him on the latest shenanigans regarding the Murdocking of the paper. Another message: Bruce Millholland, the Metropolitan Opera opening night crasher whose Broadway play became the famous movie of yesterday, "Twentieth Century," reminding Sid to attend his seventy-fourth "Star-Spangled" birthday party in a SoHo gallery. As an eminent freebie ticket getter himself, Sid has a comradely respect for the older man-about-town, who is highly visible himself, especially when wearing his gold lamé suit.

Who is Sidney Bernard? The reader will discover and delight in the man and his sensibilities through this chronicle.

—Harry Smith

Brooklyn Heights

1969

Spirit of the sixties

THE CRY OF THE CITY GULL Christmas Day, 1969, and I'm alone in my Westside one-roomer not feeling physical aloneness so much as a kind of glacial emptiness of spirit. World of enormous gray drift and cry of lead-bellied gulls swooping east from the Hudson River. Just the right note for what's in the air this last week of the sixties decade.

The cry of the city gull. Hysteric whistler-sound, a scavenger noise. Holy, holy, holy. Hail the holy-drenched, holly-drenched season of good cheer. But no sound is heard but that of a gull's shriek. Beak tearing into dead flesh, rip unto others as they would rip unto you. City gull and city man are one in spirit. And Santa is jolly at his Salvation Army coin pot. Dreams of jingle-jingle tunes in the air. Dreams of the rape of children, row on row in cotton minis, all sucking jolly red apples dipped in candy.

And the news is a scavenger news. Rip into your fellow man, can't trust the shadow coming at you from around the corner. Rip into your fellow Black Panther, he's gonna gun you down from the parlor window, so blast him in his bed at the sleeping hour of three A.M. And finish them off with an IRS paper; ain't paid their taxes and that's bad in law-and-order country. More news, this time the jingle-jingle of transportation coin. Fare-increases on the wind. The biannual hurdy-gurdy ride where you get more riled than ride.

So hail to Transit Authority's Dr. William Ronan! All hail to the Albany Governor! All hail to the Transport Union! To begin a new year, the decade of the seventies, the troika introduces a touch of creeping money shorts. Reach into the pockets of three-million-plus riders and pinch the coin. So that Ronan in his bookkeeping can do the good

German thing: balance those books, black not red is the color of the game! And the Governor (Rockefellers were always tuned to dimes—they give it away, they take it, or they stand on it) can do the good German thing: poses stoned like a von Hindenberg and tells the herrenvolk to bend at the altar of das kapital! And the union can do the good German thing: what we think's coming to us we take like a Sam-Browne-belted corps!

The cry of the gull. And the rapacity of oil round the world. Newsphoto of duck "barely able to move because of coating of crude oil saturating its feathers...." Socony trader who was only looking for a dollar gusher: let him look at that photo and see the bird's dying eye in the mirror of his conscience! The cry of the gull. At decade's end how to break the iron collar of the four B's: booze, ballgames, bombs and boredom. Our sportsloving President (who never made the Varsity) sits before the White House TV and watches a pigskin orgy from college stadium: while just beyond his window 300,000 nonsilent Americans march to the tune of *Give peace a chance!*

The cry of the gull, the cry of city man.

Vietnam protest

THE POLITICS OF SELF-DESTRUCT The power of demonstrations. The inertia of demonstrations. You take your choice, on a day like April 15 Vietnam Protest, with happenings going on all over town. Down by financial row, hard by the South Ferry, a 1970s version of Boston Tea Party. They dunked thousands of Form 1040 IRS income-tax blanks into the murky Hudson River drink. In nets so that poor dirty Hudson will be spared more ecological imbalance. A little later hundreds of high-school students doing their "Right on's" and "Power to the People" shouts at City Hall Park. A sweet young girl in Afro hair-do, pepper-and-salt on her tongue, as she hawks the Panther newspaper. At noon outside IRS's Church Street building hundreds more walking the street. Giving Sam Moneybags shouted what-for's . . . *Can't you spend our money better ways than Pentagon handouts!*

Columbia University and a long march down Broadway starting at 116th Street, about 500 keeping pace with three prowl cars up front, as they head for a late-afternoon rally at Bryant Park. Lots of colored banners pumping in the direction of office windows, and getting the "V" sign in return. But not everywhere: from one window at Seventy-second Street, broker types in starched shirts leering at the Columbians, one giving the thumbs-down of Roman Colosseum. And a "You should be in school" shout, from matronly Westside lady who mostly glares, shakes her head. The generation gap is such a pain in the pippick!

I missed the main rally at Bryant. But two high-school girls describe the scene later at Ethical Culture. Pete Seeger was groovy, but also a little tired. (Of demonstrations?) And famous lawyer Bill Kunstler was angry, mostly, said the girls, at our Mayor. Lindsay's not doing right by the Panther 21 trial, but the young girls couldn't quite fathom that charge. And knots of Youth Against War and Fascism (and who there *wasn't?*) roaming Bryant. Ripping off the podium and shrilling away at the Mayor. Who didn't show, even though he was listed as main speaker. He apparently got the message of the bongos, and stayed away.

In the evening, a near-perfect spring evening, long candlelight procession down West Side streets. Crossing over to Ethical Culture, at West Sixty-fourth Street, thousands of cupped candles bouncing lightly, as the crowd marches past Ethical on the way to Sheep Meadow. Trays of diamond-shaped sandwiches for the marchers, and for the half dozen who held a three-day fast in the auditorium of Ethical Culture. A somber but also a light-hearted march. Light-hearted from the presence of hundreds of kids. The lit candle each holds is the bright eye of their future; they see it as a small flame of togetherness, as they march along with their parents. You think of other kids, in other parades. Sea Scouts, bouncing away at drums, in para-military marches. Growing up is a tough nut.

Nighttime on the Meadow, bursts of song from hundreds, blots of orange flame going deeper as sky darkens to purple. *Before I'll be a slave/I'll be buried in my grave. . . .* There's a small visceral shock of pleasure, on hearing massed voices, ringing out a song on the big Sheep Meadow, the song rising to a kind of adrenaline high, the very public voice of New Yorkers who, for a fleeting moment or two, shuck off their numbing tough personae, revealing on the flip side a core of what they truly feel. And yet was it a mirage? A solo voice, icy against the chorus's warmth, breaks like a tremor among the crowd. "All your candlelight marches won't get you out of Vietnam!" The rudeness of the voice, laced with a kind of holywrit arrogance, joggles the mind. Then someone shouts: "Thank you Chairman Mao." And the singing picks up again.

Roaring over the space, at intervals of a minute or two, are the big Atlantic jets. They make good peace catapults, the jets' lights winking down on the scene, swept back wings forming giant Aldermasten buttons in the sky. Families begin to detach from the main group downfield; it's getting on to ten P.M. and the kids have school next day. The isolated flickers of candles, as paraders make their way west out of the park, give an aura of urban pilgrimage returning home to drab brownstones or highrise cubes. One family of five hails a cab, just outside Tavern on the Green, and as they squeeze into the cab, the two kids among them still nursing their lit candles, some walkers nearby chide the family mildly. "You should be using shoe-leather," one of the walkers says.

At Sixty-sixth Street and Broadway, some time later, a group of about fifty high-school students gather for an ad hoc rally. One tall young man wearing a panoply of buttons on his denim jacket—peace and rainbow coalition and Panther and others—climbs up on the corner aluminum light pole and cries out: "Let's take it to Times Square." He gets a gung-ho shouting response, and before long about a hundred begin to move down Broadway. Their voices a little more husky, and their muscles more flexed, than at the Meadow. One tried to figure the odds on the heat, so nicely quiescent all evening long, coming down on them once they hove into view of that big antiseptic sheath of a building, the Allied Chemical at Times Square.

Yves Tanguy night on the protest front, the politics of self-destruct.

Radical Chic

PUTTING SOME RED AND BLUE INTO MAY DAY   Dotson Rader gave a party, a May Day extravaganza that *had* to be the New Left's answer to Truman Capote's at the Plaza a few years back. Scene was the gymnasium of St. Peter's Church, a kind of bare-bones urban Gothic on West Twentieth, where Dotson and friends had worked all day to flesh out a happenings effect. In a room that had little more than two basketball hoops and some children's game sculpture, they installed puffed-out styrofoam ceiling pieces, poster blow-ups of Ché and Huey Newton and Paris street fighters, hundreds of tapered candles and Jewish *yahrzeit* glasses, a small movie screen for Andy Warhol's *Blue Movie*. Warhol and radical posters—decor for a by-invitation party that attracted several hundred at a two-dollar tab for such Left defense funds as Walter Teague's Committee to Aid the NLF and his own court battles. The mix of people from such diverse groups as Women's Lib, SDSers from both under and over ground, activists from the New Mobe, a handful of Village Independent Democrat infiltrators, *The Boys in the Band* cast, Jackie Curtis types in full transvestite regalia, and numbers of others from various strains of the dropout phenomenon was a mix only Dotson himself would come anywhere near being able to name.

The party turned out to be mind-blower and tension-raiser, in about equal parts. Drinks were unlimited, served from three tables by several bare-chested boys (hot night!) and mini-skirted girls who'd broken off their Yale-Panther protest vigil to be present. Their reports from the Eli front, and the latest radio reports at the party from New Haven, were picked up by the guests and sent around the room like stop-press flashes from some revolutionary stronghold. But the real party was right out there on the floor—rock music pounding the ears, Viva and a muscular butch faggot type making it on screen, couple of guys with cameras (which one was FBI?) shooting guests under a sinister flush of midnight-blue and liquid-red spots, two young model-type fags kissing hard and grab-assing passionately, and Dotson in clean white pants and sailor shirt greeting arrivees—famous and not-so-famous writers, young lawyers whose specialty was political defense and free-press clients (a growth practice), editors and publishers of porn sheets or Black Panther books.

Among the hundreds who attended were attorney Bob Cahn and his wife, moon-faced Bob dripping beads of sweat, eyes behind glasses rolling in anticipatory delight—a la Groucho—as he ogled the swirl of hot limbs doing Bossa Nova, and later, Bob locked in arcane legal rap with porn-sheet publisher Louis Abolafia (smothered in yards of velvet), whose bust case Bob was handling. And full-bearded Sol Yurick, out on the throbbing floor, solo gyrating and finger-snapping, Brooklyn's own rediscoverer of the 1930s novel, who took time out from his Marxian-mystery-work-in-progress, and was now moonlighting (in a way), letting out the jams on fun-in-progress. And the mystery appearance of author Bill Burroughs, moving around with help of a cane, a silent and wraithlike presence, whom several had wanted to say hello to, but Burroughs had split early. And *Ché!* producer Ed Wode, trapped somewhere between growl and bafflement, rocking from one spot to another, pissed over troubles he was having with his new production, a Women's Lib takeoff on Aristophanes: cast troubles, cash troubles, you-name-it troubles. (Wode, take another spritz of booze, and fuck the success syndrome.) And the no-shows, of whom Dotson had to repeat, over and over, "Like he didn't show." Norm Mailer, Allen Ginsberg, Andy the Warhol, and a dozen more.

Two polar moods were building, best described as puritan and

Putting Some Red and Blue Into May Day   7

dionysian. They burst in showery confrontation, like aimless clouds bombarded with silver pellets, as the party neared the midnight hour. The puritans (mainly Women's Lib) were in a stew over the Warhol movie, while the Dionysians were all wetted-lips attentive, enjoying the flesh-toned playfulness, the mimicry of fornication, first in a sudsy bath scene, later on a town-house veranda. Suddenly the movie was stopped, and a stern-faced lady activist, who had positioned herself on a rear platform, rose up and did a little number: verbal ripoff. She roasted management at Grove Press, charging (falsely) that *they* were the party hosts, and how could the partygoers pretend they were having a good time, even while "everyone knows" Grove exploited tits and flesh: Oh those *Evergreen* photos! As for Warhol and his factory, they were (her voice dripping scorn) "*outofit*," just not relevant. Cheers and boos from the floor. Dotson goes looking for Walter. Tangles with him, forelock bouncing like an exclamation point. But Walter, poker-faced Sir Bland of the revolution, *denies it all*. And to those who didn't exactly *need* the ripoff—could even be they were *enjoying* the movie—to those others Sir Bland's comeback is curt, veddy officious: "Read the leaflet!" Said leaflet being handed out, then and there, by a brace of angrier-than-thou ladies.

Holy-writ contending with holy-flesh. David McReynolds was one guest who didn't feel he had to make a choice. Said the lanky, trimly bearded War Resisters guru to no one in particular: "A party is a party. I don't need an ideology boost with my booze." He had arrived weary and bone-tired, from day and night planning sessions for a D.C. Cambodian protest rally. Two or three drinks later, and he was in a relaxed mood. Grooving the *whole number*, rapping with the Yalie drink dispensers, taking in bits of the Warhol, or making tart comment on the gay pair: "Purely a floor show. Won't be a lay between them, when they get home." He was coasting along on his own party karma.

When the libs and Walter Teague (in a swift display of biting-the-hand-that-helps-you) seized control of the 16mm projector, and hastened to replace *Blue Movie* with *Battle of Algiers*, Dave and a few others weren't buying that, either. *Great film, sure! Scene of lean-limbed French colonel, essence of faded imperialism, cold-turkey military mopper-upper, telling the press Sartre was a bum—wow! Left film for the ages! But why at the party? Ipso switcho, unannounced.* So Dave goes looking for Walter, to tell him that the showing of *Algiers*, right in the middle of a mild bacchanal, was a kind of blasphemy, reading of the catechism by forced draft. But that moment passes, too. And the party revs its way to two A.M. in high gear; lots of people looped, talky; couple of johns balling in the candlelit (and liberated) men's-women's room, Dotson rassling them the hell outta there fast; plastic drinking cups and empty booze bottles accumulating in mounds; making up of two carpools, for early-morning return to Yale; and Jackie Curtis drooling her-his stagey charms, as she-he catches people's wrists gently, urging them to "Come see our show at La Mama."

Outdoors on the stone steps, nearly three and the party unwinding, Dotson sitting around in a sprawl of long-legs, white sailor suit no longer laundry-fresh, saying good-byes but wondering (to some, confidentially) *howdiditgo*, and confessing, with a wan smile, that he "Blew a thou' on it, the advance on my novel." Followed by a weary *fuck it I think it was okay* interior sigh. And two long lean blacks, loping by from the party, on their way to their parked car, looked like a mother-bent four-door Olds, asking Dots if he wanted a lift, "Direction is Harlem." And giving him a *seeyulater* wave of hands, as Dotson shakes his head no, and off they go in a cloud of blue exhaust. Dave McReynolds sprawled on another step, nursing a fizzed-out last drink, rapping with a couple of kids, talk of love beads, which he-they are wearing, blue-night atmosphere melding with blue-romance thoughts, how relate *age-youth*, kids *fullofit* (the youth part) in their long-haired splendor, easier in politics than in bed (guru Dave owns up). And the one young man jotting down WRL's address, after he tells Dave he wants to "Seal envelopes—that sort of thing," he'll be by on Saturday to help out in the D.C. mailing.

So they gave a party, a celebration of May First, American working-class holiday that's seen better days, now that labor, and labor bossism, comes up mostly, on flip of coin, the other side of military-industrial. (Hardhats defending Wall Street ramparts, only one week later!) And partygoers, revved in *innertension*, to the shock and shlock of the outer scene, tried a few hours of fun.

Rock invades the Met

THE WHO AT THE WHAT? The New York section of the Woodstock bums laid one-day siege to the house of establishment culture, Lincoln Center's Metropolitan Opera House, and thereby hangs a twice-performed tale that establishmentarians might take with them to restless sleep. Hard-playing, hard-shafting, hard-emoting. Restless vibes from a quartet of Englishers, the Who stomping the wide and deep stage to a sound turned up tenfold, musical lightning off a rock score that spells anger, dionysian revels, gropes of body-love and mind-fuck, counterculture riffs. Message from the 1970s that says: the jugular is far point of our vision.

The crowds flocked to the fancy flagstoned quadrangle, moved round the pretty cascading fountain, packed through the glass entrances, all on an untypically clear Manhattan Sunday afternoon and evening. If they had tickets, they moved along quickly. If not they stood around and hoped for a winner. "Give you a tenner, if you have an extra ticket." Close to 8,000 for the matinee and evening performances had tickets, and easily 8,000 more did not, but the latter were not about to go away. While the concerts were in progress, rumors were floating by that some lucky visitations would take place. Out of the blue Grateful Dead or Jefferson Airplane might just materialize—on Arabian carpets?—might just plunk themselves down astride the fountain and play for the ticketless. Big culture domes do not our music make. But alas the visitations were stacked up there on high, never made it down from the sky that day or night.

Evening performance. In the thick-carpeted orchestra alcove, sallow and magisterial Rudolph Bing stands around unnoticed (and unknown by most) as waves of kids make their way inside. The kids case the premises, several nodding their heads in approval. Both Bing and his ushers, the latter all looking like captains, maintain a posture of distance, maybe even extra distance from the usual, as if the Met were grande-dame hostess to a bunch of skruffy outlanders for this one time only. One goes over and engages him in conversation. Calm face but a pinkish flush of concern shows on his aging-smooth skin. "How does everything go?" Pause before he answers, wary eyes taking in the waves. "Everything goes just fine." "And the matinee performance?" Another pause. "Goot [ever so soft guttural]. Very goot." Pause. "I am just vorrying about the smoking. Not permitted inside. But it is no problem, they are a fine audience." One is about to ask: "Is it the flavor that worries you?" But the numero uno of world opera is paged at that moment, and off he goes to another part of the house.

Seated in mid-orchestra, minutes before the start. The Met's a royal $32-million gilt-and-maroon cage, with ribwork of five grand tiers that ascend to a height, where "They fly the mail to Pittsburgh," as we kids used to say on climbing the second balcony of the RKO Fordham. There is a loud crossfire of greetings, quick darting conversational gambits, all pretty much in the vein of "Cool, we've made it into the big palace!" The dress is a wide spectrum of expensive Paraphernalia mod, and East Village cracked-leather and fading-denim. One young couple near me is aglow in an attire that has to be rated: Rock formal at the Met. The girl wears fine white eyelet cotton, a Cinderella dress, topped with wide granny shades of an amber color. Her boyfriend wears a tight white turtleneck, eight-button Edwardian black suit. The couple, and pretty near the entire house, are tense and swivel-headed as grayhounds, as they await The Who's presence onstage. Soon a cheer goes up, as the house gradually darkens, and the eight or ten small crystal chandeliers slowly rise roofward. From boxes several kids make playful lunges for the crystal, which is just beyond their reach, and the cheers grow louder. How do you housebreak rock into the Met?

Here they come from the wings, and pandemonium takes over wall to wall. Not even a Renata Tebaldi claque can hit the high shrieks of rock fandom. But only for a minute or two. The Who is all business, and after checking out the forest of amp boxes, they plunge ahead into their first set. And an excellent set it is. Short and mostly familiar numbers (and again those shrieks of recognition). The sound is crisp, delicately turned and at times near-overpowering—a revelation of fine acoustics plus nerve-ends music making. Later one heard of dead spots, or complaints of distortion, mostly from upper-box locations, but in what house do you win 'em *all*.

And the theatrics, the plain and fancy caperings, are stunningly adequate to the occasion. Watch lanky Peter Townshend, decked in white jumpsuit and laced jump boots, black middle-long hair popping over ears and forehead like some musical monk riding an electric guitar. His deep-set eyes shifting, demonic, two dark beads trying to escape their sockets, as he does another of his bounding splits, early Ray Bolger transmogrified to a hard-rock beat. And deep-wailer-singer Roger Daltray, short and wild-haired sprite, hips swiveling as if motor driven, catch the piercing song as it travels. From low inside the bared gut, up through jutting apple and twisted mouth, then rifled home through hand held mike—which he tosses around like a Molotov ready to go. And drummer-stick-juggler Keith Moon, a seated dervish who all but swallows his sticks, now faking a riff so real (as Townshend strums away) that one thinks one *hears* it. And now hitting thirteen—yes, thirteen!—instruments with an authority that boggles the ear: two foot drums, three snares, three cymbals, three kettle, Chinese gong, triangle. And second guitar John Entwistle, the look of a warlock in black leather, all steadiness and controlled frenzy, as he shatters out the rhythm line.

Under The Who's attack, Cinderella and boyfriend move in their seats like a Coney Island joyride. They shuttle back and forward, or they unlimber with deep sighs, faces suffused in a glaze of pleasure. Tension builds up and then breaks in a wave of happy howls, as Townshend announces "the extravaganza," a fifty- or sixty-minute concert version of the rock opera *Tommy*. Audience is at knife's edge as The Who go at it with driving energy, with a gutsy hauteur. As vignette follows musical vignette, the rapid choppy style hits the ear with not a decibel's waste. And when they do the short but blazing "Pinball Wizard" section, the crowd is all but levitating to the Met's roof. If there are faults—lack of strong continuity, for one—the performance itself can hardly be excelled. And when the piece ends, there are shouts of celebration, tiny fireflies of lighted joints, all through the house.

There are little downers, too. Hundreds gather at the stage, go on and on with their ritual shouts: "More! More!" Something kinky in all this Fillmore-type brouhaha, this dead-assed repetition of "More!" And one puts it to some shouters: "If they were good, why do you need more; if bad, why do you want more?" They respond in a high adolescent blank. Followed by more "More's!" Townshend reappears at that moment, he tries a brief rap on rock brotherly understanding. And they seem to buy it, but then one young dude fires away with a paper object. That's all Townshend needs! He flares up and rages at them. "Two fucking hours of play!" And he flings that hand mike, flings it at the head of a hundred or so droners. Quick rush down the aisles of palace guard, the black-bolero-shod Met ushers, and the lingerers do finally get the message.

Several remain at the fountain, till way past midnight. They review in minute detail all that transpired. They stick it out just a while longer. Hoping for those visitations.

"Revolutionary" film

THE NEW PLASTIQUE For the Eighth Lincoln Center Film Festival (Sept 10–20) management offered a slick innovation to tell the financial side of the problem: a handsome and hardsell brochure that sang the virtues of the newly formed Film Society of Lincoln Center, and asked the question, "$384,000 for the Film Society's year-round program. Isn't that pretty steep?" (The answer of course was "No. Think of the Film Society as an iceberg.") Icebergs aside, the annual festival is thus entombed as yet another display piece in the pantheon of mid-cult and middle-class sensibility that Lincoln Center—in all its corporate efficiency—represents. And while one can look at this with no great surprise—Parkinson's Law being as sure in the big-business cultural realm as Einstein's is in the physical—one is still locked into the notion that the dollar method of measuring film festival success is like measuring Fort Knox for its wealth and saying: "There's the biggest culture package of them all!"

Given the emphasis on rising budget, maybe it would be fair pool to review the social side of the Eighth first. This involves a good chunk of money, what with after-film soirees, flying in and housing directors and stars, and other such logistical chores. John Springer Associates has flacked the festival for several years now, and the pluses are an old habit: speedy releases and synopses of films for press, smooth arranging of interviews, tasteful if low-key parties. Memorable, on another level, was one Springer bulletin-board item: "*Rapsodica Satanica* will not be screened, since film has shrunk and it is not projectionable." (You can't get more rarefied than that!) All the above services, to repeat, were ready to hand, but not if you were some kind of underground kook. The radical press had to do handstands to get press credentials. The sense was of a residual fear—going back to the year the Eastside Mothers threatened ripoff of what they called "cultural imperialism"— and there were occasions at press screenings, and more so at the parties, when it appeared as if all strata of the New York film underground had gone into quiet exile.

The kickoff was a $100-a-plate dinner party, in the ground-floor Philharmonic restaurant. Mayor John Lindsay was numero uno of the film illuminati, and later that evening, at the opening film showing (Truffaut's *The Wild Child*), the mayor repeated his last year's joke, when he introduced Catherine Deneuve, who was sitting in a box with

The New Plastique

Truffaut: "They don't make babies like that, anymore. For that matter, neither do I." (Say this: Lindsay's been away from greasepaint a long time.) Later still, a past-midnight party at the graystone French consulate on Fifth, where the air was overly humid, the drinks all French bubbly, nothing for the palate but trays of bonbons, a crush of people that made the IRT at five seem roomy. One eyestopper that nobody missed, other than Deneuve once again, was diminutive and sleekly handsome Jean-Pierre Leaud's very own dish of Gallic, a tall model-type beauty in white seethrough gown, who topped Jean-Pierre by a head. And closing party, a mini gala at Philharmonic by night-letter invite. Crowd of 250 or so munching on cheese, peeling fat California grapes (compliments of Cesar Chaves), and downing highball doubles. Deneuve-Truffaut in due, she still drawing ahs; and he, somehow, the image of the man on top the wedding cake, French version. Our own la Streisand, almost severely plain in manner and dress, and while not overly the center of attention, regally cool for all that. Richard Roud, Andrew Sarris, John (the bad) Simon, P. Adams Sitney, in concert. Pleasant festival chatter on the rocks, with just enough eavesdropping on the fringes to make it curious. One observer: "Wonder who's burying the knife in whom."

Last, we come to to the films, twenty-seven major screenings crammed into ten days (for press), and one's overall view was that, so far as impact goes, last was indeed last! Constantly, one heard the refrain, the Eighth was weakest of all Lincoln Center festivals. And yet from a commercial point of view, and indeed, from the new posture of middle-class sensibility, the Center now seems to codify, there were more than a few box-office successes (SROs). The French group—which should be no news—was predominant here. Truffaut (*The Wild Child*), Chabrol (*Le Boucher*), Resnais (*Je T'Aime, Je T'Aime*), Duras (*La Musica*). All four showboated a technique, a facility for the well-made film, that was just about the end of the line. Faultless editing; ravishing camera eye; pace-movement as pristine as a Bach score. It could have been the Bayeux Tapestry one was looking at, or medieval illuminated scrolls, or the very Pyramids. But with an absence of filmic protein of the kind you get in (say) Godard, even average Godard. All in all, rarely has form-content been so glaringly at odds, so out of balance. The former French New Wave genius has, in the seventies, suddenly blossomed as the New Plastique. Viewing these one could understand a little better Godard's determination to smash-shatter the well-made (oh so well-made; and oh so empty) French cinema. Even in face of the gritted teeth, the boos, that Godard's own film (*Wind from the East*) provoked, upon being offered as a kind of off-festival screening, at Tully Hall. Incomprehensible, to many, *Wind* may have been, but the other way is the sleeps.

Truffaut's—painfully old-style, a breathless cobweb of 1930s pre-talky Hollywood cliches. With a rise in music (Couperin?), and a trotting-in of the iris (scene fading to a tiny circle), for each and every epiphany, such as: Wild Child gleans the alphabet! Audience coming up soggy as a rainfall! Chabrol's—crypto-Hitchcock in smooth, diaphanous drag, with a hero (le boucher) who does in young women because he has seen it all (murder at the front). Resnais'—man taken on a time-retrieval tour, an experiment in a huge electronic pumpkin, where he relives scene after scene of a toweringly banal romance. The freshness of *Marienbad*, the poignant moodiness of *Hiroshima*, gone to senescence and tired blood. Duras'—couple in a postmarital agony encounter, whipped up to a Cartesian froth, something in the nature of: "I stink, therefore I am." All of them, the very sleeps.

No festival—not even plastic Eighth—could be all bad, while surfacing with a new Bunuel (*Tristana*), two from Bertolucci (*The Conformist* and *The Spider's Stratagem*), and a couple of tries—however flawed—at left-political cinema: from France, Marin Karmitz (*Comrades*), and from England, Maurice Hatton (*Praise Marx and Pass the Ammunition*), both directors newcomers to the festival. Bunuel's was at once mellow and strongly iconoclastic, not to say incomparably "well-made," but a well-made that mocked the plastique kind in numberless ways. As for Bertolucci, suffice to say that he's back, more so in the *Conformist* entry, to the enormous talent (and maybe beyond) of his big one, of several seasons ago, the beautiful Stendhalian *Before the Revolution*. Bertolucci was, additionally, the big bear of the festival, in his frequent talks with the press. Most were variations on the theme: "Can middle-class filmmakers make 'revolutionary' films?" His comments were often fresh, and yet despairing of a "a solution."

Good pickings along the way. But the brochure's $384,000 question would still have to be answered with a "Yes." (The price is wrong!)

Warhol and friends

VAMPING ON THE OLD HOME BOX   *Show me a happy*

homosexual and I'll show you a gay corpse.—Mart Crowley

The factory head man—Andy Warhol—catatonic with a Polaroid—sat with not a blink of the eye, in one of those circling studio chairs. He aimed and snapped his camera—two or three times—at Dotson Rader who (with an assist from ex-*Esky* editor Tom Hedley) was moderating the show. Camera at rest, Warhol tried to relate, tried to concentrate, as Rader pressed him for a word or two about the factory. The color studio box, about ten feet above and behind the action, showed Warhol in a state of speechlessness, lips distended in an effort to make words, hair a shock of powdered white, ducktail a mouse-brown at the back of his neck. Warhol's blinkless eyes, his cheeks almost pinkish, along with his stammerings of nonspeech, made a scene at once poignant and sadly distant. A kind of loss—of youth? of wasted art?—the image not unlike that of Eric Portman in *Red Shoes*, who sits in his Monte Carlo hotel aerie, very much alone, trying to measure *his* loss (of Moira Shearer), locked in motionless pain before he, Portman, charges off from his gloom to pursue new young Moiras. Image fades—back to Warhol and his leaden sadness on Channel 13 "Free Time" one Monday night.

The billing: Warhol Variety Night. Top banana aside, there was plenty of motion, forced chatter and laughs, very "in" boffos and tag lines, as Rader gathered before the cameras a large cast. Second Banana Paul Morrissey (ever-talking Morrissey!) was fourth man of the immediate group, and it fell to him (he needed no urging) to fill in Warhol's silences, so that the more Morrissey spieled, as Warhol played endlessly with his Polaroid, the stronger was the impression of myth gasping to stay alive. (Rinds of the apple only, shriveling in a dish, and was there ever really the apple itself?) A lot of business, even if forced, was going on around the edges of the Alphonse-Gaston act. Easily first in the esteem of the large studio audience—and first in its effect on the audience's very available funny bone—was the trio of voluble and playful transvestites, each one transmogrified into a camping image of what she (he) most wanted to be, nothing less than high-flying facsimiles of Hollywood's never-never days of MGM stardom.

There was Candy Darling, tall and wiggly-assed, black lace mini dress showing off amazingly "sexy" legs, as she minced her way up the short gangway to the tiny stage, where she performed a heated-up torch number, sibilants and throaty caresses in her voice, a touching (and not untalented) parody of one of Candy's "most dreamy favorite" stars: the Immortal Marilyn Monroe. Second of the trio was Jackie Curtis, wildly wigged in a reddish fall, face painted like a Kewpie doll's, body of a natural light-heavy, she hisses back hard at some friendly audience razzing, like a roving bulldyke not to be messed with lightly. Third was the new factory super star—drag-queen division—Holly Woodlawn, dressed in frilly grown and klutzy-heeled green shoes, a feminine dervish who can put on more "airs," unleash more facial flutters and piping calls, then a stage full of queens gussying-up for the big number at the annual costume ball. Rounding out the cast were a hayseed-type warbler (straight of straights), redolent of Jack Benny's Dennis Day, and a rather tiny dyanmite-laden rocker-singer with Latin charm and bosom enough for a Borden's roadside display. After the latter two did their fillers, moderator Rader brought the three "girls" and Warhol-Morrissey back to the main arena for a final go-around.

The sense of a plangent lostness, of a once-with-it gone sour, kept coming across from the circle of swinging chairs, where almost every gesture, every attempt at *shtick*, or even "communication," brought from the in-grooving crowd hollow chuckles of joy. Andy Warhol shooting his Polaroid (in quiet desperation), speed-kid Morrissey running on about West Germany's groovy response to the factory's films (five years behind?), Holly caressing the moderator's hand over and over (the "on-the-make" bit), Jackie *hallooing* and savaging the audience by turns, and Candy explaining her "sense" of herself as being ". . . well, *androgynous*." The heyday of the Warhol style, we know, served (as in *Chelsea Girls*) to drain off some of the swamp fire of mid-American masculinity phobias and hangups. Now it all seemed like self-parody, clever and suacy on the surface, but who was vamping on whom? The enigma of camp.

Near the end of the show, some talk of a factory work-in-progress, a women's-lib film with Holly, Jackie and Candy in the leads. "Why do you think you can do it? approach the subject with the seriousness it calls for?" Rader wanted to know. The three reared up in a tizzy, giving Rader sly digs and disapproving looks. After which Candy, arching her body high in the chair, offered a crisp "Darling, *we are the exploited ones.*" Theatrical pause, audience filling in with cooing ripples, then Candy purred "We know the subject *in our hearts.*" She easily won the round, if not the politics. Out on the street later, while waiting for the two hired Caddy limos (to take them to the Library bistro for drinks), all declared they were *just sure* the show went well. They compared it with one they had done a week or two before, a tapped session with David

Susskind, who, in the words of one factory member, "wasn't exactly *kindly*." And, in the words of another, was sure to come up "blipped as a Swiss cheese." Which would hardly be stoppress news, seeing as how David's sensibility gap, so far from behing on a par even with the Germans' (i.e., only five years behind), was somewhere off in infinity.

Moratorium

DAY OF STAR SAPPHIRES & CANDLES An aerial view of the Boston Common from Associated Press. Moratorium Day had brought out an estimated 100,000 people, and six long converging lines on a field of white, or a spokewheel of aisles in a surrounding sea of white-shirted bodies, had made a perfect star-sapphire design. Was it a symbol? Star-sapphire to show the way to a turn toward sanity, conscience and new beginning in an America wracked with crisis perhaps greater than any since the Civil War? In the midst of a World Series fever, with plenty of cheer for a ragtail Mets team going Cinderella, Moratorium was fielding its own teams who would turn defeat into victory before the day was out.

In New York City the day was filled with an air of VP Day: Victory for Peace. Wherever you turned, in almost any section of the five boroughs, there were assemblies of thousands who had quit jobs; stayed away from schools, absented themselves from supermarkets, canceled appointments, turned from the routine of the calendar to concern for peace. In the quadrangle of Low Memorial at Columbia, a squeeze of ten thousand or more students, faculty and neighbors fanned out from the Alma Mater statue, and under a bright sunlight cheered each reference to the guilty thing in our national closet, a cheer that at the same time was a release of conscience now out in the open. It was softsell all the way, a consensus attitude of the right way at last, a stretching of moral muscle in the streets that dwarfed the words of President Nixon, who only twenty-four hours before had proclaimed that national policy could *not* be made in the streets. And to Vice President Agnew's warning that such assemblies and actions could be very close to treason, to the Governor of California's words that yes just such demonstrations might have implications of treason, speaker and lawyer Arthur Kinoy rang out the word that if this be treason, let them make the most of it. A little later these ten thousand slowly left the quadrangle for the Broadway streets, and the police were split-second in stopping and then rerouting traffic for them, and the thousands had the downtown lane to themselves, as they began the long walk south to Bryant Park, where they would join up with several times their number in the largest of the many New York rallies, at twilight.

Measured by beads counted and genuflections made, Judson Memorial's six-p.m. service may not have been as impressive as some. But the church's two celebrants—Reverends Howard Moody and Al Carmines—had more in mind than the surface trappings of worship: a prayer-song-dance hour that involved the five hundred or so Greenwich Village peace witnesses in community singing, a "Prayer for Morning Headlines" by Daniel Berrigan; a "Liturgy of the People" sung by Lee Guilliatt, "The Peace Dance" choreographed and danced by Arlene Rothlein, and a vivacious musical set tinged with humor, by Al Carmines, a sort of cantata that gave equal time to Ho Chi Minh and the musical rouser *America*. Here, once again, the mood of the crowd was open, hopeful and life-affirming. Later many in the audience, and hundreds more from the Village neighborhood, joined in a candle walk for peace, all making their way to Washington Square's waterless fountain, glass-encased tapers, and hand-held ones, throwing light-cones of orange on the night, and soon maybe one thousand people were bunched quietly at the fountain, and then some singing was heard, along with discussions on what Moratorium Day meant to them, and some began to plant the glowing candles in circles at the fountain's center, circles and more circles, moving outward from center, teardrop flames going deeper, and before long the fountain area was a wide blaze of flickering candlelight, and the crowd was looking into the glow with meditative eye, as if there at the fountain's downward core, and hard by the alabaster Washington Arch, a penitential bonfire of candles would show the way out of the tunnel, if all could but ingest (as if through the skin) the fire deep enough. Later still, as the fires burned low on the wicks, there were rounds of singing, roistering tunes on marijuana, prickly ditties on the military mode, and the late-remaining crowd had their own Mets-day of celebration for peace.

Even the Wall Street area had Moratorium observances, with thousands gathering at the Sub-Treasury building, and in the long shadows of the money temples, they listened to words of peace. How could they help not making the linkup—between the workings of the marketplace and the ongoing obscenity of that faraway war? The business day of these thousands was dedicated to the anatomy of trade among the Blue Chips, the General Motors and Chase Manhattans, so how could they *not* get the linkup between Blue Chips traded on the Street and red blood shed in the cities and the rice paddies of Vietnam? They listened on long lunch breaks, and most took in the scene with a fitting sobriety, even while a clutch of tinhatted construction workers tried to razz the message down, at which point the police asked the workers (invited rather than muscled them) to step back so that the ceremony could go on uninterrupted. Later many of the demonstrators marched north to Trinity Church, where twenty-five business leaders read out names of the war dead, the church itself being packed to an overflow, with hundreds more coming together at the church's historic graveyard (*circa* Revolutionary War). Here again the linkup would have to be made, or at least thought about.

A chemical change was in the air on Moratorium Day and the President's words of the Tuesday before would fade as in a strong wind on the Thursday after. And to the Aldermaston March symbol of peace, a new one was added that will not fade. The star sapphire that rose from the huge assembly on Boston Common, on the day of Moratorium.

Abzug goes to Washington

BELLA VICTORIA The National Maritime Union Building on West Twelfth is a tubby, neo—Frank Lloyd Wright tribute to men and ships at sea, and on election night the building was all Bella Abzug's. The Nineteenth C.D. faithful, plus hundreds from outside the district, gathered early and were entertained by a rock trio giving off musical splurges in one hall, while two banks of TV screens were flipping results (and the usual election pundits' chatter) from the walls in the second hall. I got there about ten, walking a line between caution (NMU-Bella togetherness?) and slight euphoria (not *all* unions buy Attorney General Mitchell's "trend to the right"). The halls were decked in Bella posters, stage klieglighted brightly as the checkers posted latest returns. Beer was being pumped from metal kegs, and the drinkers sat under the screens in powwow-like clusters, now voicing cheer ("Agnew's not grabbing 'em in———"), now expressing mild lament ("Looks like the

Castle Irishman [James Buckley] is gonna make it").

Quick chessboard talks, here and there, on the "What if I'd switched to Ottinger?" dilemma. Surprisingly, most who had faced this choice, and were now in the process of going down with Goodell, had no deep angst over it, no wail of second-guess blues. I, personally, was among the latter, and at one point, in arguing it out with a Village Independent Democrat couple, who were smug but who stopped short of the "knee-jerk liberal" accusation, I owned as how "Principle is better than opportunity," whereupon a second Goodell voter sprung to my support, with the remark: "Goodell would have won it all, if *Ottinger* had quit." A third pressed the point, soberly rather than belligerently: "We've got to fight the *whole* trend, the whole overturn of human values, and one Buckley more or less doesn't change that."

But the local race, the imminent Bella victory, was the main focus of interest. As each new lead for her was posted, plastic beer cups were raised, cheers were sounded, and the rock trio came through with a crescendoed riff. During one brief lull, I got to talking with a leathery but well-dressed NMUer, a former seadog and now a local official. I expressed the view, trying not to sound coy about it, that the NMU-Bella marriage was a nice switch from hardhatism. To which NMUer coolly replied: "It's easy; we don't believe in beating on heads, just because people want to march against Vietnam wars." And so the evening moved on, Bella at around midnight pushing to a comfortable, near—ten thousand lead, and a little later, a rise of extended cheering, as the man at the mike announced: "We're gonna have Bella here anytime now!"

Her entrance onstage, shortly thereafter, was a wowing, noisy and not entirely dry-eyed moment. Bella, her face tense but happy, beneath the wide-brimmed floppy white hat, pleading for a chance to speak, finally getting it, then crisply boiling it down: "People in the Nineteenth, people in lots of places across the country, *do not buy* Nixon-Agnew's law-'n'-order loss leader!" She went on to thank "the many who worked for this victory," and while she spoke, a long-stemmed bouquet of American Beauty roses (redder than Mao!) was handed up to her. Silence fell over the crowd, as Bella removed the card, and read the message: "From all of us at the National Maritime Union." Near-exhausted, misty around the eyes, Bella whispered into the mike: "My heartfelt thanks!"

And it's off to Washington for the Nineteeth's fighting Jewish mama. Or as the campaign shopping bags put it: "Carry Bella Abzug to Congress."

Abbie pursued

TALES OF HOFFMAN Nearly the very first time I saw Abbie, back three or four years ago, I understood in a flash the meaning of "freak," that special ambience of mood and that special air of inventive play that baits the bourgeois, unsteps the locked-step factotum, baits both out of their pose of righteousness. The occasion was a benefit for scruffy street people, St. Mark's Motherfuckers among them, all of whom were attempting, at times with their own mistaken self-righteousness, to inject some small dose of humanity into a street scene ridden with violence, with police hostility. The place was the Electric Circus, that weirdly whitewalled wind tunnel of rock explosion (mostly inferior), and *oops* Abbie was loose on the premises, making his pitch for good bread to fight busts, while on the Circus's oddly cantilevered stage, a then-little-known rock quintet out of Detroit, called MC-5, was infecting the rather tight acoustic space of Circus with its own brand of (feverish, funky) sound. Abbie was in his usual Hoffman dress: denim street clothes, Italian grapepicker bandana around neck, hair a good mop of natural curly black wild, eyes buttony sharp and dancing shiny glazed. The haze and molasses-sweet aroma of grass was thick as a cloud and odd Abbie was either taking joints himself (and on the sly) or he was by now consumed enough in that free layering whiff of dope to be getting a high (as others were) by merely being there and letting his nose do the rest. Reason for the walking-on-eggshells caution: Narcs allegedly were all over the place, and the word, not entirely paranoid, was that the good clean Rogers Peet-suited ones were out to earn their pay that night, were hot on the stick for making busts, not least on old Abbie himself. But Abbie, super-gaited as usual, bouncing around from here to there, up dark stairs, and down to orchestra floor again, was playing this beanball chasing game, shouting his gruff jollies of encouragement, or doing his "What's happening, narc?" number to backs or fronts of those alleged NYC and/or Federal narcs, who could no more admit the stakeout, to Abbie or others, than they could prevent ironjawed mouths from cracking into smiles, as Abbie happied the evening away.. Many, many tales later—Chicago piggy trials, flag-shirting on TV, steal-the-book happenings, variety freakouts—and this tart grizzly welterweight is still with us, climbing the ladder of antic imagination, his own and that of his fellows, pleasuring most of us, doing it daily and nightly, our permanent floating crap game of laughs in the steamy void, turn-on kid of the USA asylum. Abbie Hoffman has nine lives, all being shadowed, all giving the word. *Fuck the gloom, fornicate in broad daylight.*

Women's lib vs Norman Mailer

NORMAN & DAVID & GERMAINE & JILL & . . . The Women's Lib-Norman Mailer talkout-shootout at Town Hall and the Andy Warhol preview at Whitney Museum—on the same Friday night—were the two hottest tickets in town. I was shoutout on both, waiting until the last minute (decisions, decisions!) to make my press requests. First I got an earful from usually unflappable Leon Levine of Whitney: "You haven't been to the museum for *what?*—a year or two? Now you and hundreds come out of the woodwork for *what?*—some kind of cocktail and smarts gathering? Thought you were a serious journalist?" Levine had a point, though a bit overstated, so I put the phone back in the cradle: "Thanks a lot!"

As for the Lib event, I did attend the party-after part, held at a barebones Westbeth loft, crowded and shuffling full of high gawkers on the litry-feminist-polit fronts. The affair was catered by Nathan's, the hip new prole thing, three or four ruddy-faced guys in Coney Island striped uniforms of red on white, dishing out the fat frankfurters and canned beer—all you could handle. The prole touch was faultlessly correct, all those highflyers in mod dress, and finely tailored Eastside swingers garb, rubbing shoulders with the angries of lib revolution, the menu nothing less than the great U.S. feedbag of TV and ballgames and prize ring: hotdogs and aluminum-canned beer.

Norman & David & Germaine & Jill & . . .

On my way over to Westbeth, I ran into raunchy East Village rocker David Peel, of Wanna Marijuana hit-tune fame. I asked David if he'd like to join me, hedging the invite with dip of skepticism, after all the bash was not exactly—I told him—his "cup of tea." Followed by his own touch of skept, "Intelec*shuls* are a new scene for me." But he'd give it a try.

We got there about midnight, and we were both soon swallowed up. Swirls of people moving around to their own cicadalike hum of "*Who* said *what?*" at Town Hall earlier. The stars hadn't arrived as yet, but sides were being chosen as if Germaine Greer's or Norman Mailer's or Jill Johnston's words were palpable presences, or "the message" made flesh. The consensus on Germaine, "adorable"; on Norman, more often "clod" than "hero"; and on Jill, about even between "outre" and "ballsy." (clitorally ballsy, that is.) I became separated from Peel, he himself surrounded by a circle of intellecshul admirers, faintly mod costumed "I'm in publishing" people, who reminded him as how they "caught his gig" at Bethesda Fountain, in Central Park, and David meantime trying to sniff out the trend: weigh the balance between the "lib politics" clout and his own no small clout of grass-and-rock outrage. Through the dark shades, and throaty holler of his St. Mark's street lingo, Peel's image was coming over rough but salable.

I myself became encircled, or rather was lassoed singly, by a tall blond actress-model, who seized me by the lapel of my lib "knowledgeability," a kind of weak lapel, at best, but actress-model insisted, flatly: "You've given the subject some thought; I can *tell.*" So I yammered one or two cliches, and then shifted to *her* thought. "Tell me how it hits *you*," I demanded. Adding—what with all the feigned toughness afloat—a quick: "I mean, *gutwise.*" Eye-fluttering revelation or two later (example: "Sure, I'd grope-sleep with a sister; no big deal!"), and the actress-model was off on another tack.

The word by now was that Germaine and Norman and Jill had arrived. And blond friend was pawing for "Introductions—I'm sure you know them all." And so, giving in to first causes, even while regretting the break in our so-recent friendship, I then delivered actress-model to, first, Jill Johnston; and then to Mailer. (As for Germaine, she was besieged one hundred deep, easily.) Delivering her not directly but to within a few feet of their royal presences, mobbed as they were by chatting tens, twenties. Angry chatting, or happy chatting, or just plain chatting. Me saying to actress-model: "That's Jill—" and "That's

Norman—." And then adding: "Now you're on your own." Not too gallant, but maybe wise, in the circumstance.

It was a bearpit and holyroller love-in by turns. Norman was deep in the pit, most of the time. The baiters surrounded him, he bulging a little in conversative blue suit and mod tie, his steelwool gray hair curling out on his bobbing head. The girls were Barnard types in jeans, plus a couple of jetsetters with lacquered green nails. Most delivered mild tentative shivs, but an occasional "Sexist pig!" retort, which Mailer fielded with mock comatose calm, lent the encounters an air of tension. The love-ins were for Germaine, who had the pose of regal talky beauty; and no less so for Jill, who was garbed in patch-encrusted bells, her style a quicksilver mix of butch bravado, hideaway tomboy looking for a friend. The two left the scene early, leaving Norman the field. He performed with a deft belligerence, save for the downward scowl of the lip, now and then.

A very special scowl, on their first encounter, was served up to David Peel, whom Mailer tried to "figure out behind your shades," after Peel put it to him: "How do you stack up this meeting with the Washington May Day demos?" which on first blush sure did sound like a boggler. Between the hotdogging and beering, and the heavy lib rapping, who had time for demo talk! So Normal passed, scowling it.

Several hours into the party, dragging near to two in the morning, some few of us still hanging in there, including the sharp but tiring Mailer. When the stripped Nathan's crew yelled for some clearance, so they could haul the tables and stuff onto a waiting truck, he held them off to the extent of two more cans of beer, which he then pocketed with a boyguilty grin. David Peel, also among the late ones, squared for a second encounter. He chinned up to Mailer: "You know, the next President's got to be a rock-n'-roll star." The other man paused, his tired eyes dilating a little. Then, in a rapid and hoarse delivery, Mailer countered: "I like you, shades and all. But a rock President, *never*! Couldn't hear the man's words, for all the background noise." It was a standoff, with some winking goodcheer all around.

Other late-stayers were into him, too. The young Barnard girls, who kept upping the lib count of numberless dilemmas, even as Mailer feinted them with each anxious query. I spotted one woman, somewhat older and more "dressy' than the Barnarders, who was speeding a ballpoint pencil across a flat yellow pad, looking to cram in the pearls with a minimum of loss, and I asked her whom she was covering for, to which she replied, while Mailer was in a temporary quietus: "I'm covering the event for the Social Page of the Washington Post." She was very cool and dandruffless. No doubt the Post would display some variety, along with the page-one demo news, come the Sunday edition forty-eight hours later.

"Law and order"

WE ARE ALL PART OF ATTICA   The roving editor has experienced, in the past fortnight or so, an input overload of moog vibes. Not all of it moog, but enough to throw him off stride. In making the rounds he's drawn too much of the wammy of that bad feedback—and he pauses along the way to wonder at the insignificance of it all. We are of course all in the time of now—the Attica time of billionaire liberalism with its embalmed, cloying smell of law and order in the state and national capitols. At the very moment of cries for help in the prisons, ghettos and numbed neighborhoods, and the response from on high is little more than a stony rectitude that stabs at the heart. It is in this context that roving's rounds seem (at least to him) to take on the shape of a feckless dilettantism. Yet we all move from where we are at in everyday habit—and so roving herein reports on several of the fortnight's happenings and gut involvements in the time of Attica. Moogs and all, last event first.

The Ninth Lincoln Center Film Festival, also known as So What Else Is New?, found roving left out in the cold. He was disinvited to the event, denied a press pass after covering and writing about seven of the past eight festivals as a freelance. This was the so-called new "austerity," the excuse being that only press "bona fides" were qualified for passes, the codicil excuse being that the Film Festival hoped to lure some extra loot by this exclusivist arrangement, so all non-bona-fides please move your ass over to the box office and do your bit for old Lincoln Center. With a budget of close to 160 thou', it can be seen that the Society thinks in pennies, but blows its image around to the tune of crisp dollars all over the joint. On fatty PR fees to the likes of John Springer Associates, on director and associates starting with the perennial and trilingual (English, French and Bureaucratese) Richard Roud who gets a reported eighteen thou' to mount the festival, on wholesome fringe doings like opening and closing parties. For the

Ninth, the Society took the Vivian Beaumont dungeon, with its paltry nine hundred seats (as compared to 2,700 at Philharmonic Hall). The seats on a teetering and wraparound rise from stage center, fine for theater in the round but more than a little ass-upwards for movies. Add to which several dozens of seats to the sides that are in a near, or even total, blind. If you don't come up with attack of vertigo, you still get the chance of seeing the movie in all-profile. The Society generously pegged the blindies at a low buck, but no surprise if all or at least some in those blind spots up and make a holler: "Stick the seat up yours; I want my buck back." The Society by the way is really a one-man influential named Martin Segal; it's the businessman-gone-film-esthete who's the *macher* of the Ninth.

And so I took my disinvited self to the first press screening, at (for me) a dummo twelve-thirty in the afternoon, not so much out of past habit, but to check what the new austerity had wrought. Everything in that lobby was icily correct, and roving got the impression that a bunch of medical technicians were filing into Beaumont for a boring anatomy lecture. (And where has all the fun gone, Marty boy?) Yet there was a bone of satisfaction, as when a couple of the bona fides told roving they were teed over his treatment. Also another bone, this one with more meat on it, when he ran into two young film writers from the underground Creem and the East Village Other, both holding in tight fists their bona fide passes, photos laminated-over and all. (One of the choicer yocks in Springer Associates's press invite went: "This time we won't ask for fingerprints.") Whether or not due to past agitprops from roving and others, it was good to see underground on equal terms with the Andrew Sarrises in their right to cover the moog. The fact is Sarris is a moonlighter who—mixed metaphor or not—carries pails of whitewash on both shoulders: he covers for the Village Voice even while he serves on the film-selections committte for a thou' "honorarium." Another committee moonlighter is Arthur Knight, who covers for the *Saturday Review*. There's even a slight case of incest going on—film-critic-wise: Molly Haskell, who is Mrs. Andrew Sarris in private, weighs in with her own *Village Voice* comment. That may not be the entire lot, at that. (And so back to roving.) He even managed to get to the craw of the snotty Beaumont factotum, as when he aimed his cigarette roach for a nearby ashtray and missed, factotum (factoady?) then snapping at roving: "Do you do that in your living room?" *Fucking-A I don't,* said roving. *Besides, this living room of yours is a public heap, nicely supported by tax dollars.* And when the screening buzzer was sounded, some ten or fifteen minutes after his arrival, he made his way out of Beaumont's thickly carpeted lobby, not sure but what he felt no pain at all over his personal diaspora, out he went into the crisp air and pale sunshine of a late-September day. (The sun a burnt-orange splash, mood sort of birch-foresty among LC's hard travertine and polished glass.) And he recalled the closing line of a past festival report of his: "Maybe they ought to hold the Eighth Festival, next year, in John D. Rockefeller III's Chase Manhattan vault." Give the Sprung Associates another year or two, and they'll get the festival to that vault yet!

Party at Claudia's pad, one flight over (would you believe) a "florist college" storefront, on Ninth Avenue in Chelsea. No-special-reason party with accent on publishing, rad activists and hot young freelance writers. A trio of the latter are ladling sangria drinks from the wide punchbowl and sharpshooting their barbs at "Pig editors who fuck over our copy." (It should be mentioned that the same three had met with several other freelancers, a week or two prior to the party, the meeting held at a Westside apartment, where they discussed ways and means of resisting, in the words of one writer present, "our vassalage to dumb editors who drop the truth from our stories, our reporting." They ran down other problems as well, the meeting ending with resolve to build "an organization of freelance writers with clout.") At the party roving meets up with Dotson and his Raiders—among them hot Tom Seligson, who for starters hits *Evergreen* like he owns them, and who for continuers has a new book out called *To Be Young in Babylon.* Talk around the room is sharp, but edged with a kind of black-crepe anger. The now writing and politics are shadowed by an unnamable bluepencil and bluenose hotbreathing, lurking around the next demo and next trip to the typewriter keys. I'm turned on by the vitality in that room, as if I'm the eye at the center, while all around me are those soundings of hurricane winds. (At sound of the gong, it will be Attica hour.)

I meet and chat with John and Amber—John Wilcock and wife Amber back from several months of poking around the counterculture in Europe. John, a finger or two heavier at the gut, but his tongue lean and biting-sharp as ever, as he does inventory on "piggish New York, piggish USA." He says: "I'm apeshit tired of the whole mess . . ." He says: "I've tried in my small way to bring reason to the beast . . ." He says: "We're splitting for good, taking off for Europe and elsewhere, before the scene [here] goes fully apeshit mad...." Roving catches the winds, and though he's heard a good deal of Wilcock's kind of rundown of late, Eastside and Westside and all around town, solo and a cappella and in mass chorus, he's sad and a bit uneasy scared. Yesterday's "paranoia" is today's paranoia, with *real* blood in the caldron. But he gives his rebuttal, what he thinks of as roving "pollyanna" defense line, oft repeated but lodged in him deeper, he hopes, than just whistling dixie past the yard. He says to John and Amber: "The beast is apeshit made because its bowels are outta control ..." He says: "The sure way for the beast takeover is for people like yourselves to opt outta the scene ..." He says: "Nixon will be eighty-sixed in seventy-two, my crystal ball reveals it.... By a clasped-hands of the George Walds, and the Leonard Woodcocks in labor's ranks out there ... and by hardhats and new voters, black and bluecollars, fleshing out the win ..." Roving's been pushing that line, Eastside and Westside. And he wonders if the catechism is going down with John, with Amber. He looks into the man's eyes, and the cold anger in the Wilcock bluegreen orbs is still there. John says: "It's the same old election-politics hype ..." And roving: "It's the only politics we've got ..." The nada and double-nada, like the echo of E. M. Forster's Marabar cave.

DEAR ARTHUR & GLEE*: The Mailer film premiere-party was less than banner headline, so maybe your missed trip (from California State College, Pa.) was no great loss. The film "Maidstone" is a curious melange (cinema verite, Pirandello, Mailer genius—but genius in the realm of *what*?). I won't go into detail on film here, might want to do some comment later, so I'll keep my confusion open for the moment. The party itself was unexpectedly softsell & the setting likewise glossy soft. Picture a big, high-ceilinged Whitney gallery, crawling with some great (some indifferent) Edward Hoppers, up and down the walls. In the midst of which, a long table with white-on-white linen, three huge bowls of, the biggest, the pinkest, shrimps this side of Four Seasons, shrimps winking up at your palate to a tickle. (Roving winked back, dove in with a toothpick.) A crowd of about 100, all Mailer or Whitney invited, but an easy gate I'm sure, had you decided to fly in. (Whitney Museum is coolly civilized, next to the Hessian-horde security at Lincoln Center.) The host was front and center, doing his brief turns with his usual rough-roguish aplomb. With at least one exception—me. Roving's record vis-vis Mailer remains unblemished, he zapped me with curled-lip grunts, when I put a couple of questions (re the film) to him. Norman sizes me up with Mailer-aforethought look, and he groans "Ho ho ho, he wants to know if . . . ." Really minor stuff, so I save you the details. On with the party: Around the room the small clusters, palming tall highball glasses, talk about the film, but all seem to avoid *in depth* comment (not easy for some, *too* easy for others). Several present at party are also in the film—but roving draws a blank trying to guess who is and who isn't. More so with the display of good-looking and chicly gowned ladies on the floor, a confusing number of whom are "identified" as "One of Norman's former wives." The absence of Rip Torn brings on some comment, no surprise when you remember that most had just come out of the screening room, and were still fresh with the image of the mindboggler last scene from "Maidstone," where the Ripper (in as spooky an improvisation as director Mailer *didn't* call for), lurches along the Gardiner's Island green towards Norman, and then does a sudden tattoo on director's skull with a toy (but indeed damaging) hammer. The impromtu madness of the incident, the no-holds-barred denouement, with Mailer trickling blood and Torn nursing a savaged ear, keyed me to one likely ambiguity (call it even a basic fault), in the Mailer film gestalt. That whereas Mailer is an obsessive talker on the existential film he *thinks* he's making, that last scene throws into bold relief the hollowness of most of what went before. Add to which this irony—the masquerade backfires, and director claims the backfire is *part of the genius*. Meantime, back at the party, the Ripper doesn't reappear, so we are denied what might have been a face-off, a second-act spook.

I run into Dotson, running into him often in that fortnight. He's wearing his surrogate cowboy duds, boots and leather and big red kerchief, and he moves around the polished Whitney floor in that cowboy lope of his. With him are close friend Jack, and D's number one upfront Raider, Tommy the hot freelance. Earlier I caught a view of Dotson and Norman doing their "confrontation" thing—a bullish little mime of elbows poking into ribs to the tune of prizefight rumblings. The script goes like this: From Norman, "This one's for a quarter-million purse, winner take all, for the left benefit named by winner." Sentimental or not, it's a warm little number, hinting at good two-way vibes, between older king-of-the-hill writer, and young "challenger" who has notched some impressive early wins. Now Dotson and company—after an hour or two of the party—decide to split and they ask roving if he wants to join them across town to Library (the West

Side pub). It's a little past midnight, Norman's belting last drinks with half-dozen admirers, they're all more or less happily squiffed. A taxi ride later we're at Library, and Dotson says: "Tommy tells me Mailer was rude to you. I don't like that and I'll tell him when I call him tomorrow." Well, that's all right, says roving, but I'd rather you don't. You see, you'll blow my game that way, blow my unblemished status.

Love to you and Glee, SB

*Prof. Arthur Knight is *not* *Saturday Review*'s Knight.

Roving is a bookstore freak. He does New Yorker Books, Eighth Street, East Side Books, Papyrus (Columbia U area), Parnassus (oldies but goodies), Gotham, Scribner's (establishment, but in good taste). He browses (buys now and then, but a helluva browser!) like a kid turned loose at the FAO Schwarz toy shop. He's also done the selling side, as in eight or ten past Saturday nights at New Yorker. You don't know depth of curiosity, of your serious book and magazine buyer, till you've visited that top-masted store on West Eighty-ninth Street, with its firehouse stairway that links mags-dailies with books. And you don't know a bookman's commitment—to the kind of author whose name, say, is *not* Irving Wallace—till you've met Peter and Madalyn Martin, and by extension, the New Yorker's sharp young regulars and bench, Allan & Janet & Bob & Kenny & Jimmy, who are not in a Hollywood movie, but out there live and in longhair on the bookstore boards. It's the kind of shop that affixes "Neighborhood Author" tags on new books—by such as I.B. Singer, Murray Kempton, Rosalyn Drexler, Jules Feiffer, Guy Daniels, Gil Orlovitz, Dotson Rader, El Sid, and others. Nabe authors who may come by on the moment, after trip to local greengrocer's, and they scan the racks for some "quick read" material, not forgetting to ask: "How is my book selling?" There's a sturdy wicker chair off to a corner, for those who get footweary while browsing. All told, a pretty good New York version, or maybe the other way around, of San Francisco's City Lights, which figures when you learn that Pete Martin was founder of the Frisco hillside shop.

Roving came by one recent evening, to check out the autograph do sponsored by Dutton for Jack Newfield's new collection, *Bread and Roses* (which has to be "Sean O'Casey title of the Year"). A tight squeeze in upstairs rooms, drinks coming at you from risky angles, author Newfield (wearing bright mod tie) swallowed up by the crowd. Pete Martin is playing the outer circle, a big drink in hand as he lays on the Martin "rap." And what a unique bookman's talking-tongues it is! If Newfield's comments are pointillist—quick dots of greetings and "thank you's"—Martin's are ex!plos!ions! of Jackson Pollock—overflowing anecdotes, splashes of politics satire. The Right gets the brunt, but the Left is not spared. "When we were kids in Pittsburgh, fifteen-year-old Leninist adolescents, we sat around planning how to take over the *steel industry!* You understand, *the whole goddamn Pittsburgh* steel industry, for god's sake! We wanted to capture it *for the people!* Boy were we dumb!" (And more such Martin riffs.) I get my drink, bourbon on rocks. It loosens me as I chat with bearded novelist Sol Yurick, more than chitchat, as Sol declares: "The repression will come down on all radical media, and very *soon!*" So I blink, I've heard the weather report before, but I ask Yurick to flesh out some gritty for *Newsletter*, and Sol agrees he will do it. Minutes later, a hairy bustout, swift and unexpected. Writer Rosalyn Drexler, whose downer on Feiffer's *Carnal Knowledge* had appeared in the *Times*, is confronted by Judy Feiffer (Jules' wife), who then goes on to pole-axe Drexler with some choice carnal knowledge of her own. "Cunt, ungrateful bitch, after all Jules did for you!" Very heavy verbal rip-off, which left Drexler shaken up, and Judy Feiffer leaving the scene. A few days later I'm at the bookshop, and I see Jules Feiffer riffling the stand for the London newspapers. No show—Fleet Street's on strike. Jules tells roving: "Wanted to see what they say about my film." And I get a balloon flash: *from the worried look, Jules might be expecting the worst, even while he's hoping for a saver. Just like in a Feiffer cartoon.* We discuss the party, which Jules hadn't attended, and I counter his defense of Judy's blast: "That kind of thing hits all writers where they live: the right of the coldprint putdown!" So saying, roving chalks up another friendly score.

Thus some turns on the bigcity rotisserie, during the Attica fortnight. Plus a surprise phonecall, from the Attica prisoner who sent an over-transom job appeal to *Newsletter*, on the eve of his parole from jail, the letter received and then published by TN (August 3, 1971, issue) some weeks before the law-and-order shoot-in. It was Daniel Sokol on the phone, roving pressing the earpiece closer, and saying to Sokol: "I hope you're calling from *outside* that jail." And he was, having gained his freedom, and having found a job in New York, in the meantime. He found a job, let it be said, *not* through the generosity of any one of TN's publisher subscribers, or any one of the other bigbiz subscribers, none of whom deigned to take a minute to write *Newsletter* in Sokol's behalf. Yet there were several who did—to tell TN that his appeal moved them. Poets and writers and little-mag editors—all expressing concern and sympathy. William Childress and Alexandra Garrett (from California), Arthur and Glee Knight, Collette Inez and others. Collette writing that she had photocopied fifteen sets of the Sokol letter and mailed them to people she thought might help. We are all part of Attica, but some are more aware of it than others.

Leopold Stokowski

THE AMERICAN TUNING FORK   At least once a year, I must catch Leopold Stokowski. Master builder of concert hall, in his very late eighties, to watch him is to learn again, call it ecology of musical soul. Music as mirror of inner harmonies, contrapuntal tensions, aging master putting a hundred musicians in "touch," sculpting with sound the grand design of those inner voices. The program is all-Wagner, at New York's best acoustic shell, cream-gold and steeply tiered Carnegie Hall. I second-act the set, arrive just in time for the "Liebestod" from *Tristan and Isolde*. On the scenery-less stage is Doris Jung, relatively svelte (for Wagnerian heroine) in flower-pattern gown, she meshes those serenely difficult vocal passages with Stokowski's magic with an orchestra. (The *Times* called him ageless Klingsor of the podium.) And it *is* an ecology pattern, a washing of the sands of glop, all the turbid juices, we're trapped in, the day's accumulated downs brought into the Hall, and then having them wiped away by the music (that most natural cleanser of grease-spotted egos). The soaring last notes are sung by Ms. Jung as if from outside herself, her tall body and slightly heaving chest being dowser that intuits a cycle, a cycle of love and death hitched together, timeless and regenerative as in all nature. Next the "Forest Murmurs" from *Siegfried*, which Stokowski offers as sumptuous orchestral feast, but with that controlled grace that is his hallmark. There's a soft humming of violins, picked up and intensified by deeper cellos, rounded finally by froggy-voiced tension of double bass. And the more than twitterings of woodwinds—which to the ear (as

Stokowski urges them on) are nothing less than songful mimicking from the very beaks of woodlands. In the forest primeval, there's a greening harmony, soundings as the ear of genius conceives them; thus are we restored to balance once again. For concert's end, Brunhild's immolation scene from *Gotterdammerung*, or twilight of the gods. Rising-falling waves of massed violins, trumpets and English horns in forte, convey the hero on last journey home. Leitmotivs that scale to the heights, ease down to below-treble depths of lament, Ms. Jung's big voice limning the score to shadowy and transcendent close.

The immediate bravos and sharp rattling handclapping, from top tier down to front of orchestra, are a kind of music by itself. Carnegie Hall "owns" its audience, whereas Philharmonic Hall's is a mere "lease out." The first is especially true for a Stokey concert, where you get a fairly even mix of young people, many of them students and musicians themselves, and an elderly band of concertgoers whose faces are lined, not simply with the toil of years, but with (additionally) the soft indentations of musical fandom itself. Of the Lincoln Center clientele, let's say that they shuttle their musical evenings, the Philharmonic being a more or less "other stop" in their weekly round of smart things to do. *Literally* a shuttle, from fashion-conscious Upper East Side, to Lincoln Center plant on West Sixty-fifth, making it there and back on the ML crosstown bus. Back at Carnegie, there's no end to the applause. Through it all, Ms. Jung maintains her regal pose, betrayed now and then by a warm flickering smile, both hands extended in a wide arc, as she acknowledges the loudest cheers pouring down from the roof of the hall. But mostly to Stokowski are the cheers directed, Ms. Jung herself, on her third or fourth call, signaling with her hand the object of everyone's pleasure. He, the Klingsor with flowing mane, stands at the podium guard rail, looks on with patrician composure of years, takes the applause with a wide—and dimming—twinkle of eyes. But he takes it only on "loan," as he repeats the gesture of directing the crowd's response on to others. First to Ms. Jung herself, then to the full orchestra, then to the first desks, and finally, he "signals" the cheers back to the audience itself. A large bouquet is handed up to Ms. Jung, and later on, after the fourth or fifth call, she returns from backstage, and hands two of the roses to Stokowski. He, on his part, quickly hands out one each, first to the lady at first-violin desk, then to the lady at first-cello desk. On her very last call, Ms. Jung returns with still another rose, longstemmed and redder than the deep red of Carnegie's seats; she clutches it to her bosom, and then hands it up to Stokowski. *This* rose is indeed "ticketed" for him—Ms. Doris Jung, members of the orchestra, and the shouting audience, will have it no other way! Still, they will not leave, but they quiet down somewhat, as Stokowski edges to the mike. He announces: "If you loved the Wagner, you'll also love the Bach." And he goes to the encore, velvetsmooth passage from one of the cantatas; the audience settles back under a wand. Leopold Stokowski, tuning fork of American concert hall.

Charles Henri Ford

THE MINOTAUR COMPLEX The handballcourt-sized Bleecker Street Cinema is packed to orange walls. Small alcove hung with art erotica—from heterosex to homosex to unisex to groupsex. *Johnny Minotaur* film delayed past eight-thirty invite time, latecomers meantime buzzing the art while waiting for second screening. It's a tunedup crowd known as the artsy in "gamut." Poets & painters & filmmakers, Max's Kansas City watering-hole faithful, friends of Charles Henri Ford, friends of Ms. Ruth Ford, friends of Dotson Rader. Call the latter "Dotson's Raiders," scouts-out activists/scribblers on the Movement scene, and hot number in the litry-polit raffle for its "growth potential" in counterculture surge of late 1960s & early 70s. Nor do we mean "growth potential" in bullshit Blue Chips, in bullshit Gross National Product, what we do mean is GP for radical change in TFS or This Fuckedup Society.

All just about make it in a squeeze, tight up against the walls & All. Program opens with Jean Genet's *Un Chant d'Amour*, the 1950s two-reeler and a tough act to follow in avant-homosex genre. The reels spin on and out, audience tension sort of layered like slowmoving cloud, one viewer caught in web of *Chant*'s roughtrade sex inside wrapper of lunging/daydreaming lyricism. Jean Genet, the streetfighter Janus of gay. And the crowd murmurs its appreciation. Next the promise of Charles Henri's flick, with long trailerlike sequence for openers, lots of splashy color & velvety seascape, couple of bareass Crete Island boys in quick tableaus of Minotaur theme, two bronzed male studs playing in surf, lovely girl (Charles Henri's niece) snaking away nude in hammock, Charles Henri's voice-over trying for "story line," but the reach for legend and phallic appeal, as film wends along sluggisly, gets further & further beyond the grasp, a case of high-low camp meshing with high-low voyeurism. That plus, now & then, a funthing or two.

The crowd settles into seats as if in cradle, innocence awaiting its reward, like kids getting their bath rubdowns by mums with educated hands. But soon they begin to stir uneasily. Just lost two up the aisle, as bronzed studs make out on beach, cocks dangling like toll of bells as they swap spits on the brilliantined sand. Two more lost up the aisle, as horny beachboy plays with his bared erector, then cuts open lush melon and fucks the fruit to a come. And two more up the aisle, as still another horny dude, crazed by the in-heat of it all, carves out his balls (symbolism, you know) with a carving knife.

Charles Henri probably had Bunuel & Cocteau in mind, but his takes are more Bellevue Castration Ward than skinchilled avant-garde. And so it went, and so went several in the audience, as voice-over briefs us on Theseus & Minotaur thing once again. We did up-the-aisle about two-thirds into film, and when Bleecker Cinema owner Lional R. asked why, we could only think of Warhol for answer. "Andy's folk are pure passion flower, next to Charles Henri's cold-turkey masquerade. Or cock on ice, if you'll excuse the punpun." But there's still the party on tap, several of us hike the seven or eight blocks to Soho loft desert in fresh spirits. Charles Henri's *live* happening has to be a winner, the Minotaur film's not necessarily the man.

Two flights up from dim & deserted street, waves of rock sound splitting through the hallway, through high-ceiling & near-bare studio, the party's in progress with reawakened energy. Gathering of the arts funky, the leather-boots-caftans-jeans Mod draped bodies, you've seen them at gallery openings, at pop and underground watering spots, at Bethesda million-cameras Fountain, at peep-the-freak Sheep Meadow. But *who's* the dude with lace up to his chin, and the cool-cucumber dame in soft boots up to her thighs, and the fiercely bearded cat with scowl to match! Not to worry, Dotson & Charles Henri'll have the line, they'll tip you as party moves along. Meanwhile, a fineboned & fiftyish lady comes by, shy "Where do I know you!" in her eyes, and you make drinks & *eh-eh* party rap, then memory clicks on like camera shutter: "How forgetful of me, you're Ms. Dwight M., how's good ole Dwight doin'!" Two distanced bodies closing in the crush, but a small wave of regret afterwards, there was more to say, as bodies get sundered in the fast-word-&-out scene.

Dotson larrups by, he wants you to meet, Tennessee. Next moment you're in a tight little knot, *the* playwright smack in middle, he stands about five-six and pigeon pouting & healthy, wellcut-suit-modshirt-&-tie combo from (maybe) Finchley's racks; he's very alive for man who'd been touted DOA, back a year or two by bible New York *Times*. (He recalls: "I was at this redneck Florida Hospital, fightin' off the nightmares of a bad ticker, and some bad shakes. Whiskey shakes, not malted ones.") When you give him a nudge, that the *Times* item was slightly exaggerated, he foxes a broad smile, under tight & gleaming mustache, but then he eyes you with pixie playfulness, as he fends off a query on work-in-progress. He says, "I'm surer than hell, working on a new play, that Ashley Famous (or Famous Ashley?) agency of mine would nail me to a cross, if I didn't come up with one a year! *You know it!*"

You stay in there, nosy for detail, but all you can get, in response to a new tack, is a cagey "It's about two people . . ." His index right & left fingers held high, rolled at you in thickening haze like couple of exclamations. "Two people . . ." What he *will* talk about, is Charles Henri's film ("Adored it!"); the pretty picture gloss of Candy Darling, who's right there in our midst, a steamy and wrungout image of Jean Harlow put-on ("Take a devourin' look at her!"); the gliding presence of Rader, stop-motion and D.'s off to another klatch ("Dotson, let's do a light fantastic!"). Minutes later, the playwright wanders off & out, he's bound for Italy by transatlantic liner the next day. (And a bon voyage, hope your "two people" enjoy the sea-change.)

More ripples on the party surf. Dotson keeps active book on high knowables present, tips you with quick bio strokes, and next thing you know, you're in a *ho-ho* rap with this goodboned (lots of good bones floating by!) conservative lady, wife of God & Man at Yale writer-—editor—TV heavy, only through D.'s nogap friendship roll, would such as you & the lady cross social-polit lines, and come up smiling. He introduces you, "Movement man before Movement began," and you force a *ho-ho* chuckle, while lady herself does a *ha-har-I-see!* A polite exchange, but you don't ask her about Minotaur flick. You're pretty sure that she didn't ungap the gap that far, as to sit in Bleecker Cinema cradle & glom all that unbleached erotica. The hunch checks out, when D. confirms Pat B.'s no-show at movie, but he's sure she would've shown had she not been "delayed at airport." And he adds: "She would have dug it." You slip him a *no-no*. Not with all that fineboned conservative aura. Pat B. carries it like Helena Rubenstein before-after treatment.

And others, from Dotson's and Charles Henri's datebooks. They minnow back & forth, a round of conversation here, slosh of wine or booze there, deep puff of dope in another corner. The traffic's a blurred, runtogether circus of jawjaw faces. Handsome & lowkeyed Jack W., sturdy friend of Dotson's, takes in the action coolly, with just a pinch of "seen it all" remove. Two from (ha ha) the deviate theater groupies, playwright Ronald T. who sleepwatches all, and does it keenly at that, as if he's soaking up some new shtick for next play; and equally sleepy Taylor M., he of the near-spastic drawl, and softfast bon mot, graces party like a Harry Langdon with smarts. Two from the jet-set list, young blondish & elegant Prince Egon von F., whom *Daily News'* Suzy Says blueribbons as "Prince Egon von und zu Furstenberg"; and veddy British stage-director whizz Peter G., who's a sort of arts-jets-flower hero sandwich of a celeb, if you hobby with him you partake of the whole three-course feast. And the Raiders, D.'s playpals from off the Columbia campus, some of whom planted liberation flag on Grayson Kirk's rooftop, back in the heady days of the troubles. Tommy & Kathy; Dick & Louise; Craig and Frank, solos. They have their own party thing, their this-side-of-gap highs. Toking joints & women libbing & counter culturing. Not flagwaving this time around, just laying it down lightly & bitely.

And finally Charles Henri, himself. It's well into the evening, the crowd's thinning out, you catch him on the bounce for a chat. He's survived the *hellos* and the "Loved it!" salutations, southerndip composure still intact, tiny lines around seablue eyes only sign of wear. His voice a soft baritone, with hint of magnolia-speak from ole Miss days still there. And, after years of Paris-Crete-New York, painting & poetry, editing surrealist little mag, middleage suntanned goodlooks still there too. You last saw Charles Henri, only a day or two back, at his topfloor Dakota digs, a shadowy but cozy space, sunk right into the eaves of that darktoned manse, the building itself a sort of mini Versailles for showbizzy people, rich name authors, and camp followers with heavy wallets. He showed you to the roof, for a *real* picture-postcard of Central Park, and then back to digs, where Charles Henri served up, for you and three others, an offcuff dish ("CakeMasters' caloric bummer of the week," he called it) of banana cream pie and espresso coffee. His own paintings-collages on walls, big steamer trunk filling up with gifts and things, for annual trip to house in Crete. From Dakota hill on park, to Cretan hill on sea. As we left the apartment, he reminded each one of us: "*Yu'all* be at the premiere; for sure, now! It's Johnny *Myn*otaur night!" Light curlicues of speech, that trip off the tongue of Charles Henri.

Back at the SoHo loft, you swap a funword or two, but how say to CHF, in the latehour glow of Minotaur evening, that (ha ha) you "Loved the banana cream pie; not sure about the film." So you back off, but you do tell him, that the party's an upper. Relate that you got a thrill, not mushy but "warm" thrill, in chatting with *the* playwright, and that you're longtime admirer of Tenn's swinging gifts, his glass-menagerie-honed humor, all wrapped in that muslin craft of his. (Okay, you continue, the craft's worn a bit thin of late, but you feel a good half dozen of TW's plays are gonna stick out the wear-tear of time, maybe even as long as old Tut wrapped away in *his* muslin shrouded image!) As for Dotson, you tell Charles Henri further, he's the party's hellon-wheels outrider, introing you to this & that celebrity, old Tennessee among them, wereupon Charles Henri smirks an imperious smirk, and lays the message down slowly: "I'll put it on the burner, for *yu'all*. Who do you think introduced *Dotson* to Tennessee, one guess!" His voice dripping southern acid that allows, of course, for no mistake as to *who*.

From Suzy Says's column, two days later, you pick out the Minotaur party names. Her list includes, besides those you had met, playwright Mart C., actress Sylvia M., author Hortense C., socialites Mrs. Willima Rhinelander S. and Mrs. Goddard L., set designer Rouben Ter-A., Broadway and London West End director Burt S., and several more. Suzy's whole bag delineated in a scant three graphs. Which shows you what *real* nosy will get you, next to which yours is only *timid* nosy.

Out of Vietnam now

THE UMPTEENTH RALLY What to do at an OUT OF VIETNAM NOW rally? Umpteenth in a long series, this latest one (November 6) on New York's big tramped-upon Sheep Meadow? You fancy the ground's hallowed by tens of thousands of "votes with your feet" from past demos, but you know too that there's no bank in the Nixon land that will negotiate those votes, none that will accept trade-in at the politics

The Umpteenth Rally

window for an end to the bloody affair. ("Come back on Election Day '72," says the White House chief teller, "and we'll see about cashing your protest on that day.") But you show up at the Meadow on a blustery fall day, the sun sitting low on your eyelids as it breaks from the fleecy clouds, and you view the new batch of ten thousand or more with that *deja vu,* dry-cheer-in-throat feeling. Sisyphus rolling the stone up the hill once again! Yet you show up for the community of voice, knowing that if protest has no magic ring of illumination, neither does the hole in the dark protect you from the angry time of day. On the Meadow at least, you are full-fathoms deep in people, the waves moving this way and that. A strange corps of Jesus shouters, up from Texas to announce dangers that need no announcing. Better if they took their show to the Pentagon, where the buttons of peace-war are pushed. Now some twenty of them move in single file, round and round on the fringes of the rally; they're shod to the ankles in a rough brownish twill, each one holding a long birchrod stick, each tapping the ground in weird cadence. Moody silences alternate with sudden cries from their lips, a kind of speaking in tongues that doesn't sound like "Out of Vietnam Now," but might well offer its own illumination, *if only they would tell us!* And they carry those bible-quoting placards, each one holding across his-her chest *this* word from Corinthians, *that* word from Sermon on the Mount. . . . But we all know the holy word to infinity, from one Sunday session to the next! And the young Jesuser-than-thous can speak in tongues and tap their rods—but nobody up there at the high listening post seems to be getting the message!

And the hardcore group of some fifty North Viet flagwavers, they're toting the yellow-star standard as if they *owned* it! And does General Giap know his battles are being won with the aid of every last boy and girl fluttering their flags . . . out there on the Meadow? They've read the Mao book, studied the Trotsky canon, argued hotly *in re* the Tito fault. And they mistake the book of ideology for the book of life. With energy and passion to burn, they'll invade any demo on the horizon, but they can barely raise a corporal's guard on their own! And when Senator Vance Hartke is introduced on the speaker's stand, the pavlovian shouts (from the flagwavers) rip across the Meadow like a chill wind: "Off Hartke! We don't wanna hear his shit! All Senators are pigs!" They form a tight phalanx, move on the rally in a snakedance, flaunt banners as they edge closer to the stand. Hartke is not fazed; he lays down his peace rap, crisp Indianian nuance rising above the ripoff shouts. A short time later—after the Senator returns to his seat—hefty

Beulah Sanders (the welfare battler) projects her booming voice over the rally like a thunderclap. Her words are piranha sharp: "You all try to mess with this meetin' . . . this peace agitatin' meetin' for *all of us* . . . and you're gonna feel my righteous wrath *right down to your diapered asses!*" She means it so bad, that a loud cheer goes up from the crowd. The ideology boys and girls hold off, then take their snakedance back out from the stand. And to even *louder* cheers, they next troop out of the Meadow, and head towards the zoo.

There's electricity in the air, Congresswoman Bella is next speaker. The Abzug message is direct as a homing pigeon, sharp-taloned as a feeding eagle, as she targets at House Military Affairs underbelly. Bella's wearing a big halloween-colors chapeau, which she loses to the sudden gust coming off the trees, followed by the hopscotching chorus of *oooos!* across the Meadow. But she belts on and on with the good jab, losing not a moment's pace over hatty-hat taking flight. The quick recovery of hat, Bella's thank you and her smile, some seconds more to pin it back on, and she's again zinging the military with allofit! Bella— NYC's Rosa Luxemburg of protest. And tall applecheek Peggy with camera, flew in from Bowling Green campus for a visit with friend Tommy (newsy freelance writer), and doubling on the Meadow now, for a pic-story for her college daily. She snaps the Jesus people, calls it a sure turn-on in Ohio! She catches Bella in the hat incident, the before-after sequence. And she's busy trying to keep up with the flags, the placards, the streamers. It's a fine unity day, with a wide spectrum of banners, including the Latin, the Black, the jobless . . . and of course Nam. Also the unexpected, the breezeblown blue-white Israeli number, and the giant fifteen- by ten-foot black silk display with red lettering: OUT OF NORTH IRELAND UK. Peg, Tommy and roving are unanimous: The Irish number is the whammy of the rally. And though cheerless in terms of OUT OF VIETNAM NOW, it was a good afternoon in terms of TOGETHER NOW.

Fillmore East

COLOR IT RASPBERRY Rock impresario Bill Graham's farewell, plastered in full-page ads in the *Village Voice* and elsewhere, must have sounded (to some) as touching as Napoleon's farewell to his legions,

Color It Raspberry

and very near the grandeur of Washington's spartan charge to his troops at Valley Forge. The sheer modesty of those words of his! And Graham all these years so misunderstood. Could very well touch you to the quick.

Well, it really might be a cracked crock. The authentic Bill Graham, as opposed to a Graham Cracker image of innocence assaulted, was a persona of hothouse suspicion, a man full of noisy and people-baiting rages. *That* part of him was on display, for several weeks running, back a year or two ago when the neighborhood freaks, in a great leap of imagination, came up with their free-Fillmore-on-dark-Wednesdays plan. Much of what happened in those weeks has been amply hashed and recorded, with pros and cons enough to confuse the issue to a standstill. And yet one aspect stands out, at least to me, and I followed the events closely, for it struck me that the idea had great promise. Both as symbolic act of togetherness, and as viable handle for an upswing in life-style in a neighborhood that had (and still has) little but downs.

Briefly stated, Graham came down on that idea with an overkill of hostility, not to say raging paranoia. He trusted no one, when in the very essence of those days, he should have been alert, indeed *right up front*, for the chance to build connections, the chance to reach out beyond the call of "I'm running a business." With just a mild offer of empathy, in his own backyard and space, he might have been instrumental in creating an environment of change, from the sleazy pill-down drags of weekly cash-register gains, to one of connection in and of "our own thing," if that's not too vague and sociological for the hardnose maven. (London's Roundhouse and the West Village's Judson Church come to mind, if Graham should ever poke his head outside his Fillmore-Ratner's yardage.) That he didn't do it, but instead saw fit to clobber that imaginative idea, even while he was tokenly allowing some dry runs (the attitude being "They'll muck up their own parade, wait and see"), is more a measure of the man than the innocence-abused of that full-page blurb.

Nor could one miss, as well, the picture of Graham the toughie, taking a defiant stance under his own marquee, stalking his narrow turf in green jumpsuit, chin at a forward tilt, as he tells off the freaks, junkies and kids, all with no bread for tickets, tells them "Tough shit—you're not getting in!" Hanging in there and showboating his boss clout, through (one supposes) the workings of some weird attraction-repulsion button. All of it hanging way out, a perfect snap of the people-baiting thing. I saw that steamy side of him, as I'm sure others have, on more than one occasion, while roaming by that angry corner, on my nightly roams of Second Avenue.

"Balance," some will insist. What about Fillmore's benefits, for this and that cause? What about the Central Park gigs, for the masses? The man sprang for space, for mucho expenses. Agreed, but there again, the presentations were the man. Hectoring and bossy. And always with a glum, doing-'em-a-favor benevolence. Like the time he gave us Airplane (or maybe it was Dead) on the Mall, reminding the thousands at the close, as how he "bought all the new trash cans," and as how the Park Department rated a "great big hand for their cooperation—let's hear it again!" Hairy display of noblesse oblige, king coming out of counting house to lay goodies on our heads. Color it raspberry, call it tokenism.

Meanwhile, let's all wish Bill Graham good luck in future rounds. So that when he next has the sad duty to close down on yet another great enterprise, with lots of loot in the pillow for the in-between times, he'll be sure to come up with a farewell notice that will be up to, and maybe even beyond, General George Washington's.

Non-sexist revolution

WOMEN'S LIBERATION: ANOTHER VIEWPOINT Women's Liberation! They shout it from rooftops, the new battlecry. The rebels at Columbia started it all. Back in the April-1968 sit-ins the commune at Mathematics was doing the heaviest homework of all. So no surprise when the cry went up among some Barnard girls in rough denims and red armbands—after the boys in the commune put together their battle-plan for defense of the sit-in. *Here's the way we do it: You guys man the fire hoses! And you guys barricade the doors, and let 'em have it when they break through! And you girls hit the kitchen, keep the coffee-and coming and tend to the first-aid kits!* The boys were playing Che to the hilt, and the girls in the commune were slighted. *Piss off, we ain't playing Florence Nightingale while you make with the Winter Palace heroics!*

And that's how Women's Lib was born. And from that start the

Women's Liberation: Another Viewpoint

movement has spreadeagled all over the place. With sharp talons at the ready. The ideology of the Red Stockings Brigade and sister brigades have a book on males that makes Bernard Shaw's *The Intelligent Woman's Guide to Socialism* a set of revolutionary fables in a playpen for children. They are kicking us in the gut. Or more accurately plowing knee into genital with the ferocity of an Amazon guerrilla attack, all on the premise that male sexuality is a form of imperialism in the bedroom.

And if that sounds overstated, from a male view—gelding the lily, sort of—just look at the Lib text of a Miss Robin Morgan, whose talent for the piss-off polemic is so large as to qualify her for Minister, pardon, *Ministress*, of Propaganda of the lady revolutionaries. Robin Morgan says: ". . . So they'll [males] have to make up their minds as to whether they will be divested of just cock privileges or—what the hell, why not say it, *say* it—divested of cocks." She wants to rip off cocks, but she doesn't have the balls to admit that one phase of Lib is snatch hankering for snatch. (Jill Johnston in the *Voice* puts it, ". . . encouragement of latent homosexual needs is the pivot upon which their liberation as woman would turn.") And to state my male view so crassly only means that Lib's penchant for escalated attack using a lingo right out of some sex-sadist-fantasy handbook engenders (gender being *all* to the simplistic Lib mind) a response in kind.

From bedroom the malaise—as women's Lib sees it—spreads out to the social, political and cultural fronts. Male supremacy is pretty near hydra-headed. It pops up in so little an act as the man hailing a cab or the larger act of Jane taking care of the wash while Jack is futzing around with a blown TV tube. Jack is no doubt thinking—why not say it, *say* it—of Jane's fallopian tube as well, which Jack would no doubt like to futz around with soon as Jane gets back from the wash. And that's really small potatoes. It's the politics of Lib that gives off the real smoke of feminist rebellion. The girls in the revolutionary band want equal but separate rights. To seize and run a newspaper, say, and then to bring forth a style of journalism that's as screechy-boring as the one it supplanted. One example was the seized newspaper called *Rat*. Playing the role of ad hoc editor, the same Miss Morgan stomped all over the copy of Paul Krassner, even though Paul seemed to be doing some heavy Mea Culpas, re the charge of male chauvinism in *Realist*'s flying nun and other such insults. The interdiction of editor Morgan's spaghetti-like tracks of comment, right onto the margins of Krassner's essay, was as sleazy a case of Stalinoid journalism as you're going to find. Underground or above ground.

Another phase of Lib is its rampant revisionism, or Tuesday morning quarterbacking. They are on the trail of no less a group than the Fugs for what the latter has done to the image of Hilda Highschool in the Fugs's number of a few years back called "Saran Wrap (or after the prom)" and other retroactive heresies like "Slum Goddess." Forget that Sanders & Company has freaked-out and radicalized more kids from the crinoline country of the middle-class mind than a shelf full of SDS tracts! The ideology of Lib dictates that any day now they'll be holding a public burning of Fugs records so that the male-supremacist image of Hilda being erotically smelly under the armpits and below will be wiped clean from good Lib consciousness.

Lib stresses the new stridency and separatism of radical woman, from the Weatherwomen to the female Palestinian Commandos. They want to put the powder puff inside the revolutionary clout, and while they're at it they might want to explain if the fedayeen lady guerrillas are ready to overcome not just the Israeli lady sabra but a thousand years of Arab male dominance by taking off the veil. Fat chance with bossman Arafat calling the tune! Fact is if Women's Lib were reading its Marx, Lenin and Sylvia Pankhurst straight, and not through granny shades, it would see that the slouching beast of male chauvinism is a posture right out of the bourgeois menagerie, and of course, right out of the dominant class structure. And conversely, if you take class rule out of the society, you might have a prayer of evicting the slouching beast from the bedroom. And there is this gem of Lib euphoria, from Lucy Komisar (komisar?) in the *Saturday Review:* "If the 1960's belonged to the blacks, the next ten years are ours." *Belonged*, yet!

So right on, the revolution has no gender.

The muggeries

SCENARIO FOR A BADASS NIGHT Main Character is middle-aged, hair on wild side and graying. He's an obsessive walker of city streets, daytime or nighttime, with hardly any concession to foul weather. Gets his "lifts," his amateur athletics, in mile-long jaunts

Scenario For A Badass Night

around town, most always solitary. Coming home late at night (two-ish), swinging buff-colored plastic book bag, mags and stuff inside. Turns into his street, turns west on Broadway, in the Seventies. Nobody out—you could shoot off a cannon. Bitter cold night (below 10), congenial to neither man nor beast, but a showcase for creamy bluewhite moon, doing a rounded slow dance on black sky.

Earlier (about one) Main had pint or two with a friend, at East Village's Phebe's. Friend, who's just up the street from Phebe's, had asked: *How come you're out—badass cold out there and no police.* (Cops were on a "job action.") Explaining, middleaged had put it, he's a man who trots with the clock, from one part of town to another, running the hours down, finally wending back to Westside pad at hour when most of city is lapped in sleep. (Yes, his "lifts.") Besides, said Main Character, how nice the streets don't seem to need the truant cops. Knocks on bar softly (jinx is a jinx is a jinx).

Main Character recalled that—before the two had hit him—he was vibing with the puffball, which lay high over the Hudson River shore. He was tracking its luminous smoky aura, as he walked briskly (make that "half"-briskly) ahead, with less than a hundred feet to go to his entrance. When they hit, they hit him instantly. And like the lurch of cats, silently. Big Blackie, huskier of the two, hammerlocked him from behind, and spun him toward a parked car. *Mother, your money!* He forced Main Character up against the car, while his partner, Medium Blackie, laid a hundred hands all over Main. *Your money, and no shit!*, the shorter man hissed. Not hurt, but shook-up a bit, hero repeated: *It's in my pants pocket.*

For a fleeting moment, and no more, Main Character had the flash: *How do you squeeze out of this!* But hammerlock was strong, and Main found himself going into a mini collapse, a kind of untensing of body, making him into a bundle of nonresistance. Made it easier, under the heavy worn Brooks coat Main wore, for Big Blackie to fish up the swag. Two pairs of glasses, small leather key set, dog-eared wallet, all of which Big inspected, and then replaced. Medium Blackie, meantime, had the dough.. Small roll—fiver and some singles. Main Character, a moment before the money surfaced, heard himself saying: *Dig it, I'm a poor man.* He said it twice, and he thought later, that *had* to sound like a cop-out, even if a true audit of his bank account.

Cold icy silence, all along that street. Out of the blue, a bottle is thrown from an upper-story window. Hits a snow bank, a soft thudding smack, and the muggers go into a freeze. Big Blackie stares on high. Nobody there but he hesitates. And then Main Character meets his gaze, as both lock in on one another's eyes. Hero feels a momentary easing, almost a rush of sympatico, as he senses an "equalizer" pull. As if hero's desperation in that instant meshes with the desperation of the two. It passes, and Medium Blackie, palming the dough with one hand, jerks Main's arms outward with the other hand. He feels for wrist watch, for rings on Main's fingers. None there. Medium then steps back calmly and counts the money. He sorts one bill on top another neatly, like an Automat man straightening out his pile.

The denouement is speeded up, like a movie suddenly doing quicktime. Big growls to Medium: *Let's move out*. Hero (hardly knowing why) yells: *I need carfare for tomorrow*. With half a smile, half a snarl, bagman comes up with a quarter, hands it to Main. (Nickel short, Main lets it ride.) Both go winging toward West End, they are swallowed up in the dark. Panic for Main Character: he cries out *my fucking keys*. He strides after them. *My fucking keys* he groans on the night air. Retraces his steps back to the car, kicks the ground as he looks for keys. FINDS THEM. Small leather clump on snow bank. He draws in a big breath of icy air. Cool flow, like a resuscitation! Gathers up his plastic bag, and his dumb *Times* newspaper, which he forgot he had. Beats it fast for his apartment.

Main Character stands motionless, once on the safe side (ha!) of his bolted cubicle pad door. Stands for what seems like an hour. Does he or doesn't he call the fuzz (for all the good that'd do)? He calls and lips it to them: *You don't have prowl-car or prayer out there, and it's all useless anyway, but I want to report a mugging*. Man in Blue: *Sir, your department's doing its best, in these rough times*. A'hemmm. Main gets into bed, nursing bruise on his lower spine, and bruise on his upper ego. And contusions on his brotherly love.

1972

Demolition job

WHERE HAVE ALL THE HOUSES GONE? This is no hymn of praise to urban living. Yet my side of town, the 70s from Broadway to Riverside, has a thing or two going for it.

Narrow it down to my street, 75th bordering West End and Riverside, and I believe we come upon a unique vein. A street dense in turn-of-century houses, a dozen or more of those solid vintage manses with clinging vine, long since turned into apartments at manageable rents, which give the street its special flavor of casual if faded elegance. The "feel" carries over even to the problem of muggings, 1970s analogue of meeting up with highway leper of medieval times, for something there is about a spruced street that blunts the rawhide stance of mugger. All by way of introduction to a worm in the apple: Bulldozers and wreckers are here!

They've been doing their thing for several weeks, tearing apart a superfine 1890s residence, whose first and long-ago owner was a tobacco millionaire. One rounded wing and peaked mansard roof to go and the wreckers will have leveled to an open hole another example of chateau space that can't be duplicated for money.

The skills that built West Side's baroque showplace Ansonia, or the ruggedly handsome Dakotas two blocks east, are vanished beyond recall. Now we have new skills by a real estate fraternity, who bulldoze what little craft architecture remains to make way for their pyramidal phase. Down go houses we pleasure in, up go poured concrete boxes, those fortresses of nuclear living that more and more assail our skyline.

I live across the way from the doomed graystone. I have gone off each morning and returned each night for some fifteen years, always with that welcome view of form-elegance to greet my eye. As the house has been toppling rip by rip, I've taken notice of the high curving windows, all gracefully embossed in laurel-wreath patterns, the sheer roominess of each apartment, the carved Greek Revival columns that gave entrance to the two wings of the building. But to wreckers and contractors no detail is worth a second look. They have been hacking away as if the chateau itself had a kind of stubborn will to survive. Yet stubborn as its sinew and bone has been to sledgehammer blows the battle of course is foredoomed.

Like so many kings of their hill, the men are more than competent in the arts of cannibalism cum salvage. Sorting out miles of twisted wire, piling up tons of bruised brick for hauling away, loading on open trucks hundreds of thick wooden floor beams, stacking yards on yards of lead pipe and shiny brass, sorting it all out with the diligence of magpies in a brush. The name of the wrecking game is salvage, and with the cry for recyling, maybe a case can be made for bulldozing the old, so that space can be hacked out for the new. Calibrating for progress, real-estaters call it. And yet watching that good house go, cornice by molded cornice, graystone by heavy graystone, window by embossed window, room by graceful room, day by day, makes you wonder about language gaps. Our paragon of progress, behind the stance of ripping efficiency, looms as a new-old breed of Luddite in our midst, or disposer of the good.

The demolition was easy-going at first, with an infiltration of twenty or more hardhatted sappers, half of whom began to pick away big slabs of brick and plaster with long iron pokes, from fifth-floor roof and down. Later came two loudly chugging Caterpillars, which took huge bites out of the building's hide, like sharks going after dead tuna.

From my fourth-floor digs across the way, I was awakened each morning by the Cats' huffing groans. Now if the West End grid is a bowling alley for jets, and if I at times feel like a pin going down in their wake, the sound of jets is as stereophonic music next to a Cat's, at that early hour. Fact is my jets are a welcome counterpoint, since the wrecking crew showed up.

One day I was bounced out of bed, at a dreamfoggy 6:30 in the morning. Though I've tried cotton wadding for ear-stops, and hitting the hay at midnight, which is early for me by about two hours, I was thrown way off my time-synch.

Where Have All The Houses Gone?   49

I checked the clock (6:30) and then dialed 911. I yelled into the phone: "They're thieving away the house. And will you look at the hour!" The police informed me (too calmly, I felt) that seven A.M. was legal. So I had the wreckers by at least thirty minutes. I've made no effort to stop progress, not even illegal progress, since that first try.

Now the real *big one* is due, the earth-chewing mastodon. I'll be hearing those spiked teeth and iron tracks, badmouthing the air from hell to breakfast. Soon after I'll be bouncing off my narrow walls, as dynamite goes off in the bowels of the Manhattan rock. Split the block in a hurry? I go out on my small extension roof, eye the canopy of new-blooming ailanthus in the back yards. Splurge of 10,000 oblong leaves with that peculiar, gummy soak running in them. The lift of this seasonal bonus is not to be denied. And where the hell do you move to, anyway! So you take it all in with a little froth, if you can get some. As in two recent scenes, staged right out on the near flattened turf.

Scene One. Wreckers lay out a pathway of green sod, or instant grass; they throw up a tepee of yellow-tinted, see-through plastic; they mortice together some bricks and a plaque, for a cornerstone mockup. Street is closed by police, for groundbreaker ceremony. Rainy morning and mayor doesn't show (and see how that tepee sags, grass turns to muck). Some forty or fifty "community leaders" do show, they listen to short pep talks given by "leaders" of the community leaders. Flowery praise all around, for "philanthropist and industrialist Sam Korns." Ceremony ends with reading of plaque: "Our Very Own Faith Day School dedicated to the foresight and perseverance of SAM KORNS philanthropist and industrialist by a grateful community. 1971 5781." (Names are fictional.) Instant immortality, even before they've carted away the whole house!

Scene two. A bright Sunday afternoon, four or five days later. About a dozen young actors—a sort of city gypsy troupe—improvise mini mimes and playful games. Two others with 8mm movie cameras catch footage from close-up and distance, as "actions" proceed. Six of troupe are sitting in a musical-chairs row, chairs awkwardly planted in among the rubble. They are costumed in flowing black shrouds, and huge headpieces in the shape of lemons, headpieces moving in a weird astrally unison, as if on the wind. One tall gangly actor, apparently the "lead," who's dressed in Columbine clown's outfit, spins in and out of lemon-headed sitters, or he darts up daringly to top of rubble pile, back and forth he goes, a kind of banshee howl coming from his ruby-painted clown's mouth. One time he drags himself and chair to the highest mound, plants himself on chair and puffs away on a big cigar. He sits on top of beaten shards of that mansion on 75th and lets out his banshee howls, all in a kind of mocking appraisal of the destruction "he's" brought down on us.

Touch of Felliniesque froth, cropping up from a ruin.

Second city lit

"LITERARY TIMES" DOES A LAZARUS DEAR JAY NASH: So the *Literary Times* does a Lazarus, rising out of not-so-pristine Chicago River, typewriters blasting as of old, as befits what used to be known as "Second City" journalism genius! And you know, it's not too soon, because those 2d-city boasts are now being heard elsewhere, for one from (I'm sure you've heard) the city that sits on the Fault, the town of seven hills and the book shop called City Lights, San Fran and its announced 450 writers, poets and other litry swatters: More writing-editing talent than "we have garbage collectors," as one Frisco cynic puts it. It's way past the time when Chi should have come up with new evidence of 2d-city, because as you know too, windcity's been going the route (writing-wise) of the one-shop town for too long: Hef and his manse & his dunking pool, his *Playboy* writer convocations; or lit so-called on the pearly halfshell, and oh those pinkeyed shrimps, the good prime beef on table. And what ever happened to good honest fare like bread-on-table, knife-carved apple & pear and jug of vino, and you stay home and do *da writing*, crapola on those Hef *con*vocations, never proved a thing 'cept that writers respond to the money gong, with the best & worst of em. So let's see if *Literary Times* restores some balance, picks up on some outrage, livens its pages with the newly discovered writing clout, and gets it back to where it was, the Fitz & Hem (and dozens more) lightning freshness of yore. Can't be that all your Chi (and midAmerica) writing talents are hotbreathing it to shake windcity for the cracked gems of funcity (some fun!), or for the sudden allure-shmoor of west coast (weskit) writer nirvana. You stay home and do *da humwork*, do the hot flashes of poetry-prose-&-whatever, and you showcase it in the *Literary Times* scratch sheet. We all getting a little

"Literary Times" Does A Lazarus

tired of the glazed Hefmag, the polite Hefpuff of non-brushedout crotch shots (daring, wow!), the whole fantasy sell of Lit-&-Living sprung from the brow, and the bellybutton, of the pasha of the prairie. Thar' he blows from O'Hare, winging his private 707 to some new remoteness of turf, and coming up with one more lollygogging hutchery! and hey Hef, next one's got to be the Bangladesh city of Dacca, what a gas when you bring the green to that dark, etiolated (yeah!) & hurtin' town! And hey Hef, if you take some time with the Mao & Lenin texts, after Dacca comes Peking & Moscow! What a wipe-out for OUR WAY OF BUFFIN' THE NATIVES.

You see what I mean, Jay. The Chi image has become a *Playboy* "only wheel in town." Now with your buffcolored 16-pager off the press, maybe we're gonna see a few surprises, as indicated by Ray Puechner's dandy little satire, which pulverizes Charlie (the Don) Reich's consciousness greening game to a turn. (Old Charlie's dice throw, after the Peek has done with him, comes up a lowly snake eyes. And the color's not so much green, as a livid vomit.) And as indicated by Curt Johnson's "worm's eye" poke into the litry mag grocery list. There are of course some misfires, in this first issue of the reincarnated *Literary Times*. For one you're gonna have to put more muscle into your "New York Publishing: Bombs & Bombshells" column feature. As it reads the first installment comes up more like "Creams & Creampuffs." As for 5 Beekman, I'm still on the roving beat, clocking the curbstones for material, and looking over my shoulder at the shadow I've just passed, in some dark alleyway hard by Gem's Spa terrain. And lacing a lotta stuff together, for my 2nd Apocalypse book, which agent Mary Yost is high on, but she warns: "It will be a tough sale. They (publishing houses) want pornography, nowadays." And I say to her, "I see what you mean; they want *high grade* porn." And she informs me: "High, middle or low pornography. It doesn't have to be Government Inspected." So again Jay, thanks for laying the reborn LT on me, and let's do an exchange, starting with the enclosed set of TN's. And to end it with Hem: Shit-detecting can be a lonely pastime, but when the detecting is good, the game takes on essence of hayacinth.

all the best,
SIDNEY BERNARD
February 21, 1972

Handel and superstar

"SLEEPER" MESSIAH   It had to be the sleeper of the year, a vivid mixture of "participatory" dance and record playback of Handel's *Messiah*, Christmas Eve at the Washington Square Methodist Church. The offbeat environment all during the long evening, with its very dense (at times even hallucinatory) melding of moods, was its own not small reward. First there was the sonorous, marvelously agitated rounds of what is probably the most dramatic score in all Western music. Rounds of near gossamer serenity one minute, explosive outbursts as the Passion winds to miraculous end, the next. Drape those long, continuing flashes of voice and orchestral rapture with the cloak of a sort of black mass, and what rose from the misty near-dark of the church was a duality of winter solstice, weaving in and out of the carapace of those holy rounds.

Washington Square Methodist is a "poor" church, stripped down to the barest of accouterments. Small gilded organ and choir loft, narrow and wraparound balcony, mini altar and modest-sized carved wooden cross, six arched stained-glass windows of less than grand design. Likely it was just such a hall in Dublin (Music Hall, Fishamble Street) that offered the first performance of *Messiah*, a benefit for a poorman's hospital (and for the Society of Prisoners) back in the 1740s. Washington Square Methodist is also "home" for activists and peace dropouts, the basement offices and basement meeting room being occupied and busy pretty nearly around-the-clock with some form of protest or art-theater-film showing. (*Battle of Algiers* is an odds-on favorite.) Washington Square Methodist is also a church with no steady parish in the usual sense, most of the older and more conservative-leaning parishioners having drifted away in proportion as the church has become a sanctuary (and 24-hour witness) for dissenters. Including, no surprise, more than a few dissenter AWOLs in uniform who wanted out on duty in Vietnam.

I got to the church about a half-hour before midnight, and people were already settling in, athough there was no sign of activity as yet. Except for a beam of white coming from a weak spotlight near stage right, a tiny aurora of orange rising from two lit candelabra on the altar, and more orange flickers coming from the altar's small cluster of glassine candles, the church's open seatless space and newly polished floor were locked in a thick hazy darkness. The holes of light at the altar, besides putting the jagged wooden cross in a bold relief, also lit up a medium-sized mosaic of two brilliantly painted butterflies on black-lacquered ground. Early-comers found seats on two long cushioned benches to the sides, treading to their places softly and a bit cautiously, almost as if they were swimming around in a dark pool. Soon the benches were all filled, and each new arrivee, not sure how the evening was going to shape up, stood around and simply watched for a clue, until several young couples among the standees began to ease themselves to the floor. After that a pattern of "seating" was established. As more people arrived, they would thread their way forward, then sprawl down on the floor, and soon you had "terrace" on terrace of prone bodies, reaching about half-way down to the altar, all sitting or lying in a meditative quiet, for the most part, one person hard to distinguish from another in the heavy dimness. No one paid much attention, at least for the first hour or so, to two rear tables that had been set for a simple holiday repast, including nuts and cheeses and bottles of wine.

A little before midnight Reverend George Hill—a tall bulky man in non-clerical blue suit—came to the altar and made a brief announcement of welcome. He said at one point, "This is an open church and all kinds of people wander in—so please keep an eye on your belongings." Said neither in sorrow or anger, but more like a tone of resignation, which brought a few mild chuckles from several of the sitters. He then read brief passages from St. Matthew Passion, taking each in a cadence that allowed for moments of silence in between. All the while the candles shone steady in the gloom, the Reverend's bulky contour meantime being thrown up on the organ loft in slow-moving shadow. After a further brief interval, of solo singing with organ accompaniment, Reverend Hill and the two performers disappeared through a side door.

The altar and "stage" area, to a depth of about twenty feet, was once again clear of people, but more room was needed for the main event, the dance-Messiah mixed media, so one of the dancers came forward, and asked the crowd to shift a bit. At his direction, they moved their bodies closer together, like an accordian pushing slowly inward, and space was made for the group of dancers waiting in the wing. At that point I found a spot near the middle of the floor, after standing around just inside the big church doors, earlier. Earlier, too, I had recognized a rather famous Broadway—New York City Ballet choreographer, a slim balding man wearing jeans and tennis sneakers, and guessing (wrongly, as it turned out) that he might be participating, I had asked him for a hint on what to expect. He gave me a thin smile, which I read as, "I wish I knew . . ." He then said, "We'll see what pans out." Flopping down to the floor now, I found myself rubbing shoulders, at my right side, with a moody-looking young man in leather dress, who was arching his body in a downward bend, and thrusting his knees outward in a sitting V, all told a fairly vivid if snug picture of the lotus position. He, along with pretty near the entire audience, was vised together in a wheel of seated and lying bodies. Except for a murmuring of whispers here and there, the near-darkened church was layered in an expectant silence.

At the first sounds of the Overture, those rapt velvety sounds of massed strings and bass, call them undulations of the Baroque writ large, the wheel of bodies pulls even tighter. From a small room at stage right, a processional of dancers make their entrance. The lead is a dark-haired boy (age about fifteen), bare chest painted in silver streaks, youthful face rather solemn as he walks past the spotlight, he's pushing a wheelchair in which is seated a motionless figure. The people up front gasp, as boy and chair move slowly by. Is the figure *live*? Is it an *effigy*? Draped in yards of black cloth, hair and face dappled in chalky gray-blue color, gloved hands wound firmly around a glassine candle at her lap, the figure, at that first instant, and throughout the more than two hour event, imposes itself as a kind of feverish vision, a moving (both in locomotion and "spirit") life-in-death caricature. The processional is completed by three torch bearers, two men in dark cloaks swinging censers, as they go, and a half-dozen more dancers in black tights bringing up the rear. The smoke and flame of the torches, the sweet cloying incense smoke from the censers, swirl up in gray ribbons to the church's peaked roof, a fiery and smoky touch in a bacchanal of black mass lapped with holy rite.

As dancers channel through the seated audience, the pace is just short of funereal at first. Soon little patterns of mime are offered, a kind of seesawing of choreographic burst of energy one minute, and slower figuration of near ethereal step the next, the group taking its cues from the swiftly changing moods of *Messiah*. First the measured solo voice of "Comfort ye my people"; next the rapid rise-fall of "Every valley shall be exalted"; later the joyful release of "He is the King of glory." When the "Glory" passage is repeated, over and over in celebration, the meld of chorus and orchestra densely rich and incantatory, many in the audience get to their feet and unlimber their bodies. They soon join hands in a big circle, weave through the dark hall in a jump step. A roar

"Sleeper" 55

of thudding feet rises from the floor. Dancing shadows are thrown up on bleak walls. As the tape spins on with "God gave the word," pretty near the whole room goes "participatory." So many blithe dervishes, rollicking and clapping to "word's" lusty beat.

While all this is going on, the first group of dancers, those who had come out of the side door, stay close together as a unit, and act out their own tableaus of fast changing mood, the effect being a "looping" of minor and major improvisation, or smaller happening swallowed up in larger audience happening. Only the wheelchair motif stays constant, boy in silver streaks doing "court" before the effigy, lady in black glued to her chair, her eyes heavy-lidded and spooky in the candlelight, as boy leaves off dancing and wheels her around slowly (almost in regal step). As tension builds to the high peak of Part One, there's a long moment of surface calm, a winding down of pretty near all dancing, as if for a recharging of energy. The hall is just about stock still, the crowd seems to gulp breath as one.

It changes on the first joyous outburst, the ecstatic four-note *Hal/le/lu/jah* for full-chorus and orchestra, succeeded by those endless and richly varied repeats. And a breakout of driving bodies! They whirl through the dark hall in a spirited free-form, break the calm with staccato handclapping, join in their own round of Hallelujahs. (All so marvelously singerly, one has need to shout it out.) At the same moment, boy and wheelchair come to a stop, just about at the eye of the crowd, where he offers his own mime of celebration. Taking hold of a long thick ribbon, which is tied to an arm of the chair, he reels back from the seated effigy, reels as far as the ribbon will go, and then bounds forward in half-dozen great leaps—the expression that of a penitent, mixed with joy of beatific release. He flies back and forth, in capering homage to our Lady of Death, ribbon an umbilical (?) that joins end and beginning, or regeneration in the guise of black mass. The glassine candle all aglow, burning hard and steady at her lap, burning its warmth through the heavy gloves she's wearing. Later, at the end of the Hallelujah passage, several wander over to the food tables, they pop handfuls of raisins (or Fritos) in dry mouths, or chew on slices of cheese, or down cups of white wine in thirsty gulps.

The audience was nothing if not "Greenwich Village." From longhaired, unsmiling activist and his clan of five or six (they do the Vietcong-flag-at-demos bit, and they appeared to be paying homage to the music, if not to the Nativity itself), to the tall Botticelli-like donna

Anne and her bearded poet escort (she's donna of poetry readings at the other, more easterly "poor" church, St. Mark's in the Bouwerie), to the grayhaired Washington Square wino in out of the cold (he kept looking for the exit, couldn't make it for the tangle of bodies so he settled for a couple of quick belts at the back tables), to the several hundred others. Participatory to the full, sans self-consciousness. I myself—Villager by way of roving visitation—felt it all the way. At around two-thirty A.M., and just before the start of Part Two, and with fifty or more remaining at the church, I came down the stairs and headed for the west side IRT. It was a fine clear night, star-studded and streaked in blue-white, as on the night the three Magi came joyful to Bethlehem. The echoing music, all the good tidings, are still in my ears. And suddenly my memory comes alive. And I recall a different roar. Of North Atlantic gale, laced with strains of *Messiah*, the oratorio coming in over the troop transport speakers, from the London wireless, on Christmas Day of 1942 or 43. I'm far aft on the main deck, where you get the full bellyroll, and the low growl of the ship's prop, as prop hits (then misses) the long swells. The Handel now wafting in loudly, now fading out over the watery expanse. Another transport GI is with me, and he sours back at the gale: "Helps pass the bumpy time of day."

It was my first hearing of *Messiah*. At least my first bumpy hearing.

Town Hall and Felt Forum

VOZNESENSKY/YEVTUSHENKO Andrei Voznesensky on stage is a shorter Russian Barrymore of the muse—poised at the Town Hall mike, right hand extended roundly like a suction cup, as if to scoop up to his spare body an audience wrapped (and rapt) in moody silence. He sings the hard-soft Slavic syllables in theatrical style that allows for no response short of implosion of warmth-empathy. He can do spine-tingler changes up and down the register of moods, too. But the fuss and feathers of an unending showiness is in his muse, along with the winning of his quick talent.

Are the words and imagery lost in the showiness? Do we need the high decibel count, along with the loftiness of line? In "Moscow Bells" perhaps yes, in some other poems it skirts, on the ear's slippage, the *hup toop thrup forp* of the corporal guidon on overnight camp march.

The readers and translators are William Jay Smith (made possible by the New York State Council of the Arts), who looks and reads like uncorked champagne that's lost its fizz; W. H. Auden, a gramps of poetry whose sureness of craft and modulated playfulness with a line (like cat stroking ball of wool) are the vintage other side of Andrei's rumpus-room precocity; and Barry Boys, an actor in a frilly white shirt, who has the aura of a Byron without bite and over-pretties a line to the point of flutterings in a dovecote.

Later, backstage, it's touch-eminent-poet time. Voznesensky in his Carnaby-type cardigan, shiny blue garment zipped just down to the waist, fine white wool turtleneck showing not a crease, modified blue bellbottoms falling neatly to top of patent shoes. (Gone the embroidered peasant shirt and the tough leather boots of the Essenin-Mayakovsky days!) Midst the homaging crowd, the poet's sea-smooth eyes are inward-looking, cherub's face titled a little upward, a study of famous persona taking in the crowd's licks of adulation evenly.

When the saucy girls from campus, several of them clutching paper copies of "Anti-worlds" to bosoms, run the poet down with requests for autographs, he complies with a sunburst (and very near private) smile for each. Other greeters are translator George Reavey; *Up the Down Staircase* author Bel Kaufman; American-Russian poetry umpire Stanley Kunitz. Famous East Side, world-traveler, poet-colleague arrives, with a splash of followers in his wake. Looks tired and wan as an overcast winter sky, long trailing orange-white muffler lending a touch of *brio* to his entrance. As if on signal, they and Voznesensky run the back-stage crowd a chase away from Town Hall, to private rendezvous at a "bistro on West Forty-fifth."

The chase is more solemn than merry, past this knot of well-wishers, that slow moving line of traffic. And Andrei's "Hunting the Hare," read earlier from stage, is evoked once again. (Or "Hunting the Midtown Action.") The fuss and feathers of notoriety. And could East side poet read his own poems from the Bolshoi stage? Or even the smaller Town Hallish Mally? Now or on some tomorrow?

YEVTUSHENKO AT FELT FORUM As for Yevgeny Yevtushenko, call him a Russian Hamlet of the muse. He hit town and built up a head of performing charisma rarely matched in these parts. Ending in a double set of readings—two near S.R.O.'s of more than 5,000 each—at a sports-rock palace called Felt Forum. Very well named that "Felt," on that occasion anyway.

Picture a tall, spare-limbed Yevtushenko, tensely walking the three or four levels of the stage, he the very center and spoke-wheel of all energy, the readings by himself, and by a "few of my friends," all connected by the tissue of his passions. Running now to hot flashes of anger over crimes of state, now to soft warming lines of life and nature, or on international good will. Picture him thus as he stalks the boards, in tight gray turtleneck, and silky green trousers, and you see a Hamlet of the muse in living color.

His friends paid intimate court through the long double set, hour after hour of (mostly) Yevtushenko-Hamlet's explosive moods. First a good attentive Horatio (actor Barry Boys), alter ego of Hamlet's wide-ranging jousts; and an Ophelia (actress Viveca Lindfors), reading a poem called "Monologue of a Broadway Actress," on the need for role-playing in life, doing it with all the panache of a "mad" scene; also, a very Fortinbras of a Senator Eugene McCarthy, reading two poems (one of his own, one by a Vietnamese) on the war, voice and bearing giving an image of new beginnings; and a Claudius in the guise of U.S. doing wrong (in Vietnam), partnered by a Gertrude in the guise of Mother Russia, adulterating the best hopes of the revolution, by her neglect (and worse) of such as Mayakovsky and Essenin. And by extension, by her ill treatment of poets and intellectuals today.

So much for parallels. As for the performance, it was dizzying in its up and down waverings. Whether doing his own Russian lines, or doubling with Boys in a sort of down-home English, or backstopping the Bijou Singers, who had put some of his verse to music, Yevtushenko, poet in motion, was at times a moody bundle of action *in extremis*, so that lines of even some of his best poems became blurred. Drawn inevitably to the "theatrics" of his reading, one nevertheless had a sense of a "washing" away of some of those peaks.

At times, a big head of steam was built up, only to vaporize to the very roof (as it were), as in the offering of such a line as: "America, your stars are bullet holes." (Or maybe it went: "The stars in your flag are bullet holes.") Not that the line was *all* that bad, but rather that when sung in chorus by the Bijous, it had nowhere to go but to vapor.

Other and perhaps lesser distractions: Boys, decked out in Pierre Cardinish (or Bill Blassish) finery, elegant shirt made of yards of posh black silk, tight black pants that wouldn't be amiss at the ballet. Matched by Richard Wilbur and James Dickey, both resplendent in a similar (though less ballety) Cardin style, to a point where one wondered where poet left off and fashion-plate began. And the crowd cheering Senator McCarthy as if at a convention—a sort of hankering on their part for that "*pop* hero" role of so many *déjà vu's* ago. And the Senator perhaps not too sure of his own image of himself: "Politicians say I'm too much the poet, poets say I'm too much the politician." And bringing it back to Yevtushenko, who's even more of a road-show than Voznesensky. Mounted near Barnum & Bailey aura of TV, upper East Side parties, New School dinners-testimonials, slick-mag interviews. Some of it good and tempting—no doubt. But at a price of the fuss and feathers of notoriety.

Pablo Picasso

MIRACLE ON 53d STREET, THRU EYEDROPS Maybe it was an optical miracle. One moment I'm walking around with blurred vision, due to drops administered a couple of hours earlier in an eye examination. The next moment the blur disappears, and my eyes feast hungrily on those walls of paintings. Picasso's paintings at the Museum of Modern Art, and that might have been the difference. Anyway, the incident made my day, and I'd like to retrace how it happened.

But first a word about my eyes. From way back to about age five they've been a source of worry that one tries to ignore, such as the more or less common worry that one might be walking around with cancer (or call it smokingman's gray shroud). My worry is over blindness, more specifically blindness in my left eye, which was near-shattered back in the dumb innocence of that age five, during a romp in a Bronx junkyard. A group of us Washington Avenue kids were horsing around, climbing up and down the hulks of dead autos, or bouncing missiles off the sides of other dead objects. "Bet I can break that windshield . . ." In a flash my left eye becomes a target, accidental but real enough, as one of the kids explodes a Coke bottle against the rump of an auto. It seems 100 years since that jetted splinter of glass bloodied my eye—years of near losing it at first, painful treatments over a long period later, into the Army as a non-combatant later still (where I made "marksman" on the Fort McClellan rifle range with my good eye), and gradual loss plus fear of total blackout in the left to this day.

Now I'm at the office of a Park Avenue eye surgeon for a long-delayed check-up. He puts me through all the hoops, spying deep past the retina of each eye for any telltale signs, using the pencil-thin instrument whose beam of light can probably go through stone. Later he floods my eyeballs with those chemical drops, and after a twenty-minute wait in his outer office, he has me back in the chair for a pressure test. (He's looking for glaucoma, I guess.) On completion of all the tests, he offers me a consolation prize. "No cause for immediate worry," he says in a kind of even-toned neutrality. "You're in your fifties and a certain amount of loss is to be expected." (Only a day or two later, when I get the bill for $35, I mutter to myself a belated "Thanks a lot.") And despite the nurse's cheery "See you in a year," I do feel more than a small relief. Even though I navigate out of the office like a tugboat in fog.

Out on the street—one P.M. on a sunny pre-spring day—the gauzy liquid curtain drops plays tricks. My vision is sort of wavy overall—cars and people float by the wide Park Avenue lanes as in a Coney Island distortion mirror. Other times the effect is pointillist—as when I pick out details like the hedges along the island and they come up in bunches of green dots. I walk south along Park and then west toward Madison—a little aimlessly and with a kind of cushiony bounce that makes the hard cement walks seem almost rubbery. Soon I'm at the corner of Fifth and 57th—hugging the Tiffany window and catching the glints of the jewelry as if at an aurora borealis. (Oddly, the jewelry no longer looks Tiffany, but more in the style of Woolworth tacky.) I stay at that spot a minute or two longer and gaze in a westerly direction—attracted by one of the newer edifice complexes along West 57th. It's a sky-high building with a sort of Noah's Ark barreled base—and through my fogged eyes the building does indeed look like it's rocking in place.

I cross over to Doubleday's windows, gliding past lunchtime crowds entering and leaving the bookshop, all of whom appear and dissolve as if out of a pool of water. Though the drops are weakening, I still can't decipher one book title from another clearly, so I pass the shop by. I then head toward the museum—my usual practice when I'm in the MOMA area daytime—but with no firm notion of going in. (My vision is still jumpy, so why bother.) And yet cubism through a pointillist gauze might be fun. The big window streamer for the Picasso 90th Birthday Show convinces me. I put on my general-sight glasses—good for movies and museums and the like—and idle my way into the main floor galleries. There's a good size weekday gate, including lots of students mingling with vaguely suburban-dressed ladies. Most first take in what looks like a close second to the Picasso show, dozens of Matisse bronzes from small to full-life standing. And what bronzes they are, with or without my full sight! At least I can make out the sheer plasticity of one figure after another, whether standing or lying down, caught in poses of "weightless" gracefulness. My appetite whetted, I move on to the inner galleries, for the Picassos, bumping one or two shoulders in the narrow passageway as I go.

There's a double magic at work, in the richness and plenty of the four or five rooms of Picassos. As I look around the walls, I find I'm able to intuit the shape—the very iconography—of the paintings, *despite* my visual haze. It's as if I see them clear, by virtue of the very "memory" of each piece, a memory that seems wedged somewhere inside my head deep as a brand. (I can no doubt close my eyes altogether and see them too!) But the sensation of clarity goes even a bit further—to a point in fact of the earlier-stated miracle. Standing about ten feet back from the big *Night Fishing at Antibes* oil—suddenly my eyes clear up as if out of a Biblical tale of scales falling from their sockets! And the whole nocturnal panoply—of speared fish, distorted yellow moon, recumbent fisherman in white, two hooded girls in corner, squiggly crablike scrawls in another corner—stands out in full perspective. One moment the scramble brought on by those drops. Next the *un*scrambling of my sight, and I take in *Night Fishing*'s marvelous scramble *as it lays*. The others were clean as a whistle after that.

The second magic is in the crowd. Take the young lady—no older than college junior by her looks—who is busy with pencil and notebook. She's weighing each painting, and taking notes as she goes, as if the Picasso imagery is as immediately translatable as a thermometer reading. Or, to paraphrase Robert Frost, the Picasso ambience was hers, before she even became exposed to it. So too perhaps with most everybody walking through the galleries. For them motif and period—from classic to blue to cubism to the rest—all must have seemed alike in their immediacy. And all could trip the hammer of that "memory." Which brings the thought that Picasso remains—all else added up—the number one shaman cum spook in our 20th century arts closet.

As I say, it made my day.

Vermeer quartet

WHAT ARE THE VIBES OUT THERE? I go to one concert by design—Vermeer Quartet at Washington Irving High School, part of WI's Saturday night series that (at a buck admission) may well be the best buy in town. I take in the second one by accident—a noisy and even menacing rock benefit for the Hell's Angels clans, at the Academy of Music just around the corner from the high school. Leaving at the end of the Vermeer concert, floating on the Franz Schubert which is still humming in my ear, with its deep poignance so redolent of late Mozart, I take little notice at first of the police bus parked a few feet north of Fourteenth Street. When I get to Fourteenth, and turn the corner so I'm facing the Academy, I see the flashing marquee: HELL'S ANGEL BENEFIT   JERRY GARCIA AND GANG   BO DIDDLEY. Up closer I observe that most of the cops remain in the bus, and that four or five are stationed just outside the barriers at the Academy's box-office. The benefit at that hour—about 10:30 P.M.—is apparently well on the way, but there's the usual bunch of shutouts hanging by, twenty or thirty longhair boys and girls who cheerfully—and by turns—hawk for freebies or unused tickets and then hang by some more on the hope that the trio of big security fellers (in producer Howard Stein's employ) might get generous at one point and let them in. The night is cold for March—it's blowing an unusual 20 and below—and I notice a party of three well-dressed, well-squired ladies, all wearing Easter Parade fur pieces, their escorts similarly well-groomed in silk mufflers and fur-collared coats, leaving the stained-glass Luchow's restaurant at that moment, the six then getting into a waiting black limousine, and pushing off into the night with hardly a glance at the Academy of Music doings.

I cross over to the marquee, edging sideways through a long row of bikes parked at the curb, a kind of bigcity hitching post that attracts passersby who give the scene an over-shoulder look. The bikes are mostly heavy road-runner models, full of shine and bristling appendages, about thirty in all, with mini license plates from all over—New York, New Jersey, Connecticut, Florida, Ohio, California, and other states. Ten or twelve of the Angels are standing around in the lobby. They all have that macho-tough stance, all are wearing pretty much the same leather studded jackets, with the embroidered Hell's Angels emblem, along with the city they hail from, splurged on the back of the jackets. One of the Angels comes out of the lobby, looks over to where I'm standing, sort of casual time-of-day look, then approaches me and asks: "Can I help you?" He sports tinted dark amber biker's shades, his manner is cool but not unfriendly. I tell him that I just stopped by, upon seeing the marquee, that I'm curious about the benefit. We chat a while longer, during which I mention that I'm a freelance writer, and that I think the benefit is the kind of offbeat story that I want for my newsletter, and he asks if he can see a copy. I hand him a copy and after he does a quick read of the four-pager his face breaks out into a smile . . . a cracked smile as it were for he has a deep healed-up wound running from the edge of his lip to just short of the top of his eye. He says evenly, "You say an 'offbeat' story but I wonder if what you mean by offbeat is that we—the Hell's Angels—are so very different from other people. Because that's the way some people out there have us pegged: different in a *funny* sort of way." The tone is still this side of friendly, but now there's an added touch of irony, a touch of rhetorical challenge. Well, I say to him, trying not to make it sound a cop-out, I meant offbeat in a story sense, in a journalistic sense. He seems to accept that, and he asks me my name, and he tells me his is "Rex, of the Cincinnati Angels." He adds that he thinks I ought to catch the benefit, and then he leads me past the ticket-taker to whom he nods and says "Okay for the press."

The big barn of an Academy lobby, and the big innards of the house, are not unlike the former rock temple Fillmore East, with more seats (about 3,400 to Fillmore's 2,600), but with pretty much the same parish crowd. Yet with a difference that I spot almost immediately—the longhair shimmying in the aisles, the potting sweet smell of grass in the air, the applauding of eager hands like drumrolls, the loud calls for favorite Grateful Dead songs ("Uncle John's Band"), and the highkiting euphoria of the scene, all had a diminished—and somehow mimetic—energy quotient. It was as if the lost question of the hour were: *Where have all the good vibes gone?* But the kids were out in force, were out there trying. And Jerry the Garcia, chief Dead of the Grateful Dead, was certainly getting to them on target. He plays with the same deadly vibrato, the same soft tingle up the spine at other times, as of yore. He's just about the sole surviving rock trotskyite of the times, the permanent revolution of dazzle and clout put across by him and his cellmates. So that the kids (for all the slippage since the hightime of the yipgeist) could and did take it all in as if the rock rebellion were still riding the blue sky of the nirvana.

And the Angels got to the crowd through some golden filter that displayed the bikers as knights of the same high-riding nirvana—and never mind the hairy rep earned, or bad rapped, as the case may be, at that blood-on-the-moon doozie that was Altamont, near a century ago! Old Rex and the others, lounging around, but not lunging, in the lobby. With a wink from one Angel or another, here and there, to some kid who maybe's thinking he (the kid) wants to make contact; and the Angels at other times, just shooting the breeze, or uncorking the cork, or relaxing in the penned-in aura of an Academy, that's full up wall-to-wall with the mostly white (and "wasted"?) middle class youth; most of them hot down from suburbia, or the uptown campuses, and wanting perhaps a little of the rough-salt ambience of biker; meantime making do with the wash-wave of the Grateful Dead sound, wafting down and round and highup to the topmost balcony, all of it coming off the blue-lighted Academy stage in pulsing, sinuous drafts.

Me, wandering by the lobby, or doubling back to orchestra rear, to catch the endless spasms of rock, the spasms of the longhair kids, who stand six-deep with bodies going in jello-like perpetual motion. I have all my stops open, trying to clock my own response, and it's coming up blurred. (There's no denying the gap, *my* schoolboy music was Bells of Saint Mary, sung in assembly at old High School of Commerce, before Lincoln Center—part of which stands on former Commerce turf—was even a gleam of dollar-signs in the eyes of its big-name planners.) I can't make out the numbers on the dial (*what* is the time out there?) for the blockage of the bad Angel rep. Reports, only recently, of East Third Street Angels laying rough hands on the nabe. Or noising-up the streets at early A.M. hours, rub-a-dub-dub and away we go, the monster bikes flying. Or hammerlocking a stray dude in the moonlight and relieving him of the groceries he's carrying. And the like. (Are only Angels into that?) My stops are open, taking it all in. And thinking on Rex's earlier rap, his "offbeat story" scam. But now Rex and the others are in clover. Toking on a butt, or gargling some ale, or walking the glassine lobby. A scene that has its own straight-arrow purpose. Raising bread for Angel busts that just might not repeat not be fair pool. "We're all minorities out there," Rex had said with a throw of his arm, a wide throw that seemed to take in all the mid-Americas you could name.

I run into Chuck in the lobby, bouncer's bouncer from the Fillmore nights, he's hefting his broad shoulders, his long straight hayseed locks,

What Are The Vibes Out There? 65

he's walking his cocky walk, as if on the wind of a hurricane. The menace of his stance, the ripples of muscular bravado, are cut somewhat by the rinse of his smile—planted almost permanently on his rounded face. A smile that's raucous and growling, at the full tilt, but more often than not, it's just a tickle that appears to be stitched at the corners of his wide mouth. Chuck's modus operandi: He gentles the rock fan down, rather than muss him up, if and when the rocker gets a bit too boosty for public decorum's sake. He tells me, the Hell's Angels or not, there is no real trouble tonight. The boys and girls are grooving, the bikers are together. I interject: "And Bill Graham is miles from the Academy." He picks it up, like an old sore of debate. And he walks the fence, saying, in effect, Bill Graham's got his bag, Howie Stein's got Stein's. He taps me over to a corner, where we can see a good slice of the stage, Jerry Garcia and the Dead are lost in a haze of midnight-blue lights the whole house layered in a kind of ectoplasmic sheen, and the music itself laying on the ear its own ectoplasmic ooze. Chuck loosens a pint from under his leather wraps, domestic Georgia corn whiskey which he calls "Dixie vodka," he twirls the top off and hands me the bottle. One quick belt each, and he stashes the bottle inside the leather folds.

Only a few minutes later, the bottle comes out again, this time in presence of Steve Ben Israel, street actor and Living Theatre wanderer come home after years of circuit-riding around the globe. (From European tour to Brazil to a dozen waystops in between. Le Living churning the street juices, leaving behind blazes of controversy wherever they go. Pols and police on one side of barricades, people and Le Living on the other.) Now Steve sort of hovers by, well-built dancer's body in slow glide across the Academy lobby marble, the look of vague disinterest fooling you, even as the hooded gaze takes it all in. Chuck greets Steve with a wraparound shoulder hold, and thrust of the bottle with his other hand. I round out the hellos, and the three of us swipe a mouthful of the Dixie vodka, one fast gutwasher gulp that sharpens the head and opens the ears wider. And the sounds and flashes let loose in the big-bellied, darkened arena hit with a kinetic frenzy.

Steve says, "First time I'm hearing the Dead live, they're really another thing." He talks about the bikers, wonders about their sudden turn to "status." He clips the word off at the edge (the "us") so that it comes out in a kind of gurgle of irony, mixed with appreciation of the new Hell's Angels image. He tells us that he and Beck-Malina, and several more new and old Living members, are into a commune thing. He says, "We've moved to a house in Brooklyn, we're working up some new formats. For Pittsburgh, Detroit, Ann Arbor, Indianapolis. We'll perform for factory people, ghetto youth, and students. In the streets, outside factory gates, on campus . . ." Once against the zinger of direct action, theater in the crossfire of the streets. But his words come up strange to my ears. I'm hearing it all clear, so maybe it's a case of jumped time synchs. Mine kind of blurred by stoppage of the clock, tapering off of rock-'n protest, from about the time of Cambodia and after. And Steve's running in a continuum of energy, a renewal of the "Anarcho theater genius," as Living's been described in the past.

Yet as I look at Angels and kids locked in a momentary free-wheeler, both groups with antennae out and probing, both making contact through the fog of their different life-styles (one are the shaggy howlers of the open road, the other the wised-up stepchildren of the urban shuck); as I sense this it dawns that Steve's theater-action reality is both possible and translatable, a new creative wave out of the 1970s bleakness. Sometime past midnight, I get ready to leave. I bid Chuck and Steve goodbye, head for the windy outdoors, almost levitating on the Dixie flit, the sounds and spasms, as I go. I see biker Rex in the outer lobby, walk over to him to say thanks. He's into a rap with two of Stein's young ushers, they're arguing the violence and badtripping at Altamont. (Trying to sort it all out, makers and explicators of their own scene, both.) I tell Rex so-long; he says, "All good vibes, man." The river of his wound, up and down his left cheek, disappears in the crease of his smile.

Thus my Saturday night of a split musical happening. Soulful, out-of-it Franz Schubert. Out-of-it boys and girls. Out-of-it Hell's Angels. All tacking to the rhythm of the Dead's rock. But then again, look at what's in.

Barrymore and black Hamlet

NAME OF THE GAME IS "ROOTS" There is a need to define the past. By doing this we affirm that no movement—cultural, political, or whatever—comes to us full-blown out of the blue. And while this is axiomatic, it needs reminding at a time when an "under-over-30s" litmus is used, said line in the spectrum advantaging neither unders or overs. There is a sign of an opening out, or in the lingo of now, a welcome bid for "getting it together." Say that we are "trapped" in history, only to the extent that we ignore or forget its lessons.

I saw a movie the other day, a silent in the New Yorker's revival of Hollywood oldies; bouncy John Barrymore playing, circa Fourteenth Century France, the role of François Villon; and while the film was an antique from the '20s, there was a freshness in any a frame that was little short of revelation. Barrymore, in his wondrous high jinks, in his fool's garb of rags and quail feathers, in his devilish funny baiting of Bourbons (those Agnews in 14th Century finery), was doing no more than our own Villon, our hairy man of the "Steal" book. He was doing Abbie Hoffman in medieval drag.

Or take Isadora Duncan, come alive in Karol Reisz's film biography called *Isadora*. Flawed though it was, the persona of rebel in arts, and of hauntingly free life style, came over with sharp relation to now. No Ti-Grace Atkinson, no Millett or Friedan, not even a Jill Johnston, better evokes the kind of commitment that spells Women's Lib, and this in the 1920s when Lib meant not much more than "give us the vote." As to liberated sex "roles," not even a Germaine Greer could top the passion, and quirky independence, of Duncan's romantic liaisons, first with stage genius Gordon Craig, later with that monied Singer sewing machine tycoon, and later still with the revolutionary poet Essenin. The beauty part for me, bonus of bonuses, was Vanessa Redgrave's portrayal, lank and flame-haired and dancingly awkward, and yet how true a meld of then-now, hence how very alive the feeling of roots.

Or take another example, a mod street *Hamlet* produced by Joe Papp a few seasons back, Hamlet played by a lean young black actor named Cleavon Little. With slight change in text, though stripped down to under two hours, his *Hamlet* nonetheless gave off joyful waves of relevance. Wearing tennis shoes and basketball outfit, Little took care of "business" with such brio as to transform a classic into a roaringly apt masque for now. (Polonius: "What do you read, my Lord?" Hamlet-Little: "Ebony, baby." Prince Hamlet into black hipster, at a spread of 400 years.)

And surely the Beck-Malina Living Theater, during the late fifties and early sixties than which no force was greater in terms of radical and challenging themes. Holding forth at a small upstairs loft on Sixth Avenue, Living was mover and shaker not only in its avant-garde productions, but in the way it opened us out to some gut concerns. From Living's early-on search into the drug experience (*The Connection*), to its pre-Vietnam tackling of the US military mold (*The Brig*), to its highly dramatic European tours (after being chased from Sixth by tax federales), the group practiced a communal style in arts and politics and life, the impact of which I believe had no equal. Put another way, it would be hard to imagine the freeform nudity of *Hair*, the youthful messianism of Woodstock, the orgiastic fury of *Dionysus*, to name but three mindblowers of the sixties, had Living not been on the scene earlier. And, specifically, had *Paradise Now* never surfaced. As to the purgatorial theater of Altamont, how to look at that bummer except in the context of Living's *Frankenstein*, produced some years before the Mick went "bad," hence as good an example of life imitating art as the 1960s brought off? And Living still makes waves, as witness the recent busts in Brazil. Something there is about the arts—as when a connection is made such as Living's with a community of artists, students and poor people—that causes politicians to yell "fair is foul."

Lastly, and for a kind of topping out, in this mini look at roots, I'd like to roam way further back, first to my boyhood when, standing on Bronx streetcorners, I'd listen to strong political appeals, avowing LaFollette progessivism out of the Midwest, in the bonfire twenties. Or later on, during the Depression thirties, when America was a whipped dog scrounging for bones, and I'd be vibing to the anger of those same streets. Or to the heady call of internationalism, heard in the neighborhood as the Lincoln Brigade was being formed. Or responding to the pull of labor's cause during the early New Deal, when the magical militancy of the C.I.O. was in the air. (Today the militancy seems not out of the thirties but out of another century, if not another country.) All of this was *très formidable*, and kicker to my (as yet) unformed sense of justice. And a calling to mind (I suppose) of Wordsworth and others. To wit and to paraphrase: *Life is short, art and revolution long.*

Mining Haiphong

THE WEEK OF 100-PROOF NIXON & KISSINGER The week of 100-proof Nixon & Kissinger, otherwise known as "Mining down the war," began for me on a deceptively blithe note. The Obie theater awards at Village Gate with Groucho Marx doing honors. He came onto the tiny apron stage with help of his flame-haired companion—pretty 30-ish lady who watched his moves with concern of a mother hen over her chicks. His physical moves only—the Groucho repartee was bold as ever and needed no help. From his first "Are you *really* a virgin?" drool to sensationally see-through actress Madeleine Le Roux, who assisted Groucho in handing out awards, the 81-year-young survivor of the Marx Brothers legend was as swift in delivery of barbed one-liners as ever did rain down on the patrician head of the late Margaret Dumont. It was bad dirty fun-&-games for a couple of late-afternoon hours; mixed with a cavil or two over beret-wearing Groucho's "male chauvinism"; laced finally with some tears and warm exchanges between Groucho and the long list of winners. Quick as the two-hour ceremony went, that's how quickly the overflow audience of 500 or more disappeared out of Village Gate's basement and into the night at show's end. To catch Richard Nixon on TV, many of them? Some whispered the word even as the Obies were in progress: Nixon was going to announce "something" from the White House at ten. That left time enough to get home and get comfy by the box—with cans of 6-packs and whatever ashes off the tongue of the President at the ready.

I hadn't forgotten about the speech. It was more a case of having numbed out to yet another round of "Let's make one thing clear." I was alerted to same by David McReynolds, big Dave rolling-walking on the plastic cups of vino he'd consumed, as he came out of the Obie to tell me he was going for a quick one at Phebe's, then home sharp at ten for the "lecture to God" that the President would be giving. I couldn't join him (and Shirley Broughton and one or two more) at the moment but I told him I'd call and maybe come by his place later. Meantime I wandered over to West Eighth to make a couple of calls, and to down a grungy Flame Steak for my parched gullet. Nixon's thing was now in my head, a sort of mental tapping in guise of blue-suited (flag-in-lapel) woodpecker chipping away at our tree of politics, even as I walked the near-deserted Village streets. (No doubt others were getting the taps, were gathering at home boxes to monitor the imperial voice.) Near to ten o'clock and Dave not yet home on my call. Going east toward Dave's place, turning into Washington Square, a lonely beard handing out protest flyers. I take one and ask where I can find a TV and he directs me to NYU's Hayden Hall where he says there's a set going he thinks. I make it to Hayden in a trot. A dingy, velvet-draped cube of a residence room. The darkened room is aglow with the powdered, hair-slicked-back image of the chief of state in living color.

He is talking to us. And maybe even to the High One on private vibe. Rounded fleshy jowls softened a touch by the TV makeup kit to contour of an aging doll. Face a cold abstraction of duty, trying to make contact with a heartbeat out there that eludes him: "... mining of North Vietnam harbors ... aggression must be punished ... we seek an honorable solution ... USSR is a *great* power; US is a *great* power...." The words come click-clacking as from an adding machine; the miss to the heart is just about global-wide. A stunned anger all through the room. Afro student in a riff of disdain: "He's into baptising gooks, even if it kills them." Others talk of demos, off-campus street actions. I leave Hayden Hall and walk over to Dave's place. Washington Square Park is gloomy, unusually quiet. But the woodpecker sound hangs in there. It's in my head, it's high up in the olden tree that shades the Garibaldi statue. In the prowling park a leashed Great Dane fends off a bothersome, waggly Pekingese. The big Dane rears back on its powerful haunches, and the little one goes waggling away.

When I get to Dave's, he has the phone dangling from the cradle. He's been trying to send a telegram and get a call through to the White House by turns. He tries again. Still no dice. "They are jammed up to the ears"—he laughs at his own pun—"an avalanche of calls." He readies some coffee for me, mixes a shot of gin for himself. He tells of the loss of cat Loki and says, "I felt guilty as hell all weekend." The cat is back now, and is in fact purring at my ankles, the smooth Siamese coat feeling like a puffball up against my legs. The phone rings and Dave hops for it. It's Grace Paley, she tells Dave she can't get a telegram off. He says, "We've got to stay with it ... we've got to get some calls in up front ... Nixon has his whole apparatus in motion." They talk briefly about Wednesday's demo, only two days away. It was hatched several days before the mining speech and plans are set for a variety of happenings outside the ITT (International Telephone and Telegraph) at Park Avenue and 50th and 51st Streets. Off the phone Dave tells me they (War Resisters League) look for a minimum of one-thousand demonstrators at ITT and that he personally would settle for that. He sprawls out on the floor bed for a breather, to shake off the tension of clogged phones, the uneasiness (it's still with him) over cat Loki's lost weekend walk. Sometime after midnight he gets through. The White House operator makes an apology, but believe you-her, calls are coming

The Week Of 100-Proof Nixon & Kissinger 71

in by the thousands. Dave says, "Against the President I hope." Indeed no, four to one for. Dave coolly, "I'm sorry to hear that, *indeed I am. And do tell the President, he should be impeached.*" He spells out his name and does likewise with mine as I nod and raise my fingers in a *V* sign. A short time later I say so-long to Dave and head for subway and home.

Next day, Tuesday. I leave my West End pad around noon, go over to my Greek greasy spoon at 80th and Broadway for eggs-coffee-and. Spring day with rosebud promise in the air, a bracer that wilts the moment I see the black bold headlines at corner newsstand. Screaming interdiction, or game plan of pop goes the mines. At the Texas (read Potsdam) ranch of John Connally (von Hindenburg) didn't the President (Adolf) tell the big oil-men and ranchers present (Krupps) that he didn't rule out mining or bombing of dams (Holland) in his sincere quest for peace! Because, you see, he's not the scrub in football helmet on the Whittier High bench anymore, lordy no! He's now chief and he's telling all rad-comlib-campusbum-eastern-effete-intellectual folk that politics ends at the waterline, yeah! So the day drags on, and the woodpecker is chipping away.

That evening I go to Carnegie Hall, to hear Leopold Stokowski—American Symphony in their last concert of season. The Shostakovich Fifth. (What if the Russians send minesweepers?) A massive symphony, lyrical and stormy by turns, oasis of extraordinary sound. Stokey at ninety the magus who drowns the woodpecker, vaults my head beyond the waterline of danger. To a standing, shouting acclaim at the last notes. And the end is the beginning. He leans forward on the podium rail and says over the mike he's happy to be with us and hopes to see us again next fall. Meantime he'll play some Chopin. After that, he announces a Schubert that "we haven't rehearsed but we'll play it for you if you're game." It's *Marche Militaire* and it's performed in a crystalline Stokowski that makes you forget the blarings of jack-booted war. And loving him and his orchestra, the audience won't let him go. He bids us mark the fine playing of this young man from horns, that young lady from strings, introducing each and "delivering" the audience's cheers on to the full orchestra. I wait around and later I tailgate to the reception room. His face close up is of two worlds. Mortal maskwhite skin drawn in tiny folds over high cheek bones, lit up by animated blue eyes that mock the dark tunnel. Stokowski touches our day.

Wednesday at ITT's twenty-story, glass-graystone cube at Park and 50-51 Streets. The trick of blocking the machine, zapping the insane rush of traffic, piercing the white-collar 9-to-5 ceremony at its office lair, invading the plastic space to say no, if only for an afternoon! I arrive at two and Park Avenue is being laid out by police and WRL monitors like a ball field with appropriate foul lines. So many wooden horses this side of ITT's entrance; so many that side of Park's corner islands. And a conference of do's and don'ts before the "Play ball!" Cloudy, rain-threatening day, but the game is on. Students arrive from City, Hunter, Barnard, Columbia. They tote their own signs; yell off-the-cuff greetings. "We're here because we're here...." Street theater freaks—those young ladies from staid Sarah Lawrence!—warm up their act for early comers. In front of St. Bartholomew's big, iron-frescoed doors which are shut tight. Nightmare of painted, writhing bodies; offertory of blood-on-white-bread sandwiches; taste of "the enemy flesh, eat and be saved." A tall young man with bullhorn tours up and down Park announcing on-the-minute happenings. "At four-fifteen Park Avenue will be bombed. Watch for the barrage of parachutes coming out of the sky. They are simulated bombs...."

Hundreds of people are now pouring into Park. Watching, mingling, participating. The police are cool, in more than one sense. They are cool inside the expanding pockets of theater; and cool inside their Captain America vizored helmets. All the slow-moving, slogan-shouting demonstrators. And traffic between the island slowed to a crawl both ways. At the four P.M. height the crowd has mounted to thousands. The mood is a mood of vigor and freeform expression, of both light-hearted and somber street carnival, interweaved with sober-sided political witness. And a company of young, mainly white and army-surplus-clad Vietcong flag bearers, they are grim but disciplined. The New York Congs (many of them wearing red headbands over shaggy hair) have posted themselves on the steps of St. Bartholomew's, en block. Picture parody of rebs versus establishment. And a white-haired man of about seventy, walking through the crowd in a solo demo, his step very firm and his home-made sign held high: NIXONIZE THE WAR, SEND HIM. And a theater freak in Vietnamese conical hat and pajamaed suit, doing a prayer ritual at the 51st Street downtown island. He goes down on his knees, and intones a Vietnam prayer to each passing driver, followed by a plea: "Won't *you* end the war? Won't *you* stop the killing?" Most drivers look the other way, on pretense of having

The Week Of 100-Proof Nixon & Kissinger

a closed-ears policy. And from one wrathful cabbie: "It's the likes of you that keeps the war goin'!"

Out of the welter of noises comes the voice of the announcer on the bullhorn: "Three minutes to go for the bombing!" Heads crane up to the skyline. From the jammed steps of pink hued Romanesque St. Bartholomew's (which could easily serve as the Bastille for the day), from the crowded windows of the ITT across the way from St. Bartholomew's where a good 500 are watching (Pentagon contracts suspended for the afternoon), from the narrow jammed green-hedged Park Avenue island (packed to the very trees and branches with people), from each of the four tight corners of the blocklong quadrangle, the heads tilt upwards. A sudden howl of sirens—off a tape and amplified—bursts through the canyon. Moments later a roar goes up as a stream of puffed-out toy parachutes descends at a point just south of the main assemblage. One jumping student yells above the din: "*Outasight* . . . it's coming from the Waldorf!" The cry is picked up by others as more parachutes are launched from a tenth or twelfth floor suite looking out on Park. On the dot of four-thirty the young man with the bullhorn announces: "The whole area is now under saturation bombing. GIs from Vietnam Vets for Peace are rounding up prisoners. They'll be taken to Concentration Camp Tri—at the southeast corner of Fifty-first—and they'll be put under arrest . . ." Like the "explosion-of-roses" scene of ecstasy described by Count Ciano (the Spanish Civil War scene where Ciano and his Italians bomb the Loyalists in the open), sudden waves of bodies go limp on Park Avenue and the victims are then hustled to their feet by half-dozen GIs packing M-1's. Down go the bodies in waves, the Khaki-clad GIs handling them "roughly" and belaboring them with "obscenities." The clouds thicken just about then, and a light rain comes over. And the agony of One Day in the Life of Vietnam is completed by a theater of pantomime at 7,000 miles "distancing."

I bump into Dave McReynolds—near five P.M. as I'm leaving—and we run it all down for a minute or so. "You said 'one-thousand' and you lose. By at least five or six to one." Dave replies, "I should lose that way, *always*." I ask him about the Waldorf-Astoria, and the parachutes. "No doubt it was a salesman from Dubuque, up there in the suite." And he blows the cover, with glee. "Not a salesman from Dubuque, but a 'newly wedded' couple from WRL. They reserved the suite forty-eight hours earlier, with loads of 'honeymoon' baggage that came out of the windows, today." I tell him good-show, will be seeing you, and I head out of the war area for the subway. As I'm leaving I see four mounted cops who are in a close-quarters' tangle with the main body of Cong flag wavers on the downtown side of Park. No clubs are used, in the tight ebb and flow of bodies, there's no outward sign of violence. All in all, the battle looked more like a rugby go than an out-and-out confrontation for blood. I learn later however that two or three arrests were made. And that the redbands, after their rugby go with the horsecops, chased over to Times Square to do their thing.

That evening I catch Ed Sanders's reading at St. Marks church. After the reading Ed, his wife Miriam, and myself, along with two or three more, repair to the Remington for drinks. Ed asks me about the demo, which he and Miriam had missed. I tell him: the only thing lacking was a full-fledged Fugs performance as of old. And that he was parent—along with the likes of Tuli the K.—to a lot of the stuff that went down. Ed protests: "Shit, that was years ago, but I won't fight you." We all have a round; and pretty soon Ed's calling for another. "On me," he says with a grunt, as he draws a new 100-dollar bill from his wallet. "Book royalty loot"—points to the bill—"Ol Ben Franklin shines down." He got it fresh out of the bank via his publisher's check book and hopes there's more where that came from. He orders a new round and when it arrives he says: "Everybody drink up, the honcho may have us on the ropes, but there's heavy cavalry due round the bend soon." He reveals to me great, orgiastic, nonviolent mobs of joy freaks, promised for the Miami conventions. He says, it's not Chicago-68-time, shit no. It's get the man outta there, before he stuffs the globe into his shredding machine. At the ballot box, with maybe Georgie McGovern. He says, "If the world were a cafeteria, Nixon would be eighty-sixed without even a glass of water."

Thursday, Friday, and beyond. I burn candlewatt till 4-5 in the morning, reading the Late City *Times*'s dispatches. From the battlefronts—Quangtri, Anloc, Kontum. What is the lesson of those, class? Answer: General Giap is to Saigon as General Grant was to Richmond. The world knows it, interdiction notwithstanding. And the mines dropping in the harbors. And the splinterings from 30-thousand-feet up. Not just bridges and railheads. Schools, hospitals and dams—in the bargain. A mighty show from the man who brings, "Peace in our generation." Lord believe him! And he also brings—this very week—the backlash. Cambodia, say hello to Hanoi-Haiphong. And campuses boiling. Ivy presidents—as at Amherst—who say: *Arrest me along with my students.* And the streets boiling. Your friendly local bank, with the picture-window front, is a Coney Island "knock down the bottles" prize. All they are saying is: Let's mine our own business, Mr. President.

Cosmep Inc.

THE SHORT HAPPY LIFE OF THE LITTLES   COSMEP is acronym for Committee of Small Magazines, Editors and Publishers with upward of 380 members in the US and Canada—a lively if hazardous family grouping cum occupational burn whose purpose is to build the important web of little magazines, poetry chapbooks and stranger formats. Put another way Cosmep Inc. (whose monthly Newsletter articulates the littles' view) is a kind of feeding ground for the new and experimental in literary and other areas of our culture. For five days in June Cosmep met in convention in Madison, Wisconsin, the fourth such annual at which poets, writers and little mag editors-publishers exchange in detail their problems, frustrations and even hopes in order to "Get our scene more together." About eighty people made it to Madison, from all over the country and including two from Canada (poet Robert Sward and his wife Judith, from BC), a grand parade of "non-names" but a parade of talent for all that. The gathering could be described—at least off its angrier moods—as a search and destroy of all the factors in the literary marketplace that block the emergence of new voices.

Host Morris Edelson (editor, *Quixote*), ran down the obstacles early on, from mixedup keys to soap-towels in short supply, as he got the arrivees eased in and bedded down at the Madison Y. Also on hand was an advance party of Len Fulton (*Small Press Review*) and Richard Morris (Camels Coming Press), both from California; and Dick Higgins (Something Else Press) from Vermont; all three of whom are on Cosmep's board. One of the early ones was Diane Kruschkow (*Zahir*), who had thumbed a long circling trail from northern New Hampshire to Madison, making the nearly 1,200 mile journey in four or five car jumps ("with radios blaring") since her early-Sunday departure, or close on to two full days on wheels. She told Edelson a bare mattress—rather than soap and towel—was all she needed for the moment.

By time of the Tuesday opening, a count of heads showed the Midwest was in the lead. There were Bill and Ruth Wantling from Chicago; Rich Mangelsdorff out of Milwaukee-Madison who covered the story (for *Nola Express*, New Orleans); editor-novelist-poet Hugh Fox (*Ghost Dance*) in from East Lansing; a group of four or five poets and editors who drove up from the Iowa Writing School; and several poets-small-press-editors from Madison—not all of them Cosmep Members—who helped Edelson in the latter's role of conduit between Madison scenes and visitors. Others present were Allen De Loach (*Intrepid*) from Buffalo; Carol Bergé (*Center*) from Woodstock; publisher Ted Wilentz (Corinth Press) from NYC; and Alan Austin from Washington, D.C., who handed out a new spoken-poetry disc he edits called *Black Box*.

Because campus was at a near standstill, just before opener of summer classes, the town was back to a "normal" gait. Thin crowds along State shopping the late-spring bargains; knots of students doing the lakeside turns of reading-study, or sailing-boating-swimming, or just rapping on the big open veranda of the Student Union building. The SU, and other campus buildings, looking like some form of MGM 1930s classic that typifies the lake-frontage complex. And Madison itself—call it an urb, somewhere between city and suburb—is a paradigm of ecology pilot with broad streets, non-littered curbstones, low-contoured homes and business buildings, and other such environment concern. The shimmering, 282-foot state capital dome is of course a Vermont granite classic—it stares you down (benignly, you hope) like a giant cyclops from almost any direction you find yourself in. One visitor, on a nightly walk along University, did a doubletake on seeing a litup office with gilt lettering on the window: OFFICE OF EUTROPHICATION PROGRAM. (Webster's: nourishing of lakes, etc.) Although the meaning was a bit vague to him—this New York *dirty* curbstone walker—the aura of that office and the very scent of the town spelled a message: Not so much playground as proving ground for how to stay ahead of creeping blight. Also on the upbeat: Breakfasts at Rennenbohm Rexall's—good size and Wisconsin creamy—for a mere 60c; doublescoop ice cream for 25c; large mug of foamy beer for 45c.

The maverick (if not out-and-out Maoist) mode seems to come natural to Madison's campus and the three or four bookshops on State that serve it. In a brief talk I had with a bearded student-clerk in the Book Co-Op—which had a heftier display of littles and underground papers than I'd seen anywhere—he hooked me when in doing a thumbnail of the town he called Madison the "third coast." It had a ring that reflects not just the geographic openness of the two big lakes that girt the area, but the openness too of a midwest tone in politics-literary expression that (unlike the often bigwheel, roasty and grim atmosphere of a New York) comes over almost casually and is invariably targeted for humor.

An example was the Cosmep afternoon reading—poetry and prose both—held at Student Union where more than twenty-five participated in an unstructured (and unprogrammed) round of nearly three hours' duration. The clockwise reading was as casual as the work was good, with almost no physical or other separation between readers and audience, and with lots of ad hoc feedback from all over the hall—especially from the ever-present Iowans, who delivered obbligatos of bantering putdown whenever the going seemed to be heavy. And the Mao thing is part of the picture too—it took Richard Nixon's mining speech to help touch it off. Examples were the boarded-up main entrance of First Wisconsin National and the shootout between cops and students with injuries to both groups—two not unrelated incidents of mining week. Passing by the bank now one felt a kind of ambiguity of dollars lapped onto revolution—in the way the boys and girls drifted into the bank's side entrance (some in sandals or shoeless, others bouncing off their bikes) to make their withdrawals or deposits with not so much as a second look at the splintered front doors of First Wisconsin National.

A good many of us got to see (at curator Felix Pollak's invite) the unique Marvin Sukov collection of little magazines, at the university's Memorial Library, perhaps the best in the country, with something like 717 titles and 10,600 single issues, all housed behind Mosler steel doors. In the stacks were complete sets of *The Dial, The Blast, This Quarter, transition;* and complete sets of *The Masses* and its successor *Masses and Mainstream* (all quite rare, according to curator Pollak); and a precursor—going back to 1913—of women's liberation called *New Freewoman*, an individual review, to give but a tiny idea of the collection's vast diversity. There was a Renoir day in the country—just after the reading at SU—with three carfuls of us leisurely skirting the town to a point about five miles the other side of the lake, where our hosts readied a quick (and delicious) meal of brown rice, orange-cocoanut gelatine dish, cool green salad, Wisconsin beers and wines—serving it out on the inevitable treelined lawn and see-through ozone that had New Yorkers, anyway, near gasping it all in for fear that it would go away on the instant. It didn't!

And nighttime visits to local watering holes and poetry dens. Most frequented by Cosmepers was a place called "The 608" on State Street—a noisy but not boozy campus favorite where big Rich Manglesdorff (thick beard and stony gaze reminding you of a Chaplin movie heavy) cruised the tables for litry tidbits and political weathervane trends, which he'd then comment on, or translate where necessary, for edification of out-of-state Cosmepers present. Another lively spot was the in poetry den called the Nitty Gritty, where poets and audience kept chopping at each other, but more for laughs than out of the grim ego-tripping of the bigcity reading gig.

Most of the conference forums, exchanges, Cosmep board meetings, etc., took place at the Y, a four-story rectangular "modern" turned into bedroom, living room and quickmeal kitchen for five days running. Though not exactly an elegant digs, there were a few pluses nonetheless. Foremost was the closeness—members getting to know each other quickly, and even in the winking flesh, at times, though not necessarily physically, by way of common johns-janes for both sexes. (Incidentally, one noted a kind of campus-rarefied graffiti on the john walls. Such as: "Excretio ergo sum.") And the vegetarian kitchen off the main lounge called Sunflower, a cooperative run cheerfully by three Madison longhairs, two boys and a girl, who served tasty dimes'-cheap exotica, like grapefruit halves with kicker of poured honey (15c the half), or dish of yogurt with a meld of crushed nuts (25c), and more such good-for-you fare. A few trips to Sunflower had me (an Eighth Street Flame Steak devotee) vowing a whole new thing in my future. And sharing five or six joints one starfilled night, by a dozen or more of us, on the Y's second-floor roof abutment, which cropped up as a pleasant surprise as grass was in short supply all-around. Catching the California-New Jersey primary returns in the Y's TV room (color box and settees both slightly battered) on another night, with some heavy cheers for McGovern. And the kegs of beer and the Wisconsin cheeses at each of the eight or 10 afternoon and evening Cosmep sessions. And the little mags, chapbooks and hardbacks informally up for exchange—members brought along stacks of their work, and the tables were nearly bare by conference's end.

The economics of little publishing (nor was it news that most of it is bad!) was easily the most troublesome problem of the five-day meeting.

The Short Happy Life Of The Littles

Main topics discussed were: lack of support to unknowns in the publishing avant by such funding agencies as National Endowment for the Arts; postal authorities who apparently are not aware of Ben Franklin's notion that dissemination of printed matter (not necessarily on a cost-plus, take-it-or-leave-it basis at that) is the *first* business of the US post; and the near blackout of distribution outlets that keeps hundreds or even thousands of little mags and books from being seen, judged and purchased at points of sale around the country. There were the expected minor hassels on specifics but the overall thrust was best summed up by Cosmep board chairman Harry Smith (*The Smith*, NYC) when he said: "Now that publishing has entered the mainstream of Big Business, the small presses and little magazines are playing an increasingly important role as guardian of literature, call it an Ombudsman role as well . . ." He had thrown down the gantlet, so to speak, earlier—to Cosmep and the conglomorated marketplace both—when he called littles "the agents of literary change."

Prominent too was Dick Higgins, who offered considerable expertise on how littles can "beat" the post office, and do it legally. And Higgins (heir to a small Higgins Steel family business, trendsetter in avant book publishing, and Vermont farmer) must be doing something right: He is one independent who manages to keep *his* operation in the black. And there was Leonard Randolph, head of literary grants at National Endowment, who flew in from Washington one day before conference's end, and who from appearance grooved with the advocacy mood of Cosmep—when he said postal costs-regulations were just not good enough for the small press operation. He even stirred the money juices when he revealed that: considerably less than "a penny on the dollar" has been made available for the small press scene, up till now, from the National Endowment. (How much of that dollar [and it's an 80-million-package overall] goes to the Lincoln Centers around the country; or, for that matter, to the Zilch Ballet Companies, he didn't say.) Randolph told Cosmepers—individually and as a group—to bark louder for their fair share of the national arts dollar. And there was John Gill, who, in counterpoint to what might be called "the outside help syndrome," made a strong appeal for self-help and cooperative ventures, citing his own Crossing Press as one that has done "more than a few chapbooks and larger formats, at a profit." Gill all but "signed up" several members for future cooperative projects, by time the conference was over.

Two other problems (though more in the realm of soul-searching than in pocketbook) were the related ones of Cosmep board of directors and Cosmep membership. It was more than a touchy point that, as concerns the board makeup, there was but one woman member to six of men. This provoked a women's caucus that demanded, and succeeded in getting, more board representation, from the present single member (Carol Bergé), to the unanimously passed resolution that one more be added (Glenna Luschei, editor of *Café Solo*), thus increasing the board to eight. (As to whether the change was made on "demand," or by agreement of the six men and Ms. Bergé before hand, that is somewhere in the area of the chicken-egg dilemma.) On the problem of overall membership, there was a good deal of discussion, and self-criticism, as to why *no* black littles were present, and what should be done to increase (from the handful now in Cosmep) such membership, and other writer-publisher membership from third-world, gay and women's liberation, and more such groups. And some upbeat business too: Cosmep will put out a catalog—with hope of wider distribution than just its own list—of works from member publications modeled after the *Whole Earth Catalog*; and Cosmep will provide for babysitting and other facilities at future meetings, to name but two innovations that were carried unanimously. And some talk of "Next year in New Orleans . . . we've never had a meeting in the south." (Besides Madison, annuals have been held in Berkeley, Ann Arbor and Buffalo.)

Parting snapshots. Robert Sward, with his halo of trim, brownish beard—and his head and body—turned upside down, legs extended in a perfect stretched *V*, as he does a sort of American Indian totem pose, on the lakefront green of Student Union building. Holds the pose for several minutes—unwaveringly, like a piece of live sculpture—as students, Cosmepers and blond wife Judith shoot away with their cameras . . . Round and medium-height Hugh Fox, boyish in his aging 30s way, a knifesharp sense of the ridiculous, who is quickly dubbed the "Lenny Bruce of the littles," as he gives testimony, repeated several times over with variations, on the fate of "a dozen of my novels over the years": "I get this rejection note from a Vassar Doubleday editor, who tells me: 'Fox, you're a genius'; and she compares me to Joyce, Borges, you-name-it. It's like a shot of adrenaline, right? Well, let her reject Borges, and tell him: 'Borges, you write like Hugh Fox!' " . . . Fifty or so John Gill, gray hair done-up in a tight bun, up against his fine bony head, a tall angular man with snappish, hellfiery delivery; as he aims his bag of arrows at literary philistines. Fleeting image of a John Brown in attack, or storming the Harper's Ferries, of the publishing word-world . . . Easy Len Fulton, man-on-boots from Paradise, California. Has a small ranch house, where he publishes, writes and rides. He, and Glenna Luschei, plan an afternoon of riding. They leave for a Madison stable, only to be called back to the Y, for a "really urgent" board of directors meeting. Fulton by the way likes to address his mail: "Pair O Dice, California." . . . Ruth and Bill Wantling, both taking tabs on Bill's intake of starchy food, almost around the clock. Ruth says, "He's got to watch that ticker of his." Wantling is unique for his wild-line, power-driven poetry. And the soft traceries, of his arms and chest tattoos . . . Ted Wilentz is a Cosmep board member, and switch-hitter in the world of books. He arrives plane-weary, on shuttle run from Washington, D.C. where he attended the American Booksellers Association annual. Former president of ABA, and New York retail bookman, Wilentz has been batting out small press poetry and other books, mainly from unknowns, on his Corinth label, which may well be the oldest small press around . . . Joe Ribar (New York poet with a Dakotas psyche) reading his twenty-minute chapbook, a fantasia on the plains buffalo, comic-book style, the audience going to war whoops, at times, as Ribar reams out the vaguely dreamy, mad-funny lines . . . The roving editor gets himself dunked in the polemical waters, re the women's lib problem, without even knowing *why*. He returns to his room at two A.M. for beddy-by. On the mahogany door, there's a pox of white-chalk graffito that tells smartass editor what for: FASHIST.

My land, your land

A NON-WATERGATED FOURTH OF JULY, ALMOST Three years shy of the Two-hundredth, an Olde Style Fourth in downtown New York on a humid and cloudy afternoon. Thousands get together on the big open South Street Museum pier, strolling the canyon of wooden planks between the looming high four-master steel bark *Mosholu*, and the gracefully curving Hudson River dayliner *Alexander Hamilton*, both vessels part of the deactivated gallery of ships on permanent show at the South Street spot. The view at this south shoulder of Manhattan is rare for its openness, breeziness and three-dimensional depth with the trio of hanging bridge spans on the north, the three-tiered spanways for traffic and pedestrians of Brooklyn Heights farther east, and the low-contoured rise of Governor's Island one-thousand feet or more to the south, all jutting up from the swift-flowing East River basin in the dramatic, lusty visage of a Hart Crane poem.

Crowds of families, several busloads of out-of-town tourists, couples on bicycles and other couples walking by with knapsacks on backs, all in a holiday mood as they sample at a leisurely pace the various musical and other (call them short order) events planned for that afternoon. A singalong with the X Seamens Institute trio—Bernie Klay, John Townley and Dan Aguiar—held this mostly city-tuned audience in good grip of nostalgia and handclapping pleasure as the trio ran down sea chantey after sea chantey to its own accompaniment of two guitars and some crispy, salty retelling of sailors' woes and sailors' loves by the bearded, heavy-girthed Klay. An endless array of tunes, linked easily and smoothly, like the making of a sailor's knot, with the crowd swaying along to the beat, or handclapping in the right spaces, or wheezing out the mock shame at the drop of a tuneful couplet that—in the eyes of the Burger Supreme Court—might well be subject to "local" censure for trafficking in, eh, obscenity.

Another musical repast, more in the vein of pop American romance, reflecting back to good chunks of Crosby radio thirties, and even further back to rural barnyard, or open-spaces west and southland, this one two blocks west on Fulton, the quartet plunked down neatly on the stone concourse, just in front of the glass structured Cocoa Exchange building. A natural spot for the jumping kids, with its open platforms and stairways of steel, its spurting fountain inside a shallow pool of water, its brightly painted aluminum love seats, its flapping pennants in a bright-colored pop and op design. The four young musicians—guitar, trombone, tuba and drums—were easygoing, talky between rounds, swift on play, and instantly evocative. "Now a set of oldies but goodies," the guitar player announced, as he urged the crowd of about 250 to join in, and the four jammed away with "Good Night Irene," "Wabash Cannonball," "Home on the Range," and more in the genre.

A white-haired lady in her sixties, heavy-set in ungarnished black cotton dress, who stood only a few feet away from the quartet, kept up with them in swaying motions of her shoulders, now slow and undulating for "Irene," now rapidly and jerkily for "Wabash." At the same time, many of the others were also drawn in, getting off on the

A Non-Watergated Fourth of July, Almost 83

singalong, or keeping their own beat with foottapping runs, all by no means together and on-key. (And what's a few cases of tin-ear, in so high-humor a crowd as that!) And with no suggestion, not even a whisper of it, but that the Burger Majority would have approved.

The open square down on William Street, with variety of booths and other activities, some harkening back to way earlier times. The handloom about five feet by five, set up right there on the street, with demonstration by the tall, thirtyish lady who herself is dressed in authentic down-home cottons. The crowd wandering by, taking it all in with folksy interest, as the loomer works the shuttle with nimble fingers, and alternately, as she dips skeins of wool into a vat placed over a burner, to show the tricks of quick-dying to desired colors. The long-haired Chinese artist-caligraphy expert—he scrawls your name, or message, or slogan, or whatever, as you volunteer it; scrawls it across square sheets of butcher paper, in those quick, crosshatchy strokes of the Chinese ideogram; the thin long brush darting in and out the nozzle of India-ink bottle, as he completes one job after the other; dozens of requests from the crowd; among them, the name "Sophie," or "Winnie the Pooh"; and a popular request, the word "LOVE"; and finally, some requests off the headlines, such as "Impeach . . ." A very rapid turnover. All done, of course, free of charge.

And off a little ways by himself, a man who's dressed to the Colonial nines, tricorn hat and frilly shirt and velvet breeches; black cotton stockings inside buckled shoes; he hands out a thinpaper flyer, titled *Out Front on John Street*, and telling the "ordeal" of Peter Zenger, the "local newsman, and publisher of the Weekly Journal, with offices on Pearl Street, near Hanover Square, [who] was finally acquitted after having been arrested, jailed for nine months, and brought to trial." The flyer went on, "His crime, if you can call it that, was to print the truth about government officials who overstepped the bounds of the law . . ." The *Out Front* "flash" was the one overt note, in an otherwise appealingly "innocent" Fourth, of a past dark moment that's still with us to this day.

At dusk and later still, the celebrators trooped further south to the tip of Manhattan, the history-garlanded lookout on the vast harbor, and a spot that puts you at winking distance to Ms. Liberty looming out of the water a short 500 feet or so away. The main show down there, set off from a floating barge stationed just off Governor's Island, was a half-hour of exploding fireworks, with a brilliant orange crescent looking on, crescent hanging like a slow-shifting lamp high up in the dark, hazy sky. It was in one sense Mayor John V. Lindsay's parting showers, his Valentine to New Yorkers spelled out in bursting red-white-and-blue hieroglyphics, thousands of natives and visitors from outside savoring it to the full. For years many had blamed JVL for all the foul city happenings; it seemed an appropriate moment to give him credit for some of the fair. And there was the big rock-folk gathering at Battery Park's Castle Clinton, with the obligatory "This Land is Your Land" spiritedly reprised over and over, many in the large youthful crowd singing out, and shouting out, the Woody Guthrie song as if it had been freshly delivered up that very day.

Londinium way

LEGGING IT LENGTHILY IN LONDON London is a maze inside a sprawl inside a vast bowlshaped frontier. Hundreds of individual communities join in a low-profile scrape that's at opposite pole to the glandular skyline sprawl of a Manhattan. London's layout is a King's ransom of small villagey enclaves, lively variety of some extremely handsome (and some extremely tacky) architectural styles. While out walking the streets, or riding topside on the myriad chain of devil's-red buses, or going from here to there in the spiderwebbed Underground, the variety is the moving feast. At the core of it, the mysterious core, is the added sense that London's great energy and movement, the very nowness of the place, is everywhere trapped by the equal pull of its past. After a few weeks there a visitor from the States just begins to get an idea of the map. Defining the *territory* from the map is of course an even tougher job.

You find your legs early, and I was hardly off the jumbo jet at Heathrow, when I made my way to Trafalgar Square, via the mile and a half walk (I was staying on Wigmore Street) along turning Regent Street, and then on through Piccadilly Circus to Trafalgar. The warming sun (slanting off the inevitable puff clouds over London) brought out thousands to Trafalgar by mid-afternoon, a tourist tide from around the world, many of them hefting cameras and just about all moving around with bouncy eagerness to soak up English glory. The eye couldn't keep up with the variety of dress (saris, dashikis, mittleeuropa peasant costumes, leather-and-sandals guru styles) and the ear was teased by accents and speech patterns from every corner of the globe. They were all more or less playing the Trafalgar role. Feeding the burgeoning and dumbly bold flocks of pigeons from plastic cupfuls of grain, at ten-pence the cup. The great plinth of Admiral Nelson rising almost to a "touch" with a passing cloud. The two large seashell-like fountains giving off an aquamarine brightness of such intense voltage, it blurred the retina to look at them for more than a minute at a time.

The overall impression was of big crowds magnetized to this one spot and despite language and other barriers sharing a passing hour or two of light pleasure before they broke off and went back to the closets of their various nationalisms, their social and ethnic identities. Take the young Indian couple and their 4- or 5-year-old child, all three outfitted in finespun saris and cottony tied-at-ankle pants. They stand *en famille* in the middle of a swarm of jumpy pigeons, the latter pecking away greedily at the handfuls of grain thrown among the birds by the child. The man detaches himself from the other two, and then instructs the woman and child to *kneel into* the flock, which gets him a kind of St. Francis tableau effect that finally satisfies him. Only then does he snap away with his camera, all three then breaking out in laughter as the Trafalgar pigeons flutter their wings close by and peck away at the tiny granules of feed.

From Trafalgar Square to St. James's Park to the House of Parliament—all taken in by way of a circling and slow-paced walk the same afternoon. You get to know London's parks, those magical time-out's from the touristy routine, by an expectation of surprise, which quickly turns to admiration, over the way the grounds are kept, the very unlikeness of topography, one park from the other, the lush designs of flower beds and arborial gardens, all the examples of the sure green thumb working its wiles to an English finish. Walking through them for an habitué of NY's Central Park brings on pleasurable discovery and envy in about equal parts. St. James's at that is hardly more than a throwaway (a mile-long swath of green hills and duckfilled pond bisected by a smooth runway for cars) next to the hugeness of Hyde Park, the elegance of Regents Park, the lofty highrise of Hampstead Heath.

But throwaway or not (I guess it's arguable) the lacks of St. James's are more than made up for by the presence of the token Queen's Guard of two rigid and panoplied horsemen who sit on handsome bay mounts just outside the St. James's guard boxes for hours at a time, their clean-shaven faces all but hidden behind their visored and shakoed helmets, admirable targets for the camera-toting tourists who surround them. Decked out in vivid red tunics, tightly draped pearl-white pants, black patent leather boots that reflect glints of sunshine and bulge out at the knees, and holding their crescent swords in a crooked-arm position over right shoulders, the two young guards can easily be mistaken for a pair of models in a Madame Tussaud waxworks. Here the tourist set-piece is to pose in a family grouping—usually including a skittery child or two edging up to the horse and guard—with mum urging the kids to smile as daddy sets his camera and clicks it. The guards all the while remain unflappably rigid on their mounts, betraying now and then a slitted reflex of eye movement. Proving at that they are still a good live way this side of a Tussaud show.

The Parliament, that grandly symmetrical nave of English Gothic, attached to a Big Ben giving off quarter-hour gongs through Westminster, the whole buffcolored edifice grimed over by two centuries of Thames fog and soot (a kind of dream-drenched setting, given a certain shade of pale light), may well be the most dramatic setting of all for the outsiders. The very crust of English history—Round Table, Magna Carta, Richard the Third, Queen Elizabeth, Oliver Cromwell, Winston Churchill—is on display via the large wall paintings, domed ceiling frescoes, pedestaled hallway statuary, all in a pop-history that may or may not prove, the English hold on to their past like ecstatic children pouring over their picture books before they're shunted off to bed. (With or without glass of milk and cookies.) That hardly one single panel shows a Ramsay MacDonald, or some other Labor Party hero, may be its own Upmanship comment on Parliament art works. Visitors nonetheless are caught up in the violence and romance, as they're led through narrow mahogany rooms thick with pictorial event and pageantry. One visitor musing: *Oh gentle poet, gentle Will Shakespeare. You made the world drunk on your language. You sceptered and not so gentle Isle. Your heros and villains who trod the boards of the Globe.*

Myself, taking another lap in the day's marathon, I hitched onto a fifty-odd-assortment of thirsters for the English story, the group led by what I took to be a freelance, one of some half-dozen men and women guides, most on the elderly side and all more or less knowledgeable in their "trade." (Were they licensed by the government? Or did they "come with the building"? I never did find out.) Each would collect a tourist group of his-her own, jamming the Parliament hallways in assembly-line tours. Our particular guide was a brisk mover-talker in his sixties whose spiel fairly crackled with "drama." And who indeed liked to tease some caustic one-liners from an otherwise pat script: "So-and-So's head—as you can see—was chopped off clean; but that didn't wipe the smile from So-and-So's lips." His bagful of anecdotes, in boffo vaudeville-like pace and style, was to the crowd's appetite for history as the cupful of grain to the hungry Trafalgar pigeons.

At that he saved his most cutting lines for the tour's end. After announcing that a ten-pence contribution was "the usual thing," and after remarking to a fellow guide (in sotto voce aside) that he'd "lost a good half of my blokes" through dropout or end-around-run at the exit, he turned again to the same guide, and hissed: "This is the worst lot yet! Holdin' their one-bob till very kingdom come!" But he kept a sharp look, with both hands fully extended, for any silver that was coming his way. About fifteen or twenty coins at a guess, maybe one pound in all for the half-hour tour. A hard day's rap, and wear of shoe-leather? A proud teach-in that spread the Empire word around? It depends on whom you asked, guide or tourist.

The quick visit to National Gallery, no more than fifteen-minute turn on the same afternoon. The two or three walls of Canalettos, amazingly painterly set-pieces of Venice in the eighteenth-century heyday. The busy Grand Canal and grand parade (or float) of people, touring holidayers. Canvas upon canvas of pictures that are visual bridges. That connect a revelry-past to a revelry-present. The big-pond Italianate scene of two centuries ago. The stone-plaza Trafalgar scene outside National Gallery's windows of today.

When I returned to Wigmore, where I holed up for three or four days with friends, an expatriate writer-journalist couple (he an American; she from Australia) who'd been living in London for some years, one of them exclaimed: "You took in more in one day than we do in a year!" The trick was to "get lost" for hours at a stretch, so as not to impose on them beyond the need of a flop, use of the loo, the occasional phone call. They had a three-room flat located just off Oxford Circus, a snug garretlike fifth-floor walkup in an essentially posh area of town. Nearby was the Harley Street doctors' row with phalanxes of white-stone professional apartments; and Cavendish Square with its leafy park retreat and once-controversial Epstein *Mother and Child* sculpture with the hint of Afro in the features. That Sunday (my second day there) was even more of a challenge, as both of my hosts were working against deadlines and had little time for *my* London agenda. So I was up and out of there early (around ten or just about turnover time for me back home) for a stroll to Oxford Circus looking for a fast breakfast spot.

The near-deserted streets with better restaurants all shuttered, not much choice other than the dimly-lit and near-empty Lyon's on Oxford, one of the chain of London quick-snackeries not unlike the New York Bickford's bunch, right down to the plate of beans, the Lyon's recipe a bit too Englishy (served almost cold) next to the Bickford's (Boston style and hot). Fewer than a dozen of us souls in there, and me the only tourist around, the way I size up the customers, with several of the men in dark shabby workclothes who I figure are part of the small army of Sunday sweeper-ups, for the street and the Underground, who are aboard at that hour of morning. I down a light cheerless meal—poached egg with thin sausage done in vat of used-up grease (ugh!)—then I go out to Oxford Circus, where I pass the time at the pedestrian guard rail (see the busload of tourists going around the Circus; they're so brushed, eager and smiling!) before taking the long walk up Regent. My destination, Regents Park.

Very light traffic on roadway, the Sunday walkers down to trickles, the whole area damn near a blanket of silence. I turn north into Regent, and catch a distant blare of music, the sound coming louder and louder from somewhere off a side street. And moments later, the full view of a Salvation Army troop, as it hoves into Regent in a near lockstep, the cadence somewhat off but wide-swinging arms all British showy, with trumpet and drum cracking open the Sunday morning calm. The troop parades by going south on Regent, the "Onward" marching song gradually fading, as the Sals turn west into Oxford Street. My last view of them is a snapshot—a sudden mental flash—right out of Shaw's *Major Barbara*. (Call it a spectral connection, arising from one's own "feel" of the streets of London.) The interlude itself a kicker that gets me off and striding for my Regent's Park stop.

All is bathed in a morning light—half mist and half breakthrough sunshine—that puts things in bold relief of yellow and creamy-white coloration. The spotless walks and curbstones, the matched rows of faded though still elegant Victorian houses and professional buildings (Society for This, Society for That), the long crescent turn on Regent ending at the park, and then, the high iron-grill park entrance, just past which one of the most stunning, and richly varied, displays of the London floral explosion. (Ophelia would have dallied long here.) It hit my eye with the pleasure of one who back home walks his round of walks more in the muck of it than the mirth.

To complete the double, and to delay my return to Wigmore, at least till the seven dinner date with my hosts, I then made my way (by foot and bus) to Hyde Park, and I found that great expanse of greensward carpeting, with its free-speech and often freaky corner appendage at Marble Arch, behaving very much on its Sunday afternoon best. With strident and billowy gusts of rhetoric, political bombast and the feedback of political camp, the hellfire exhortations from the various Revealed Books of Truth, the Empire-baiting by Asians and blacks with smiles as big as the Ritz. Beyond anybody's shadow of doubt the freest, and the surest, pressure cooker on five continents. And with practically none aside from the Bogside Irish and friends—making their usual disciplined march to Whitehall on that tourist-mobbed Sunday—who could inspire some degree of response from Londoners in the first place, said Londoners who didn't seem exactly to hold still for Orangemen in Belfast who wave the Union Jack in their sleep.

The next day—a Monday—I got trapped in the shopper's crush along Oxford Street, a mind and body blower that put me right back on Herald Square, the five-continent lingo replacing the New Yorkese. Huge beehive department stores, and shop after tiny cubicle shop, in a tight row-on-row alignment, all of them turning over the merchandise, and the crumpled pound notes, with a fever that made the Macy's-Gimble's scene—on their busiest January White Sale—appear mild and even polite by comparison. What the hell was I doing there, when I had come to London for its charms, and there I was getting overhauled in the sweating body of mass (nay, world-wide!) consumerism, with no exit short of the Times Square shoulder shove at five o'clock quitting time.

More than a couple of body-bruises later, I was back out on relatively sane (and mobless) Regent Street, where I popped into another Lyon's cafe for a tea break. Before long I was joined at table, with hardly a wink of ceremony, by a London gentleman (Saville Row brown suit, unselfconscious "Do you mind?" as he sits opposite me) of indeterminate middle-age, who himself was having a *double* tea break, evidenced by the two cups of tea on his tray. He said for openers, "They don't brew it the way they used to." A wry appraisal, I thought, not only of the tea; but of numberless other London amenities; all of which, somehow, weren't the same anymore. He said he was a retired theater manager ("I'm seventy, you know;" which I not only didn't know; I found it hard to believe, at that), and that he liked to travel, adding that he was leaving London the next day or two, for a two-month trip by rail to Bangkok. And with a faint smile, "When the visitors move in, I move out." He then described—in a manner I'd call slow-aging British—the "quieter but definitely more pleasant living" in the years before the tourist invasions. Not really bitter over the new turn, but more a case of savoring the old nostalgia.

I changed lodgings later that week, Wigmore in central London to Muswell Hill Road in Highgate, some ten miles north. I had a comfortable room in a rather large flat, at five pounds a week. As my host was out most of the day, I also had (in her words) "free run of the apartment," including kitchen, library and telly. If at first I missed the holler of the Dilly, the West End; soon enough, a whole new scene opened up for me. North London is a stretched out web of small communities—hills and spirals of them. With lots of woodsy acres just outside your windows; the Highgate tube with escalator deep as the Matterhorn; heavy trucking of produce coming down from the Midlands on narrow roadways ("Look to your *right!*" I had to keep reminding myself); tree and flower farms cropping out in long terraces; antique bric-a-brack shops and rare-book emporiums; all told a kind of craft variety you just won't find, say, on plastic and tin-plated Oxford Street.

The apartment building I was staying at, one of those neo-Tudor redbrick white-trim affairs, was part of a complex of four or five matching four-story buildings, with shared grassy lawn at the center, and rolling wooded areas for miles around. Once again I found my legs; first in short walks through Queens Woods on one side; later in longer hikes through Highgate Wood with its manicured cricket field and quicksnack pavilion on the other. (The tea-break was fast overtaking me; with or without the slice of lemon.) But the geography was tougher than I had supposed. I got lost twice in the first couple of days— wandered through the sunless overhangs of tree and the heavy foliage— before I could finally tell north from south, east from west. And now I was ready for the big one. The two or three mile stroll to Highgate's famed cemetery.

Legging It Lengthily in London

Guided by the map my host had sketched, I climbed the long hill up from Muswell to Highgate Village, but I was bogged down over which one of a spokewheel of four or five narrow roads to take next. Spotting a bobby at the Highgate traffic circle (the *only* bobby I saw in my two or three weeks in the Muswell area) I went over to him and asked, "Which road to the famous cemetery?" He offered me the silent treatment for a long moment or two, looked in fact as if he didn't hear me at all, whence I imagined the wheels going around behind the peaked helmet and bored look: *One more of those Karl Marx nutties, come from the four corners to do a prayer at old Karl's remains.* He then pointed out; with crisp hand motions and follow-up directions; the corner book shop about 150 feet away; take the book shop and bear around to the right for a block or two; that'll put you at the high, turning redbrick wall; follow the wall clear down to the bottom of the road; and that'll put you at the arched, iron entrance way to the cemetery . . . not to worry, you won't get lost. It was a yard by yard wrap-up from, I was now ready to believe, a fellow-traveler wearing the dark duds of the Royal London Police.

I thanked the bobby with wave of my hand—wave rather than clenched fist—and made tracks once again. The corner book shop, the road bearing to the right, the high redbrick wall, down and further on down, the afternoon sun a warm 80 or more, and hardly a person in sight. And then—voilà!—the group of Chinese tourists, or maybe they were junior diplomats, coming through a break in the high wall, about 100 feet or so away. All dressed in tuniclike dark suits, all more or less trodding along in step, two by two. As the Chinese trooped past me, all in a somber silence, I told myself: "The cemetery at last, the Mao partisans visit Highgate to pay fraternal respect." Soon I was inside the gate, and walking (now at faster pace) down a narrow gravelly path, with steep banks of headstones and crypts on either side; and among which rose thick stands of trees here and there; some of the trees (and this stopped me for a minute) looking like Louisiana hanging moss. All that was missing, and I was hardly regretting it, was one of those London days of murky overcast and curling fog; the combination of which, especially while out walking on a deserted street, let alone through a deserted cemetery, could set the adrenaline going by the spookiness of it all.

But I was in a bit of a fog in another way. After a good fifteen minutes of hiking on the gravel path, during which I checked out headstones by the dozen, there was still no sign of the Marxian grave anywhere. I was about to give up the search and go back (by now the Taj Mahal couldn't have been more distant than that grave!) when I saw two young men approaching from a bend in the road. Both were longhairs and both were hefting books—by which I guessed they might be London University students (or Oxford for that matter) on visit for silent bows at Marx's gravesite. As we crossed paths, I asked the way once again. One of them pointed to a spot about 100 feet away. He assured me, "You are almost there. It's just beyond the next turn in the road." As I made the turn moments later, my eye targeted on the large granite block, with proportionately large head resting on top, the whole imposing gray-black slab on a ten-foot rise or so, just back off the roadway. I walked toward it—less than fifty feet to go—and soon I was alongside it. (Even before I was close enough to read the stone, the glaze of something akin to prayer clicked inside me: *The onliest, worldliest KM at last.*)

Now all the sculptured detail stood out clearly. The high lofty brow and thick hair, the deepset clefts of the eyes, the fullness of face and beard. The chiseled top line of the ten- or twelve-foot granite shaft read: WORKERS OF THE WORLD UNITE. The next line down: KARL MARX 12/4/1814 2/12/1881. The next several lines: Names of wife and children, preceded by the word "Beloved." And the last line: PHILOSOPHERS HAVE ONLY EXPLAINED THE WORLD. WE MUST NOW CHANGE IT. Fresh roses and other flowers were arranged neatly in a mound at the graveside; and just across the gravel roadway was the plot (a simple affair next to the massive Marx grave) of the great English philosopher-reformer, Herbert Spencer. It was all very proper, and very natively English, positioning. The nonpareil advocate of working-class rebellion on one side; the cautious reformer who opted for "pure,"laissez-faire individualism on the other; both now resting almost cheek-by-jowl in an eternity of togetherness.

If Highgate has the famous cemetery, the next-door village of Hampstead has the famous Heath. The Heath of course is easier to get to—what with its country openness compared to the cemetery's crouching isolation behind the long high wall. I journeyed to the Heath a day or two later, making the steep climb to Highgate Village once again, then taking the Hampstead road, which lay to my right; and getting a foretaste of what lay ahead, by way of the bosky lushness of hedges and trees, the tickle of pine and other scents, all coming at me

Legging It Lengthily in London 93

from both sides of the roadway, as I made the two-mile walk to the Heath grounds. (No map needed on that one.) As I entered from the Highgate side, I came upon a verdant, many-acres-wide podium of silken green lawns, with a waveless mini lake set down in the middle; all of it opening out (on a spectacular rise of some 500 feet) to the density of central London below and away. The day was very near glassy clear, with a few cottony patches riding slowly over the inner-city's distant Gothic spires and growing Americanized highrises. And I had the image—more in mood than in my eye—of the El Greco View of Toledo. A more vast and more northern version.

As for the rest, there were London kids livening the green everywhere, with impromtu teams kicking the inevitable soccer ball at each other, the sharper kids even making short—and "educated"—head shots now and then. And doing it all with a flair—at tender ages of 5 or 6 or seven!—that appeared honed into their toes and insteps. (Yes, sonny, English girls are leggier. Call it the chromosome factor. All the fancy kicking the soccer ball around, generation after generation.) While other kids tumbled on the Heath's long, smoothed-down slopes; held spare bodies tightly in a ball as they rolled over and over to level ground. There was kite flying, insect gathering (a "specialty," believe it or not), and even a token kind of yachting on the lake.

Also the Kenwood restoration, seventeenth century Georgian graystone mansion, complete with handsome rows of Doric columns, and a sweep of high arching classic windows; the whole elegant facade platformed some fifty feet above the Heath, giving a wide-open view of the Heath's green yardage and the woodland tracts beyond. And the roomful of George Romney's Lady Hamiltons, both a surprise and delight! I'd seen only one of this genre before—a kind of favorite among the Frick's super collection of oils—and there I was ogling four full walls of Lady Hamiltons. Poor George Romney, obsessed with Lady Ham to the thousandth brush stroke! And the Samuel Johnson summer house, darkly octagonal den of thatched roof and hardwood sides, plopped down in the middle of a thick stand of shade trees, only yards from the big Kenwood house. The den contained one wooden table and single chair, and tiny engraving behind glass of Samuel Johnson at work, nothing more. Here the great man wrote the summer hours away, when he came to visit at Kenwood.

If my nights were for the Dilly, Leicester Square and Soho; those noisy roulette wheels of touristy fun and tacky pleasure; the daytime was for exploration of London's more out of the way, and perchance deeper, moods and attractions.

In and Out. When I was last there in 1969, the Roundhouse was the in spot for London activists, counter culture, and avant-garde arts. Vacated by British Railways a few years back, Roundhouse looms on the Chalk Farm community like a totem, its blackened curved stone roof dwarfing the bus barns, railroad sidings and working-class flats that surround it. I went back one Friday night by tube, and found Roundhouse no longer so much in, as in the drifts. One young Oxford student I met there said to me . . . Yes, she remembered the jamming rock benefits, Living Theatre fantasias, readings on the Vietnam war. Adding that the present mood was "Who cares?" and " 'Politics sucks'—as you Americans say." Britain, she went on, "is having a fling with oldbeans Conservatism; similar I guess to your Nixon Conservatism. It puts a pall over everything." She continued, "The *new* in spot is the Arches. They feature the Liquid Theater 'togetherness' bit. It's the latest groove."(Oxford student was at Roundhouse to catch the National Korean Folk Dancers. *That's* a helluva switch, too.)

I went over to Arches a day or two later, on Villiers Street just up from Charing Cross tube, and found it to be the equal, if on a much smaller scale, of Roundhouse's sculptured feel. In fact Arches is a sort of kid brother of Roundhouse, in that it's a former British Railways wine cellar that's been converted, at a quarter-million quid of angel's money, to a busy three-level operation. All concave walls and ceilings of brick painted in a shocking white. With three or four stylish if tiny boutiques on basement level; kleig-lighted gymnasium for Liquid performances on first level; très chic vegetarian restaurant, with color TV and Swedish modern furniture, named "Food For Thought" (what else!), on top level. The Arches mood is smoothly gay. Apple-cheeked young men in karate linens showing off, with a lot of chatty eagerness, the Liquid "touch" method. *You touch me; I touch you!* The crowd was mainly Londoners and visiting trendies on the search for the *new* new thing, and doing it just as eagerly. Notwithstanding that Liquid at the Arches was at least two-years behind, as it happens, the New York touch breakthrough.

Olympic Fever in London Town. It seemed as if all of Britain was glued to BBC for the Olympics. Distance champ David Bedford, of the flame-red socks and roasty verbal comeback, along with several other crack athletes and toprated equestrians, had everybody (normally cool press and telly included) hanging on by the fingernails. The diagnosis was gold-medal fever and England, at least early-on, looked like it would capture lots more than in the past. Hence when the Arab terrorists struck down the Israelis, the outcry was more in vein of "dirty pool" than "dirty politics." One London telly watcher, on hearing BBC's prediction that the games would probably be canceled: "The bloody wogs won their first gold medal. The 500 Meter Running Assassin event." And while anger over the killings was deep, there was equal concern that the Olympics would be called off before Bedford-and-Company had their chance to cart home the gold. (The games of course were completed, and England wound up with eight or nine top trinkets. No insult, but not up to early promise, either.)

Learning My Fish and Chips. The Great American Disaster, cutesy named hamburgery at Leicester Square, I *did not* visit. But Johnny's Fish and Chips, across from Charing Cross tube, had me *hooked* (I surveyed the joint two or three times; finally I made my move.) Johnny's is a stripped down operation, three or four oversized vats handled by three countermen who dispense orders rapidly. And by the mile. There's a snaking line of customers outside, it gathers and dissolves all hours of day and night. They come by from the tube, or from British Railways at Charing, or even by taxi. Scoop up orders of fish-&-chips or chips alone. Wrapped in double-sheets of butcher paper, newsprint wrapping is out at Johnny's. The menu is salmon-chips (20 pence), haddock-chips (20 pence), plaise-chips (16 pence), heaping order of chips alone (7 pence). Customers do their own salting and condiment shaking. After which they are off and running. The shilling talks, nobody walks, at Johnny's.

I joined the line one night for a haddock-chips, got it and paid my 20, poured on salt and sprayed on condiment. I walked to a spot underneath Victoria Bridge, parked myself up against a steel girder and began to chomp away. Were the passersby eyeing me? Did they take me for a wog tourist copycatting London custom in sloppy fashion? Not to worry! I was really hungry and really enjoying the chomp. I was in fact right back on my Bronx streetcorner, out of these several past decades ago, peeling and biting into the hot mickie snatched from the blazing bonfire. But more than all that, I was finally initiated, after five or six visits over the years, into the London mystery of fish and chips. Taken alfresco and on the fly, using greasy fingers in lieu of knife and fork.

The Jesus Number. Evangelism in London is, traditionally, a dour-doughty scene of blue-bonnets and pale, baggy-uniformed male companions taking their blaring music down to the East End, or to the dreary Thames dockside. Earnest, unsmiling Sal Army fare of saving souls through hot flashes of uplift on dullish Sunday afternoons. But for five days in late summer, the new-wave evangelism hits town in packs. Armies of youthful Jesus Freaks are everywhere. Riding up and down the Thames, popping "The Message" like firecrackers on the open decks of tourist boats. Or shouting hollow hallelujahs to unhearing crowds at the Charing Cross tube. Or buttering to foreign visitors (Muslim, Jewish, Hindu, Irish Catholic, nonbeliever) at Trafalgar Square: "May we tell you how we were *saved*?" Most of the kids are English, ages from fifteen to twenty, faces aglow with the pink of adolescence, hair brushed back straight and clean. Quite a few are wearing their red, blue or navy school tunics with gold patch emblem on breast pocket. They are out on the streets day and night, rain or shine. Pouring forth a relentless din of soapy, badly parsed religiousness.

On closing night of the crusade, a Sunday, 100 or more Jesusers gather at Piccadilly's Eros statue. They have two guitars among them, they sing round after round of "Saved!" to a vaguely rock beat. The spirit is willing, but the performance is not exactly what you'd call "with it." Hostile turf (it's the Dilly, after all) laid siege by an equal number of youths from all over Europe and elsewhere, who have their own "saved" agenda: A little grass, a little body love, lots & lots of Mick Jagger music. For an hour or more it's a standoff, bible freaks holding forth on one side of Eros, the longhair outlanders jibbing to their own breezy chatter on the other. Then a gaunt man with gray-flecked beard, who has been doing his own thing among the outbackers, the pouring on of a kind of lowercase anarchism, gets to his feet and climbs to the top stair of the Eros statue. He holds up a piece of sculpture, a giantsize clay model of the male sex organs, holds it high and swings it gleefully over the heads of the crowd, and he shouts down the Jesus flock: "Here's the message from our Pope Eros . . . *make love!* Flaunt your tool, and insert it! Taste it, or jerk it! At all times, in all climes!" It's now almost midnight, and two bobbies come by. They circulate among both camps, and they offer the *constabulary* message: "Time to go, ladies and gentlemen! Time . . ."

Scene Called Because of Blockage. In my past visits to London, I somehow never took in St. Paul's Cathedral, that glowing mixture of Wren and Roman whose vasty gilded dome is (or *was*) like the giant's own stone eye on the London skyline. Going there for my first look I was told: it's in the old, fire-swept part of London; the area was blitzed by the Germans in World War II; it's easy to get there by bus or tube. I took the Underground to the St. Paul's station, got out and had a look around. Avenue of Americas, gray-glassy office buildings all over the place (London curvy rather than New York cubed) but no sign of that "second largest church in the world." Then I sighted it all at once, through the roadway cleavage that leads directly to St. Paul's vast, triple-tiered and handsomely classic front entrance. A hundred yards more and I was there, standing before an imposing structure of grace and power on the outside and Baroque splendor within. Wren, Roman *and Handelian*. But also a wounded structure girdled with miles of steel tubing. More than two centuries of wear—plus the wartime bombings—were apparently still taking their toll; and St. Paul's needed some delicate emergency repair work. Going away from it a while later, St. Paul's very soon disappeared behind the transplanted slabs of poured concrete and tinted glass sheaths. It reminded me of a similar burial, the steel-harp beauty of Brooklyn Bridge at the Manhattan end.

My London McGovern Button. I'm on Shaftsbury looking for number 58, one more West End street of mazelike office lofts, lit-up picture palace marquees. Number 58 eludes me but then I spot the McGovern poster on the glassdoor entrance. Two flights up in a cubicle two-roomer, I approach the girl who's holding down the phone. She's twenty-one and she's on summer leave from Brandeis. "We want to round up every absentee ballot in the UK for McGovern," she says evenly. I drop two ten-pence pieces in the box for a London McGovern button, pin it to my lapel. "Wear it on the left side," she suggests, "the heart side." No more than I hit Piccadilly, the same afternoon, and my button is a magnet to the supposedly "disinterested" Londoners. For the three or four weeks more of my stay, it provokes dozens of queries. In the tube, at the Eros statue, in local pubs. "Does he have a chance?" "He's the better man, isn't he?" Thus my London buttonpoll, literally a sweep for McGovern. But wait, there was *one* exception. The pro-Fatah debater at Speaker's Corner who, on seeing the button, draws on me with a beady eye: "Does McGovern believe in peace? Will he stop sending arms to Israel if he's elected?" And I tell him: "George McGovern, the other guy, or Archie Bunker himself—they'll all send arms to Israel, long as Russia keeps on supplying arms to the other side." McGovern lost that one.

Two Propositions at Piccadilly. I'm meeting a friend at Piccadilly, an American writer who flew in from the States twenty-four hours earlier for "some action at the tables," mainly Black Jack. ("I'm a winner in London," SK boasts, "whereas Vegas bombs me out.") I get there fifteen minutes early, we said eight P.M. at Eros statue, so I go to the Dilly loo to freshen up, straighten my McGovern button. In the mirror I see a middle-aging queen, ruddy of face, rounded shoulders tucked into blue blazer, hand wound tightly on rolled umbrella. In the mirror he's smiling, and flashing his tweezed brows . . . at me. As I turn for the street exit, he croons softly: "Are you on holiday? Can I show you the town?" I return his smile, and I hum back: "Nice of you to ask. Actually, I've been here for years." And I head over to Eros.

While waiting inside the guard rail for Black Jack player, I'm approached by a tall man with springy step, he's mid-20s and dressed in rough-cut-hip, he just sort of ambles by. Obviously a street operator. Obviously, too, he's zonked with the glaze of dropped acid. Or some heavy grass smoking. In a thick Scots' burr, pointing to my button: "That's a right-on guy, that McGov'rrnn, ain't he?" He bends closer to my ear, and he asks, would I "fancy some grass?" Not waiting for my answer, he then jumps to a proposition: "I deal the stuff and when you deal smart, it's the quickest turnover of quid around." Then to his agenda: Would I like to consider taking back to the States a "kilo of Middle-East grass . . . real moojoo stuff?" And without pause: "I can trust you, I can see that," he says. Someone yells over to Scotty, from twenty feet away, and before leaving me, he says: "Think about it, man. *Really* think about it." Minutes later, my writer-gambler friend shows up, crossing from the Dilly traffic circle, then on to the Eros island. He tells me, after a quick hello, that he did okay at the tables. And I say to SK: "Glad you hit 'em, man. But you know, I have just turned down, with no sweat at all, two very hot propositions, all in ten-minutes flat."

Jumbo Jet Homeward Bound . . . It Flies! At the takeoff, the jet is all dinosaur wings and a mile wide. Taxies along in tense vibration, aluminum bird making rubbery tracks on long strip of macadam. Will it ever get off the ground! Once aloft it's a smooth, soft hummingbird climb to high seas of white cloud and transparent blue sky topping at 35,000 feet. The Pan Am girls softshoe up and down the aisles, neatly attired in babyblue skirts and tiny peaked hats: "Can I get you a pillow . . ." And once again, my conversation piece, my McGovern button: Pan Am bird stops at my seat, asks me about the button. "I'm from Colorado, but I'm London based, and I'd like to vote for him." I give her the Shaftsbury address. She says she'll look them up.

The flight is good, the Captain keeps us posted. "We anticipate no delays at Kennedy Airport, weather is clear, we should land on time." Not so. About 15 minutes from Kennedy, Captain announces we're in a "hold pattern." The dinosaur is now spreadeagling round & round, somewhere over the New Jersey flats. The weird, silent turns give sensation of sky and land barrelling round your seat. "Crud on this," I say to nobody, "Hold patterns are for Piper Cubs, not dinosaur jumbos." Finally it's "go" for landing, the giant bird banking down with mild bumpiness, starboard wing unfolding in slats for braking on wind. I was back home to big apple, with unmistakable rise in adrenaline action.

The McGovern blues

TWO NEW YORK ELECTION WAKES The election night wakes around town—at least the two I attended—were not so much wakes as counting of beads for a good cause lost. The first was a gathering of mostly youngish zippies-journalists-writers held at a semibarricaded four-roomer on St. Marks Place and hosted by Honest Bob Singer and Rex ("my first vote") Weiner—the tandem editorial whizzes responsible for the short-lived, eccentrically talented, always jumping tabloid called New York *Ace*. (In seven or eight biweekly issues got out from a basement warren at the lower end of Manhattan's fur district last spring, Singer-Weiner ran some very weird, very nosepoking pop journalism and graphics.) Bob—newsmonger cum filmcrit who gets intellectual highs on Proust and Proudhon—greeted a constant stream of media rebels (D. Walley, C. Dreifus, A. Bennett, D. Meltzer, J. Wilcock, S. Krause) to each of whom he promised: "We're near to closing a deal for 10-grand; *Ace*'ll be hitting the stands real soon, believe it." While inside the longfloor cavern Rex fiddled with the tube, or described the Halloweennight gig at Washington Square fountain where zippies burned President Nixon in effigy. Nobody, but nobody, was surprised, nor were they feeling undue pain, at the telephone-numbers sweep of "Four More Years." While everybody, but everybody, owned to a conviction that, whereas voting in post-Chicago-68 was a bush thing, coming out and chalking an X for George in 72 was no insult. So they peeled the grapes, cracked the six-packs, blew some dope. All in the spirit of losing a battle, yes; but the notion that you win the revolution by mere shouting-trashing, on any given eight o'clock in the morning, *that* one went out the window that same night.

I said my goodbyes around midnight—headed over to Dave McReynolds's flat on East Fourth for my second wake, described in Dave's invitation flyer as being "without tears/for a celebration of life/and perhaps a wake/for the republic." A livingroomful of some thirty zippies of slightly different mien from those at the Bob/Rex go—more hardcore activist, most of them, on the WRL (War Registers League) barricades, hence less romantic in the day-to-day tactics for winning America (WRL seldom uses the Kafkaesque "k") back to the ways-days of peace, back to the Declaration—Bill of Rights. Whitman-bearded Igal Roodenko is there, Christophers activist Bob Pugsley, WRL veterans Ralph DiGia and Brad Lyttle. And a passel of young men and women, who are dropouts from the middle-class way, and who have now made the jump of dropping back in, to resistance, with jumpmaster Dave's help and guidance, in most cases. The TV set is raining the numbers' monsoon frame by frame; getting in turn a certain amount of fug-you feedback, as when Spiro flashes his bland golfshooter's victory smile, from some of the watchers. Mostly though it's not a wake; more an hour of comradeship among people who don't repeat don't want to stop the world and get off but want to change it. And sharing what Dave called "a bissl to nash" and "whatever bottles there are." With the incense burning, the cats Loki and Bost purring round our ankles. Plus an impromptu striptease act, followed by a kind of lost-Balinese group mime, suggestive of, but not including, a group grope; the act triggered by next-door neighbor Peter Stafford's call: "Strip to your jockey shorts, everybody; the incense smoke is just right." The roving editor, usually straight-of-straights on such occasions, pleading separate but equal right not to join the saturnalia. And when Senator McGovern flashes on screen, to make his concession speech, big Dave McReynolds loses his composure. He sits off in a corner of the couch, and sheds a few quiet tears.

1973

Nixon triumphant

THE SNOWING OF 1972 At 1972's end, we can at least say we had a battle. The roving editor had done his share of hollering, picayune perhaps in view of the avalanche of anti-McGovern votes. He'd done his share of buttonholing people to seize the opportunity of making dramatic change in America. Not since the darkling election year 1932— or was it 1936?—had he felt such urgency of choice, the kind of bold choice symbolized by FDR at a time when the country was meanly adrift. Adrift between the longitude of myopic economic despair, and the latitude of pinchfaced "prosperity around the corner" optimism.

In that earlier decade, he had pinned to his lapel his first political button. The laminated visage of the Hyde Park patrician whose insouciant smile—one part vinegar and one part honey—had the dissolving quality on our fears of warm sunshine bursting through a long gray overcast. The insouciance had other effects as well. Such as the purging of the 1930s establishment gloom upon the mere utterance of his, "Martin, Barton and Fish!" (M-B-F was the roadshow Republican Congressional "truth squad" of that day.) Or when the FDR smile had the bite of cool outrage at its edges. As in his White House fireside complaint: "I don't mind the insult, my family doesn't mind the insult, but our dog Falla does mind it very much indeed." (If memory serves, there was the charge that Falla was sole passenger on an Army Air Corps freebie flight, from somewhere to somewhere.) We could, in those days, grasp hold of a mensch, grasp hold of an ideal. An ideal that however short in delivering us to the highground of national pride and social-economic justice did nonetheless clear our minds and tone our muscles for the job of eradicating the standpat gloom of the previous decade.

Why then did it not happen in 1972? One's first thought, sending it up from the gut, has to be the mendacity of George McGovern's "friends" among the press. The eagerbeavers who covered him on the stump, and who *really covered him* with their own sillyputty puritanism. Most of the breed had the itch to pick McGovern apart— hour upon sorehead hour—whence they would announce the alarming presence of lint on "our" candidate's blue serge jacket, an itch finally that was right out of a medical chapter on the acne of political adolescence. The examples are too numerous to track down case by gloomy case, but mention should be made of several (Phil Tracy, Clark Whelton, Ron Rosenbaum, etc.) from the *Village Voice* stable, on the theory that if *that* seemingly pro McGovern journal could do no better than its weekly bushelful of lintpicking, what chance did McGovern have with the general run of press! *Item*. On the Wednesday before election *VV* ran a page-one story by Tracy which said: "McGovern is dead even as the first dribble of his supporters fan out from the state campaign office . . ."

Now even if we concede McGovern was fated to lose, the question still has to be asked: What kind of reportorial sensibility is on display when the voice that yearns to be a fox suddenly takes on the howl of the hyena? And so it went month after month in McGovern's tough climb to the summit of his candidacy. The press by and large ("friendly" press, to repeat) that covered him, cheapshot on top of cheapshot, helped set loose a thickening miasma of stumblebum-on-the-run, at the same time ignoring almost in toto the density of his accomplishment: A man coming just about out of nowhere, taking on and overcoming a decade of dry rot at the top of his party, winning an increasing share of grassroots support from labor in spite of the dry rot at the top of the labor establishment; finally and most crucial of all, sticking to his last in face of the killing inertia on the one hand, and the dollar explosion (matched only by the explosion of dumb-dumb bullets of coded electioneering) on the part of the opposition, on the other hand.

Item. The same day Tracy's howl surfaced in the *Voice*, candidate McGovern was completing a New York round-robin of walks and traditional Garment Center rally. It was an afternoon that caught fire, even for the foxes who covered him, with all the depth of feeling a man could hope to rouse from an audience; in this case, an audience of about 25,000 workers, bluecollars and assorted Macy's shoppers; many of the first-named group of whom, in the course of McGovern's half-hour address, left machines and workbenches to mount barrage after barrage—some hanging from the graystone windowsills to make the throw—of the silk and cotton swatches of their trade. Out of the windows came a skylarking display of brightly colored wedges of fabric to liven the drab Seventh Avenue canyon; leaving (it should be added) to the GOP cheerers their own very predictable showers of tickertape coming down over the drab but money-splendored canyon of a Wall Street.

To say of that Wednesday before election that John F. Kennedy at a comparable moment in the 1960 campaign was a candidate just barely out of the political boondocks is not to diminish the earlier (and finally victorious) candidate but to offer some hint of what the country lost in terms of the growth potential of 72's defeated candidate. *Item*. The contest will probably go down as the numbers shuck of all time, with the gut issues of the Nixon four-year reign, so far from seeing the light of an open contest, getting runover in the robotry (and not a little Babbittry) of the pre-election pollster; not to mention the evasions of a hide-and-seek incumbant who couldn't talk Watergate-ITT for all the cotton candy he was mouthing; and the sheer theatricality of an announced peace in Vietnam that sure in hell *wasn't*. 44 million said yes to all that; 29 million said no, not by me; and another 54 million, stuck in the political big sleep, didn't even bother to show up. Plus the most magical number of all, which popped up conveniently in the last days of the election, the breaking of the Dow Jones 1,000 barrier. The "work ethic," that holy of holies, was alive and well on the Street that week!

Item. Four More Years! To wipe from our consciousness the decade of the 60s? From counterculture to Cambodia? Watts to Kent State? Mylai to Moratorium? Well, for starters, they'll have to lobotomize the Nixon daughters' entire generation!

INAUGURATION DAY, 1973

Corso & Ginsberg

DID NBA KNOW WHAT IT WAS DOING? Come on by for Gregory Corso/Allen Ginsberg. Seated or standing in knots, under New School auditorium fish-silvery roof like hollowed out rump of beached whale, an overflow crowd of students and grads inches forward—

sideways in elbow-tight maroon seats. *This is no sitback and be mute crowd.*

The poets middle-aging, yes, but hardly into writer's senescence. It is the recouped time of their time, voices over on a field of playful listeners, as poets sway back and forward on wave of freshness, the freshness of their earlier juices and poems. The fifties, early sixties. Back to the first dips into the well that brought up the crystal *agua* of a movement, an expression at once headstrong and sophisticated and naïve.

In Corso's case, the Bleecker Street (where he was born) smarts yoked to the jester's warts-and-all precosity. Hail to young Gregory Corso, the once king of the Gotham Hill. And in Ginsberg's, the awakened roughgem sensibility out of Paterson, polished later on wheels of Columbia's Van Dorens and Trillings. Only to roll off the Morningside Heights campus, roll off and away to open road of Beats; open waywardly US road out to far Frisco, and farther still Ganges River. Ever-expanding on peyote hashish wave, ever-returning to groove music anger of the Haight, of midwest Wichita Sutra, of East Village cobblestone grit.

The fifties, early sixties. Reincarnated on a midweek night of 1973; promissory notes on early goodbet talent paidoff into one generation later. With Allen's roaring, and by-now mythic, "Howl." We missed the set for being shutout in the eight o'clock rush for seats. But we were told afterwards by a trickly bearded Columbia student who'd "cracked" his own first reading of his poems just a week or two before, at the St. Mark's Monday nights marathon: "Nobody but nobody can match him. The way Ginsberg *reads* 'Howl.' And the way 'Howl' *reads.*"

Over to Gregory Corso in the second set. We finally do get in, a tight-squeeze push of bodies down the aisle to hunched-over spot about third row left, galvanized by Allen's charged signal: "All you people in the lobby flow into the aisles and squat!" Gregory reads his "friendship" poem, with the neat opening couplet: "Friends be kept/Friends be gained ..."

He offers several more nosegays from *Gasoline*, and from *Vestal Lady*. The jammed audience of near 1,000 ripples across to him, with applause like hot tickles under sweaty armpits. Poet sort of knockabouting in pleasurable response, he leans a foot forward on slatted chair to haul the praise in. The famous cowlick, the cockatoo's spout over jester's eyes, going a little to gray now. The ribbon-slash of smile, the cutup's frown of 100 past platform reads, caved in a notch from missing tooth or three. Yes, the magic surfacing once again, out of the ruts, the wanderings into Psychedelly of years gone by.

Ginsberg, then, like a bushy-bearded Hasid, is a chanter of Hare Krishnas, partakes of *allofit*. He's seated on a large wicker settee, busted right leg in plaster cast, leg stretched out full on three or four satin cushions, his upper-body firmly planted in corner of settee. ("Slipped on ice at Cherry Valley farm.") His suit of donkey-ride blue denims, set off by yards of orange colored drapes on settee, make for a disjointed picture. The freedom-riding poet balladry maker; the platform reader at home in Greenwich Village; doing a gig on West Twelfth stage that could be somebody's front parlor. Moments of calm in the parlor, as Allen tunes up for the evening's "special," a six-part mantra to his own harmonium accompaniment, with two standup guitar players who strum out background chords. His longtime friend and lover Peter Orlovsky—bulging at the gut like Turkish wrestler in his Nixon Makes War sweatshirt—stands close by and turns looseleaf pages of Allen's verses. It's a first performance, not of the chants, but of the chants-and-verse together.

Allen looks out at the audience, a wide-scanning gaze through moons of thick hornrims that "spooks" the crowd to silence. He then describes the mantra, the six subtly varying motifs which, he informs us, come from the Tibetan prayer-wheel. The first motif is *a*, a soft and cool sound originating in the crown; the next is *ah*, a bit huskier in tone, direct from the throat; the third is *sha*, brought up from heart and breast; the fourth is *sa*, up from the bellybutton; the fifth is *ma*, a sinuous, an orgasmic sound, from the genital area; and finally there's *ha*, sort of razzing or flatulent, from way back in the sphincter.

As he chants each motif, he points to the corresponding body-part, with arrow of index finger. He then explains the sequence: The *a*-crown part is "God and the world"; the *ah*-throat part is the "warrior"; the *sha*-breast part expressed "lust"; the *sa*-belly part, "animal need"; the *ma*-genital part is "hungriest of all"; and the *ha*-sphincter part "evokes hell."

The mantra is long, maybe 30-40 minutes duration. Typical are such Ginsberg themes as "exorcism," as in the lines: "I shit hate through my asshole/my sphincter loosens the void/all hell's legions fall through space/the Pentagon is destroyed . . ." and playful eroticism, the poet celebrating: "Lust in the heart/for pink tender prick of the schoolboy/upstairs bedroom naked with books . . ." As he belts out the mantra in that soaked-in baritone, as he chants the "anatomy" sequences with good ear for mood-modality, a kindred spell builds up over the large room, the youthful audience locking on the piece's density with a kind of rolling action of its own. And when Allen winds down to the finish, very near the entire room jumps up with a shout, with a lusty staccato of applause and whistling, all of it bursting through, as if in fresh discovery and celebration of their own deepfelt prayer.

Yet unspent pockets of energy, spinoffs of appetite for more, want satisfying. A shout from the orchestra floor, "Tell us a little about Kerouac." They gradually quiet down as the Kerouac "image" hovers around the auditorium like the unseen, mystical guest at Passover table. Allen responds to the guest slowly and ruminatively, his large bushy face masked in thought, his eyes lighting up with twinkles of remembrance. Finally he uncups his hands, palms outward in a sort of "I pass" gesture, and he nods over to Gregory. Who clasps hold instantly, delivering a torrent on Kerouac's funeral in Lowell. The way "Jack looked in his box—beautiful man, that was some embalming . . ." The considerable beers he downed; and the "holy piss that had to wait . . ." Pan to a sudden aggressive shout from the left balcony pouch of seats, a thick-lipped razzing that punches a hole through the good vibes: "Hey, Gregory, why don't you go back to Lowell, *already*!" To Gregory's quick counterpunch: "I just can't do that, man. Might run into somebody like you at the local pub."

First to come off stage is Corso (he's popped on and off all night like a kid on a pogo stick) and he's soon trapped in a big circle of admirers. Some want his autograph. One young lady tells Corso she's a composer, wants to set his poems to music. And an almond-eyed student, pretty as she is vamping bold, wants to seal her delight with hugs and kisses. To almond-eye Gregory croons, "Come to me my melancholy babe." And both peck away lightly and daintily, like doves on the park green.

Ginsberg all but leaps for his crutches. As he plods the four steps down to orchestra floor, and inches his way along the slightly raked aisle to the lobby, a train of youthful fans moves along with him. A paperback copy of *Howl*—folded open at the frontispiece—is thrust right under his beard, and Allen cheerfully, if a little awkwardly, scrawls his name across the page. Meanwhile Orlovsky, moved by what a member of the entourage calls "The Orlovsky Obsession," breaks off

Did NBA Know What It Was Doing? 107

running interference for Allen, his braided mandarin pigtails flying in the rush, as he spots yet another miscreant who is into—as Orlovsky puts it—the "coffin nails of the system." He confronts the smoker eyeball to eyeball, as much in sorrow as anger, but with the true Double-O firmness, and he makes a swift grab for the cigarette, rarely missing, after which he tears the butt open (grass is something else again) and grinds the offending weed into the ground with his foot. Then a smile that's so infectious, victim and punisher are as one in the triumph. (Peter Orlovsky, our Don Quixote of the smog, riding through Marlboro Country with lance.)

Gregory now breaks from the daisy-chain of lovers, and comes by to say hello. He introduces you to a stocky man in leather windbreaker, a rough-hewn laborer type who's chewing on a stubby cigar, and who sat a few feet from you during the reading: "Meet my old man, Fortunato Sam Corso. First time he's heard me read." Like a pride of lions, they stand close and beam at each other, Gregory's wide slash of a grin telegraphing the message: "This time I really did okay. You better believe it." You spot the physical likeness; but you can sense the apartness, too.

The downhome plainness, in his New York speech and manner, of Corso senior. The faraway look of jumpiness, the restless energy of moving in bursts, of Corso junior.

You tell Fortunato it's hard to believe he's not heard Gregory read before tonight. And he assures you, "Never heard him but now I want to catch him again." Gregory picks up the mood, "How about if we do Italy and Greece, together, one of these times." And the Bleecker Street stay-at-home, who has been on the same job for nearly forty years, a printer in a lower Broadway print shop, gets it on with Gregory: "We'll do that trip; and it'll be all on me." He seals the reunion with a mushroom puff from his now lighted cigar.

Alone moments later, Fortunato confides: "There are six of us Corsos in New York, we are all pretty close. Gregory makes seven but he's *way out there*, so we hardly ever see him. Like the philosopher says, Gregory's 'marchin' to his own drummer.'"

Out on West Twelfth Street, a night of budding in the air, of slow partings, the kids hang in there. They want a word more with Allen, with Gregory. Juices are flowing, and you're glad. Tomorrow (and you'd seen it all too recently to forget!) Corso's burnt-out case may reappear. But now Allen tells you: "Gregory's doing his best work in years. Watch for it in his new collection." And the juices flowing, in Allen's own work, like an open spigot. Three new books of poems in one season: *Iron Horse* (The Coach House Press); *The Fall of America* (City Lights); *The Gates of Wrath* (Gray Fox Press, Bolinas). *Fall* took the NBA for 1973.

The joys, and the burnings, of the ongoing muse.

New Orleans

TO NOLA WITH LOVE & DISTRESS 1/When roving editor takes wing, the flight is nearly always an east-west or west-east axis, rarely a north-south one. West to the skyclimbing Chicago hub, or the nearer Madison campus country some miles inland from the Great Lakes. Or east to London's great madness, which I'm drawn to at least every other year, exchanging like some homing bird of bigtown kicks—for a fortnight or so—the original New York madness for Babylon on the Thames. But now I've been to New Orleans. It's only the second time (not counting two or three quickies to plastic Miami) I've gone deep south, the first being a wartime 14-weeks of unreality known as Infantry Training, at Fort McClellan, Alabama, in the early 1940s: tough cadre from the south and easygoing recruits from north locked in two different countries of the mind.

So its *oh* and *ah* New Orleans! The unique Nola of present-day tensions, linked with a somewhat fabled openness, two gritty moods holding in rare equilibrium, down by the subtropical sprawl where Mississippi and Gulf churn together uneasily, I came for a five-day visit (stayed an extra day), with small press editor-publisher Harry Smith, for the annual convention of little mags sponsored by Cosmep. I found it one hell of a strange place, and I left with that hole of regret one feels, when he's ticketed for a quick stay and realizes he's barely skimmed it, by which time he's back at the airport for his return home.

Coming out of the sky for landing, the eye runs parallel with miles and miles of flooded bayous and vast forests of green under water that backs up almost to the long, rounding perimeter of New Orleans itself. It's the first clue to the mailed fist of nature gone watery that hangs over a city that's two or three feet below sea level at the edges; a city whose miles of levees and dikes have to be opened every now and then to let millions of gallons of water find escape out beyond the Nola line. All is fairly under control, with luck and quick engineering reflexes; but the threat of watery devastation is always there, as is the sense of loss that comes with the flooded bayous and forests, loss of wild life and thick winding stands of trees, the city itself meantime holding its breath while Big Muddy and wide gulping Gulf gradually boil down to live-and-let-live size. (One Mississippi watcher on the Spring, '73 floods: "Old Noah himself would have blinked at least twice to see it, I tell you!")

We touched down at Nola airport two hours late, due to a foulup at LaGuardia that afternoon. We looked for our New Orleans hosts—Darlene Fife and Bob Head of the underground *Nola Express*—who'd made the arrangements for convention and housing on the Tulane campus. Nowhere in sight and we learned later that they'd been at the airport and left when they couldn't get definite arrival time on our flight. Two rubes from the big apple—large bear of a Harry Smith and gray longlocks of a roving editor—dropped down among the southern home teams. Hawking cabbie with a no-sweat approach, "Just hunker in and leave the drivin' to me; I'll get you to ole Tulane in no time *at all*." On the long ride the knarled, punchy-faced hackie is curious: "How do you call this convention of yours—Cosmie something? Ain't the same as the one checked in the other day, I don't guess, lots of bigtime printing folks visitin' this week. Books must be a hot item every durned place but in Delta country, looks like . . ." And "no time" stretches out to near an hour as we take a long drive and even longer search before we finally come to the right building on the huge Tulane campus. The cabbie says thirteen and fifty—hiked three bucks over what the meter actually reads—but Harry makes no bones out of that as the cabbie did go above-and-beyond in his building by building search.

Between-semesters' June doldrums on the Tulane-Loyola campus. We both register and drop our bags on the 7th floor of the long, rectangular pylon that will house upwards of sixty Cosmepers by time all have arrived. About eight or ten have already registered (we're told) and went off to see the Bourbon Street strip with Darlene and Bob. It's past ten P.M., and tired-out or not we decide to leg it to a spot called "The Boot" where according to one local student you can get "jug of beer and halfway okay burger if you don't mind the racket of pinball machines, miniture pool and hyped-up juke box." On the long, circular stroll we get lost among the shadowy complexes of southern "classic," the glassine square boxes, the big slumbering Sugar Bowl (smack on campus!), and lots more of what must be the biggest mothering enclave of academia in the whole fifty states.

Out of the green shadowy vistas, blue-neoned stone walks, long swards of manicured flat grassways, the sudden appearance of a row of brilliantly-lit tennis courts, at least half-dozen of which are occupied by students, all of them swatting away under the eye-hurting kliegs, a scene that was real enough (even at the unlikely hour of eleven P.M.), but one that evoked a teasing kind of story out of mind, like those John Cheever or Irwin Shaw set pieces from the pages of *The New Yorker*: emotion recollected in tranquility upon hero's return to the college sod, many years after the time of his time as college frosh. The smoothly fabricated tennis courts, the four or five swimming pools (one of them, Olympic-size), the growing number of housing pylons, the two or three relatively low-priced eating dens, the very environment of sheltered space and leisurely activity, all gave an aura of Big Mother; nearby whose capacious crinoline skirts, a freshman at 18 could toddle and play, right up to age 22 or older; in the meantime, getting all his learning, and all his necessary degrees, without ever once having to leave the graces of Big Mother campus.

Past the courts we get lost again, in densely shadowed concourses of shade trees and more such arboreal trappings. We spot three students who are seated on the portico of a southern Gothic, and we approach them. They're passing the time of night (near-midnight) with tokes of grass between them, a tiny roach that lights up like a firefly each time it's passed around and drawn on with dabbing puffs down to the end. Two young men and a young lady; all in loafing summer dress; one of the boys wearing a faded Columbia U sweatshirt that catches our New York eyes. They straighten us out on the Boot, and before we leave them, Harry says to Columbia, "Your shirt puts you pretty far south from the West End; now that school's out don't you want to head back home." Columbia shrugs it off, "Hey, you guessed right. I left West End about a year ago and found me a home at the big T. With my old lady [points to girl] laying the Dixie living on my head, there's no way I want to go back north soon." (Columbia blue finds ole reb Tulane.) When we get to the Boot, it checks out noisy, and halfway okay, burger-wise, just as we'd been told.

The four-day convention is held in a large second-floor room of the Students Center, which has a good self-service cafeteria, swimming pool with giant picture window right next door to cafeteria, colored TV

To Nola With Love & Distress

retreat with soft leanback chairs (some of us broke away from Saturday's agenda to watch Secretariat kill-off Sham and Company in the Belmont), outdoor veranda with polished wooden tables and benches topped by pastel beach umbrellas, and more Tulane goodies and grosseries under one large roof. At the opening Cosmepers wander by from mid-morning on, they exchange greetings of reunion from the 1972 convention held at Madison, Wisconsin; hit the chow line for delights of southern-style omelettes whipped to a froth with hot biscuits on request; hesitate before deciding which tap of a dozen or more crushed ice drinks to draw from; and for the really daring palate, thick cups of chicory—the Civil War nostalgia bit?—to wash it all down.

Back at the meeting room, first business is the sampling of a different kind of fare, the ever-expanding menu of littles from around the US. The mags are stacked face up, most titles in small quantities, on seven or eight tables around the room, they're up for grabs while they last. And, in a broader sense, they're handoffs of the multiple formats of the small press world, all of them together amounting to a fairly accurate portent of the state of the writing culture from below. How much of the lot is literary fool's gold, and how much the real 22 carat, will of course be sorted out on closer reading when Cosmepers get back home. But in that first hour of greedy exchange, they're all of one mind to gather up as much of the past year's harvest as they can haul.

What is Cosmep, and why is it gathered here? As the session opens with an introductory go-around, each giving his or her name-littlemagplace, the 60-odd members present from all sections, some of whom traveled long distances by thumb to get to New Orleans, appear tuned to an idea that's charged with promise: Writers and poets each with a vision, however rough at the edges; a vision that would take wing in poem and story, and thus offer alternative voice (like arrows of the soul!) to the miasma of Watergated America of the seventies. And the barriers are way up—how do you web together these visions from oil-soaked Texas to violence-prone New York; how crack through the litry marketplace, when you bear no visible gifts of kitsch, no ersatz gunfire script that will satisfy jock taste. And finally, how do you stay together, in the holding sense; white-black, in a guilt-dragging politics and economy; man-woman, in a fragmented Archie Bunker culture; and yes, straight-homosexual, in an America that sweats alienation under blankets of native puritanism.

And they spoke to all of this—Harry Smith, outgoing Cosmep board chairperson; and such women's voices as Kruchkow, and the lady known as "Ellen," who publishes a feminist newsletter somewhere in the midwest; and Judith Hogan, fine young poet from North Carolina, pacing her words to catch the silent stretches between the playful howls of her ten-month-old daughter, whom Judith had in tow from the first meeting on; and Hugh Fox, the literary Batman out of East Lansing, Michigan, who complained wryly, "I'd love to be corrupted by an acceptance, once in a while," after revealing that thirty or more of his manuscripts had been shot down "with unctuous regularity by publishing mobs in Manhattan"; and Tom Forcade, the UPS writer-editor who was there as observer, looking like a riverboat gambler in his severe black jacket with black velvet buttons, as he dealt some ace cards on the need for cooperative effort by underground press and small press operations; these and many others spoke their pieces. From Thursday through Sunday, in meeting after long meeting, at times in a querulous tone, but always with open-ended regard for the variety (100 different flowers blooming!) of the writing persona and craft. Hence this tip of the Cosmep iceberg, 60 or 65 out of a growing membership of nearly 450 had enough to chew on (Lord knows!), not only there in New Orleans, but for the succeeding twelve months till the next convention. Planned for the big apple, and that will be a first. When the vote was announced, one member spoke out, "Cosmep is ready for New York; will New York be ready for Cosmep."

2/New Orleans for Cosmepers was a geography laid out like ripe fruit for the picking, coming as they did from the cold steel of New York, the unvarying plainlands of Iowa, the layered fogland of exhaust of a Los Angeles. And for roving it was like writing a letter in his head, take by slow take, a sort of tense "To Nola with Love and Distress" missive. Uppers and downers, both. For such is its nature, so unique is Nola for its spectrum of moods and trends that roving found himself on a five-day coaster ride, from manic highs of admiration, to sad lows of reality that the lady was besieged by trouble. He had the notion that he was recording—it haunts the page even as he fleshes it out—some vibrant canvas of promise lashed by dark, knotty forces that couldn't be ignored. The full picture being a paradigm of the US at large. So a few quick strokes here, a grasping for those fleeting takes out of a hazy but mostly loving visit.

On the St. Charles trolley ride, from Tulane campus to downtown Canal, a distance of roughly five miles, the 15 cents jingle of coin in the

To Nola With Love & Distress 113

box like old music, as it triggers memory of long rides up and down NYC's old Broadway line, for an even lower dime. With me are two local poets, one of whom teaches at Loyola. As we clang through stretches of fine old homes, some almost hidden behind showers of creeping vine, others peeking out from heavy stands of palm, Loyola points out several mansion-like complexes, and relates with air of concern: "The best of these are swooped up by oil millionaires; mostly Texans of whom you might say, they're closet New Orleaners; they hedge their down-home style of Texas accumulation—ranches, oilwells, football teams and stadiums—with tours of anticipated pleasure, here in the New Orleans backyard. Wheel and deal on Mondays through Fridays; zip down in private jet to get the starch out of their bibs on weekends . . ." I'd heard the comment from others, not only the fact of oil money pushing in, but of droves of ordinary folk from Dallas, Houston and elsewhere hopping down by the planeload, or shooting over by fast car, or rolling in tourist-style on Greyhound bus. For rounds of weekend tricks, you play it as it lays, then back home to the Lone Star state till the next one. It's a mind-boggling thought, Nola being annexed by the King Ranch and Company.

Nighttime poetry reading at Jerusalem Gardens, a natural-foods warren at the rim of the French Quarter. Gardens is a visual kicker, long oaken tables and chairs you could *lean* into, aura of 1920s bohemia from half-dozen colored Tiffany lamps, thin spokes of misty orange flame funneling out of kerosene lamps on tables. (And it had to be natural food; you waited fifteen minutes or longer for each crafted dish of vegetarian exotica; each foamy health drink.) Six or seven Nola poets in a standup reading; with what seemed a forced resonance at times. Or maybe a case of tapping roots, some of the poems striding down alleyways of the Quarter's past glories; looking to meet up with the likes of a Faulkner, or a Lyle Saxon (catalyst of the New Orleans literary rush of the 30s), or even a Ten Williams. The presence of Gypsy Lou Webb, patron lady of Nola's late-50s revival, also contributes to a feeling of roots. (Among other of her valuable scores, she and her late husband Jon Webb, under the imprint of Loujon Books, were first to bring out a full collection of Charles Bukowski's poems, which has since become a collector's item of the avant.) Gypsy Lou now seated in a corner, wearing swirling black cottons and large Indian-style brooch, her eyes two bright coals of concentration that deny the onset of years (60?; 65?).

As each poet reads his-her offerings, a certain note of proudness surfaces, as if he-she were saying: "We'll build our Nola scene yet, and we'll stack it up against, you'll see the day soon, the best work of you Cosmep Huns from Berkeley, Boston or wherever." A very bold spirit indeed, and even some poems that match the boldness, if not exactly rising to heights of a "movement." With local acoustic color invading the Gardens as they read; the low ringing steelwheels hum of what must have been a 200-freightcar linkup, moving slowly through the night on a bluff of the Mississippi; your ear catching poet's lines and freightcar hum like the cacophony of a poem by itself. During all of which roving sips at his peach-apple shake (it didn't hurt at all), feeling the Ponce de Leon nectar coursing in his veins. Served up by a shy-smiling girl in caftan print who moves around the room, or near-floats would be closer, with neat strokes of individualized service; her smile not so much fixed, as bubbling up from some inside well of friendliness. Caftan to roving, "Where are you from; I must know who you are!" Roving to caftan, "I'm from cloud seven at the moment, why don't you join me, there's always room for more."

Five of us Cosmepers—Harry Smith, Charles Haseloff, Hugh Fox, Richard Morris and myself—meet with Dotson Rader "to do the town." We stop off at the Downtowner, where Rader is staying, for a round of drinks before hitting the Quarter. Rader, whom writer Seymour Krim has called "literary princeling of New York," has had a thing going with New Orleans, ever since Tennessee Williams invited him down for a visit, some two or three years back. He says, "It's the most 'yes' city in the whole fifty states; 'yes' to life and 'yes' to your own lifestyle, whether you're pegged straight, round, kinky, sado-masochist, you name it. I wanna live here [some day when he bursts on the horizon of fame-money-notoriety; or whatever it is this post-30s writer-radical-dervisher is chasing after] six months outta the year and six months in New York. It's the yin-yang of New Orleans lowpressure smarts; and New York highwire tension and creativity." Meanwhile, he slides down to Nola by jet, any excuse he can lay hold on, best of all some article assignment for good bread; and he proceeds to "milk" his way through the Quarter, and other likely spots of interest; he milks his way as if with a straw, to siphon up the juices for a novel (four or five chapters in first draft) he's doing on New Orleans.

At the moment—while all of us are downing vodka highballs—Rader is on the hotel phone trying, with that considerable "Let me explain how it is " charm of his, to nail down a reservation for dinner, nothing less than Antoine's will do; and wouldn't you know it, it's really bananas all the way, what with it being a Saturday night, and what with that touristy printers' convention in town. Anyway we decide to leg it against the odds; we have one more for the road and leave. The milelong French Quarter, as we edge our way through it, comes up a noisy circus of honchos and honchettes on the loose, all sizes and shapes and dress and patois, people tunneling past this corner ruckus (friendly ruckus), past that corner hullabaloo where all eyes are lit with voyeur's glee. It's an updated, US style "Children of Paradise," with no sure, focused mood but that of an adrenaline high; and with a near-fisty surge of physicality, shoulders and bellybuttons rubbing close, as the crowds push along the narrow, closed-to-traffic streets.

The six of us push along with the crowds; and, after some six or seven tries and coming up 86ed in all of them, Rader walking shotgun past the hungering mobs waiting out the long, long lines; we at last find a restaurant that will take us, but only after he convinces the maître: "I've been served, unjacketed, in the best four-star restaurants on the *Continent*. Let alone your four-star restaurants in the Quarter." (Rader of course hadn't been on the Continent *at all*.) Haseloff in the flash of it all announces: "I'd love to see the East Village roped off like this on Saturday nights. It would be a good time in the old town, tonight!" And for sure it would! A good time for *homicide*!

My last day in New Orleans, I'm guest at Kate and Doug Rose's house, about a mile from Tulane. The three of us do a home ballet of discovery, on what's-best-worst in the Nola image. (The Roses' furry, sleepy-eyed baby of six weeks couldn't care less.) I first met Kate outside the Student Center, two or three days before. She's a tall, willowy late-20ish poet, with the quick-shifting shyness one somehow associated with a Virginia Wolff. Though not a member of Cosmep, she came by for several sessions, confessing to roving: "After nestling in the bosom of New Orleans for some time, I didn't realize what a charge you could get from an invasion of kindred souls." At one point she invited me to stay over for a night before I returned to New York. Now I was outside the Roses' door, well past midnight of a Sunday, the whole neighborhood of Fern Street coming alive suddenly with numberless barking dogs, as I wandered up the stairs of their darkened front porch. The rows of brightly colored one-family houses looking spooky in the milky moonlight and thick overhang of trees.

Kate finally appears at the door, ushers me into the front parlor, moves to the kitchen to mix a round of whiskey and ice. "That," she tells me over her shoulder, motioning to a corner divan, "will be your flop for the night." Moments later Doug comes into the room, and after Kate introduces me to Doug, we all get comfortably seated and sip our drinks. He looks a bit older than Kate; somewhere in his middle-30s; and though over six feet in height, he hardly towers over her; with a kind of squared-off dark goatee, and vaguely remote look in the eye; all of which evokes for roving a younger, and of course less frantic, Ahab. We talk about writers and Cosmep, and the starchiness of the Tulane campus, where Doug holds down an assistant prof in Economics. We break off when the baby starts to cry, tiny broken sobbing from the large inside bedroom, and Kate joking: "All *it* knows is that *it* wants *its* mother's milk." As for the next day, she reminds me they want to show me the Mississippi and some other spots I compained I had missed, then pointing to Doug and adding as they both leave the parlor: "If I can pull *that* man away from his computer." (Doug earlier, "If we could only keep up with *all* the figures; then we might find some answers to the *whole mess.*" Ah, yes! The eschatology of Ahab and his great white whale!)

The next morning Kate shows off her Nola garden. (Doug remains inside with the baby; one tapping away at his mini computer keys, swift fingers like ten tiny harpoons striking at the imperturbable whale; the other dozing away lightly in its crib.) Roving, a city freak all his fifty-plus years, is caught in the wonder of that small but awesomely lush garden; as Kate glides her way through an inventory of various trees, flowers, fruits and creepers. On the creepers: "They're really quite a mystery. Nothing more than hollow tubular stalks that crop out practically overnight. And if you don't cut away quickly, they'll damn near choke the whole shebang to death." On our way to the airport later, in the Roses' near-waterlogged Volks, we side-tour to the top of a wide levee, and view the devastation of the spring floods, which had reached past the floorboards of rows of old river shacks, the drooping wooden shacks having the aspect of faded, emaciated limbs of old age. Then for a quick tour of the emerald green, immaculate and well-tended acres of handsome Audubon Park. Farther along into town, and before we approach the four-laner for the airport, an apparition from a good half-mile away, a gigantic outcropping of bowlshaped edifice, a sort of monster parody of Frank Lloyd Wright's graceful Guggenheim Museum, multiplied in a mushroom by 50, and as we pass closer by, I gag out at the Roses on sighting the near-completed thing in full profile: "What the hell is that Tyrannosaur Rex gonna be when they're finished with it!" And Doug tells me: "That Tyrannosaur is gonna be the Superdrome, or world's biggest car park (room for over five thousand) anywhere in the world. All at a two hundred million tab, if it costs them a penny, by time they get around to topping it out."

My farewell view of Nola. With its magical gardens, besieged by creeper blight. With its magical French Quarter, soon to be besieged by Superdrome, the cry of jocks echoing through the quaint alleyways. With its fair and far vista of Mississippi, cavalierly bypassed by Superdrome technology and dollars that could well save the bayous, woodlands and river shacks from drowning.

Labor Day songfest

OUR MR. HARDHAT MEETS JOE HILL   At a New York Labor Day songfest, itself an oddity in biglabor 1970s, our Mr. Hardhat meets Joe Hill. The afternoon sing, on the open South Street Museum pier, is a special corner of culture city. With visual assets (steelharp Brooklyn Bridge at center stage) and Upper Bay-East River breeze that "break" you out into the open. Spirit you away from the vise of perpendicular city, as you catch a glimpse of cubelike Twin Towers topouts from the pier's wooden planks you're standing on.

The bouncy Oscar Brand, guitar-wielder archivist of Americana in song, strums out "Joe Hill" in smoky style. *I dreamed I saw Joe Hill last night/alive as you and me* . . . On the unused half of the open, Siamese stage; a dozen or more children do their own strut and dance to the "Joe Hill," their parents seated nearby listening to Brand. The audience, sprawled out or standing or just nosing by, is in the grip of that same oddity: some 500 in a mostly silent picture, nostalgia on the wing of song written on faces. Several do a lip-read of the lyrics as Brand moves it along.

The locals, in this kind of "escape" setting, shuck off their everyday tension like unwanted garments. Take the two young ladies, who are seated lotus-style, on the same open stage the kids are dancing on. They're both dressed in Levi's and cotton shirts; both have their hair long and in braids, but in slightly different configuration. Not twins, you can see that; but so absorbed are they in the sing; and so absorbed in each other's responses; you might as well say they're twained in private mood that sets them apart—for the passing—from the New York swarm they're wedded to. Likewise with the others, now melding with the crowd, now unmelding back to the private stance.

Prior to Oscar Brand's set, there was Jean Ritchie's, hers suggesting a veritable Library of Congress of mountain and folklore tunes. A large woman with flame-red hair, and softly lyric voice in a contralto range, Ms. Ritchie performed on her own fish-shaped instrument, described as a "downhome Kentucky dulcimer." She offered additional riches in the cornucopia of labor tunes. A "shoemaker's song," about a mountain cobbler who has to keep an entire village in supply. And one about mining women at home; who in a shock of recognition hear the "off hours whistle" of a West Virginia mine; which means cave-in or some other disaster at the pithead. And a lament about Appalachia ecology gone wrong—how strip-mining has reduced the farming land, made terraces of mud where crops used to grow.

Opening the four-hour round was the X Seaman's Institute Four, longtime performers on the Museum pier. Seaman's unstoppable chanteys were brief, salty as the highseas itself, exuberant or sad, as in any yeoman's book of tunes you'd want to hear. And hourly raffles, at a buck a throw, with useful prizes for the winners. (Pete Seeger records; Dell books on sailing.) And reminders that the Museum pier depends on public contributions. Add to which, a break in the itchy mid-90s weather; no howling Nor'easter, mind you, but on-and-off showers enough to send the glass down a few notches. Far from chasing their way home, as is the New Yorker's wont at any hint of rain, most stood fast on the pier; and they called for more chanteys, even as the Four wondered aloud if *they* (the Four) had had it for now. And to the bonus of rain add the incoming wind, which caused ripples on the river, and had the entire Museum fleet bobbing in place. The two-master steel *Wavertree*, lashed by hawser to the four-master *Mosholu*; the Hudson River Dayliner *Alexander Hamilton*; the potbellied *Ambrose Lightship*. All of them deactivated; all gently bobbing in place. And, you don't get any closer, short of signing on directly, to the seafarer's way, than that! Not your average Manhattan cubbyhole dweller, hardly!

Heinrich Böll

A DAY IN THE LIFE OF A NOBEL LAUREATE It's not every day you meet a Nobel Prize laureate. Mine was Herr Heinrich Böll, the 1972 winner for Literature. He came to New York—which absorbs celebrities like sunshine absorbs mist—to receive a round of honors from American P.E.N. No city hall reception; no big splash in the media. The problem, if problem it is, may be that Böll "misses out with the American reader, so far as big sales and big-name authors go." This from a quality book store owner I know. Böll, he says further, is being short-changed by the American reader.

At any rate, P.E.N. did not short-change the event. First there was the press conference at P.E.N.'s roomy, bookfilled New York office on Fifth. I got a call on a Wednesday from Kirsten Michalski, American P.E.N.'s executive-secretary and roundup person for Böll's visit. She was worried lest "not enough press show up" at the conference the next day at two. I gave her the names of some book and culture people. Most of them, it turned out, she had already called, with no firm promise they would show.

Maybe the low-key response was due to the Week of the Knicks. Or the lukewarm esteem of Mr. and Ms. American Bookbuyer. Or the near-savaging of Böll's latest novel in the Monday *Times*, a scant 48 hours earlier. Or all three together. Anyway, Kirsten said she would keep trying. As for myself, I told her I would make it, though it meant a switch in my calendar.

The conference next day, the turnout is not too bad. About 25 from various media—most with pencil and pad at the ready—which is usually a good sign for "business." And, parenthetically, a near-total absence of that very New Yorkish syndrome, "I don't know about the others; but I'm here *to be seen*." With the large photo gallery of authors looking on from the walls (Neruda and Samuel Beckett and Robert Lowell and others), the conference begins as Heinrich Böll and P.E.N.'s Thomas Fleming sit down informally at a long glass-topped mahogany table. The press sits in-the-round on slatted wooden chairs. A few introductory words, and Fleming asks for questions.

Heinrich Böll in repose, as he waits for the first question, is a deceptively calm persona. Earmarks of open middle-burgher intelligentsia, in contrast to (a flash thought) the aloofness of an upper-burgher Thomas

Mann. White shirt unbuttoned at neck and tieless, eyes of a bright gray-blue that are alert for dialogue, ready crease of smile under thick brushlike mustache, full-moon roundish face with traces of balding top. He chain-smokes with crunched pack of American butts in front of him. It's the one small detail of tension underneath the calm.

As he talks on—after the first question finally surfaces—Herr Böll seems to wrap up large problems, or "concepts," in a kind of higher-journalism of brief, to-the-point answers. Not the German spiel of abstruse politics or science; but more in the key of the "felt" humanism of across-borders European. Or in the Bach mode—orderly run of notes above, depth of passion below. With more than a workable English to steer him through.

The question, which happened to be mine, was on Watergate. Not so much, I had said to Herr Böll, from this side of the pond, but rather what he and other Europeans thought over there. "I would not want," he quickly assured, "to comment at all in a direct way. The problem of Watergate—and that's indeed a mild label for it—is one for all Americans to ponder. As for Europeans, our response can be summed-up almost in a word, we feel deep *sorrow*." He goes on: Whereas political scandal is nothing new in Europe; and in fact is usually attended by "beatings, jailings and worse"; it was nevertheless a shock that Watergate could happen "in what many of us feel is still a country of great freedom . . ." He praised the American press: "This kind of broad exposure could never happen in Germany. Our journalists are much too traditional, even timid . . ."

More Q's and A's on Watergate, the media people rushing their notes across pads as Böll spoke. Soon a second big question came up, Writers in Prison. A somber black-white poster, distributed by American P.E.N., hung from the wall just inches away, a poster that gives country-by-country listing of names (call it United Nations of Shame!), and that lent a kind of black-border credence to all of Böll's remarks, even as he spoke: "I'm very occupied with this problem, as president of International P.E.N., and one thing we never do is make 'politics' out of it. We want to free writers and artists on *human* grounds; and not score political points whether on the right or left . . ."

That evening Böll was honored guest at P.E.N.'s annual dinner, held at Tavern on the Green. New York's crème de la crème literati were there, all out in mod-dressed finery, begged or borrowed or stolen or even paid for. Writers and poets and critics, senior and middle and junior editors, bluff-mannered publishers (indies and conglomerates both), literary agents by the score, and a handful of chic individuals who are the social appendages (hangers-on with green) of the litpub scene itself. All took spirited part in the buzzing, pre-dinner cocktail mix, held in the cement garden under a slate Central Park sky, a light chill rolling in from the big Sheep Meadow. It was of course impossible to tell, clothes-wise, whose was begged, and whose was paid for, what with the telephone-numbers trend in writers' contracts these days. (Hence your fatcat writer, like as not, looking a bit sharper, more expensively outfitted, than your average publisher, for all that the untutored eye would guess it was the other way round.)

The dinner was candle-lighted, roastbeefy and leisurely. Followed by business, kept down to a minimum by Fleming, who announced the winner of P.E.N.'s 1972 Translation Prize, then called on newly appointed American P.E.N. president Jerzy Kosinski. Finally Böll was called on, to a standing applause, as he came off the dais and headed for the lectern nearby. More formal than at the press conference, both in dress and prepared notes, Böll took up again with Watergate and Writers in Prison. On the former: "Law and order, whatever else it means to the politician, is a most familiar subject to writers and artists. The plotting of a story, the idea for a painting, begins and ends with strict attention to rules of creativity, hence the artist's need for law and order . . ." And on prisoners, Böll stressed the human factor over the political, with even greater emphasis this time.

As the laureate spoke, there was a sense of a "sealed pact," if that's not too strong, between him and the audience; wherein his words of concern, and his citing of specifics, such as his figure of "over five hundred who are presently in jail, country by country," all came across as a kind of shared litany, as well as a shared determination to renew P.E.N.'s efforts in this cause. Further, it's a measure of Heinrich Böll's toughness that, even on so ceremonial an occasion as this, he'd take pause to separate kitsch from seriousness, as when he said to Kosinski in a last-minute aside: "While I salute your appointment as president of American P.E.N., I must remind you that jokes about Polish coups d'etat are an insult to present-day reality in Poland." Böll's pique was brought on by Kosinski's earlier byplay—a sort of boy-to-boy thing—as told by Kosinski from the lectern: "Kurt Vonnegut agrees with me that my taking over as president is like a Polish coup d'etat; one year I'm in and one year I'm out . . ."

Add to which one last joke. McGraw-Hill, American publisher of Böll's latest novel, *Group Portrait with Lady*, calls their two-page bio release on him a "tip sheet."

California first

MAN HERE SAYS HE'S BEEN TO CALIFORN'/1 For a confirmed Bronx-Manhattan lifer, a first California visit is like the kid who unwraps his Christmas gift, and discovers that it's as least a couple of sizes too large. Take the lonely grandeur of the coastal plain—from San Francisco all the way down to Big Sur—which I saw on wheels and which had no frame of reference except the myth of California I carried around for lo these many years. The vastness of Pacific expanse, locked onto sheared cliffs and craggy-loamy promontories, was dramatic witness to myth/reality of the last continental frontier.

There was the trip south to Pacific Grove, for the 50th Anniversary Conference of the War Resisters League during three days in August. I arrived at San Francisco and contacted WRL West, whose Haight Street headquarters (a converted three-story house and overnight flop for out of staters) served as assembly point for registration and rides to the Asilomar State Park conference site. Asilomar was a beautiful resort midway on the Monterey peninsula some 150 miles south of Frisco.

My ride down was a lucky one, the driver was a home-breed San Franciscan. He knew the California coast not only by its unique geography, but by each field and humpbacked ring of hills. And he related to all of it with an expertise that came from his frequent pack trips into the Sierras, and from his journeys into Salinas country to pick—and picket—with the Cesar Chávez farmworkers. His name was Jon, a tall, longhaired and denim-clad man of 27, an engineering dropout from U of California, Berkeley. Jon was driving his Volks with one hand on the wheel, the other pointing out the window to this or that cameo of the road, as we moved along south like one long panning shot.

He would jab his finger skyward, and yell out evenly, "Turkey vulture circling out there." Turkey vulture, and there I was hoping, *bald eagle*. At other times, as we dipped past unbelievable spans of thickening crops, and rows on rows of greenery stretching to the horizon, I'd call out in unsure voice, "Those must be lettuce fields."

Only to have Jon correct me, "Not lettuce, they're artichokes. Young ones, they barely show their leaves. Takes two full years for a crop." However it lay, lettuce or artichoke, it was all grass to me. Yet I did feel the envy of your curb-stone walker, when in the company of someone like Jon, who could wrap-up the terrain with mere flicker of the eye.

We arrive at Asilomar, sloping ten-acres of cabins hidden among Monterey pine, resort with a view if I ever saw one. Barely do we drop our baggage, from car to administration building, when I find myself scaling three or four hilly dunes, drawn onward by my first up-close look at the Pacific. The lengthening swath of placid ocean, the watery carpeting of blue-aquamarine rushing in to fill the curving hook of Monterey peninsula, tugged at me like a sleepwalk of discovery; out of the royally blue pulsing of great rollers, so gentle on top but so awesomely powerful below, rose a mystical incarnation of great Balboa treading these same or like dunes all these centuries ago. Latecomer El Sid, looking out on the unfathomable Pacific. With the flash that whatever man has done to despoil and greedily abuse, one still had the image of a godhead design; and that all would go back to its original grandeur, to its wakening harmony and rough-calm play, soon after the despoilers had gone.

The War Resisters Fiftieth, while mostly this side of self-congratulatory, could nontheless boast a "bigness" that had everyone applauding. Well over 500 had showed up and registered, from 29 states in a wide sweep from Maine to Oregon. We were all housed in rustic, modern stone-and-wooden cabins; we took our three meals cafeteria style; we used grounds and meeting halls to a fare-thee-well. Yet the management's cheery cooperation had me wondering, and I put it to one California WRLer, "Today, they're being nice to us WRL radicals. Tomorrow, they'll be just as nice to the John Bircher. I guess that's a special California touch." But he scoffed, "Maybe it's the color of the money. WRL and the Birchers use the same green." The good soup of it all was the dollar-stretching value. A three-day package for $34, including meals and grounds, sunrises and sunsets, the ocean facilities.

Veterans of the resistance, among them three or four going as far back as jailings in World War I, and a good dozen others to jailings in World War II; along with a newer generation of activists, many of them from the campus and bigcity turmoils of Vietnam dissent; all got together, exchanged ideas and talked shop for the three days. The emphasis, What next for the US; now and in the next fifty. The review of the recent past, the Why of our descent into Nam and Watergate, was cause for neither self-punishment nor second guessing, nor again for the hardedge smugness that says, "We had the correct answers, if only the voters had listened." From somewhere at the middle distance came the touchstone of what WRL is all about: That in face of an illegal war that "wrapped itself up" in four additional years, fifteen-thousand additional American lives, countless bombings and jailings and homefront disruptions, the WRL could say "We didn't buy it then; and we don't buy it now." Call the WRL a political Brand Name from out of the grass-roots.

The conference had its lighter side. Larry Gara got his sequence mixed up, while doing slide projections of WRL highlights. One example was staffman Jim Peck's "triple jeopardy" arrest. Slide revealing Peck in nonviolent protest, and being collared in decidely *nongentlemanly* fashion. Moments later Gara projected the same slide twice more, *oops*! It was like the old silent movies, or like the Pentagon body counts, the exaggeration of Jim Peck's "arrests" causing nervous laughter in the hall. Joan Baez and Mimi Farina, the richly-piped siblings with guitars, gave two or three informal "sings," when not holding down Amnesty International's literature table. In the "Amazing Grace," during one of the sings, the whole assembly rose and linked arms, swayed and sang together with an esprit that was deeply moving. There were beer and wine bustouts each night, logfires going both indoors and outdoors. Friends made instantly, "actions" discussed openly. Despite the rumored presence of two FBI fuzz dressed in trademarked Burberry trench coats. (The government shoe-flies hardly missed a session, most times hanging back at the periphery of the crowd. The rumor seemed more than your garden-variety paranoia, at that.)

One particular action—it was the 2d night—stood out boldly for its directness alone. On that night Joan Baez, just before she went on stage, had received a call from an UFW organizer, who urged WRL "body on the line" support for the farmworkers' Fresno picket line the following day. (We had all heard about Dorothy Day's arrest in the Fresno area, it happened only two or three days earlier, and it wiped out her own scheduled appearance and talks at Asilomar.) Joan informed the audience about the call, adding that a meeting would be held right after her sing. And later that night, with about 150 in the hall, the informal rap began. One west coast WRL member: "If we're going to Fresno to get off some middleclass rocks of guilt, it's best that we forget the whole thing." Several of the others discussed options: "If we observe the court's ruling on limited picketing, they'll probably leave us alone. If we *defy* the rule, it's got to be the slammer for all!" The meeting ended well past midnight, with about 100 signing up for the Fresno demo.

At eight the next morning, coffee and breakfast under belts, they gathered in a caravan of twenty cars; led by one lonely, dilapidated UFW bus flying the red-black eagle emblem; and they took off for the five-hour Fresno trip. The final count was closer to 150, most of them in the under-30s bracket. And conceding the action put a dent in the last day's agenda, in another way Fresno was as dynamic an example of theory-into-practice as WRL or anybody else could have wanted. And for me a foreshadowing of what I'd run into later; the more so in unlooked for places in San Francisco; that the Cesar Chávez-UFW pull, with its emphasis on the purest form of nonviolence yet, at least in the often turbulent history of US labor, had at its core the aura of nearreligious crusade for, in the first place, many Californians who themselves are not farmworkers; and who indeed are far higher on the economic totem than are the latter. And that "la causa" and "la huelga," insofar as labor priorities go, may well be light years beyond the closed deck of biglabor-bigbusiness parlaying that has center stage today.

2/My conference action, more literary than political, was the trip I made to Big Sur. Several west coast writers, poet Bill Childress among them, had for years badgered me: "We've got a real live scene out here; it would do your New York heart some good to come out and dig it." And so Big Sur was surely a natural, what with downhome memories of Henry Miller, Jack Kerouac and the Beats, and the California poet eminence, Robinson Jeffers, even farther back yet. Four of us joined on the 2d conference day for the forty or fifty mile ride along the same coastal route. The party consisted of myself, New York Christophers staffman Bob Pugsley, and two women members of WRL West. Eyeing once more the immensities of Californ's three s's: space and sky and seascape! On the one side a vast panorama of high cliffs impacted by mile-long Pacific rollers; on the other serried ranks of baldy hill and piney mountain that appeared to hurdle clear down to the mini Datsun's car windows, as we threaded several hairpin turns in a gradual climb.

There's the scenery, and there are *scenes*, the latter often hidden inside the former, like boxes inside Chinese boxes. We came upon one such scene, about an hour's drive from Asilomar, the kind of eagle's-aerie setting that Jeffers caught in his poems. Looming on the promontory's shoulder, all broadbeamed and chateau-like, was a pub called the Nepenthe, where we stopped for a breather. Though built in post-Miller times, and more than a little touristy, there was no faulting Nepenthe's magical vistas. We took in the view (like a wide throw of fisherman's net) from our veranda table, sharing a bottle of California Inglenook red, not a bad number at four and change. And this was indeed Big Sur, at height of two or three thousand feet. And our own craggy lookout, just one of tens like it for miles around. With great stands of trees in a leafy green, gold and russet tumble clear down to the ocean. Near hidden coves brushed lightly by lazy-moving clouds. Lonely mountain cabins brushed by the same cloud formations. Then all at once I saw it, circling off a high ridge some 500 feet away, my lofty bald eagle! I called out to the others, almost upending the bottle of wine, as I raised my hand to alert them: "Bald eagle over Big Sur!" And of course Jon wasn't around to contradict me!

Before we left the Nepenthe, I asked the waitress about Big Sur. She lived in the nearby village and was as knowledgeable as she was obliging on the local lore. She told us that Henry Miller's daughter now occupied his old house; she pointed it out but we could see only a slice from where we were standing; the house jutting neatly on a rocky ledge way above the Nepenthe. The waitress, "Miller's daughter has made the house into a showplace, but she herself isn't into writing so much as real estate." And the Big Sur writing scene? It took her only a moment, "There's hardly any of that around." She then pointed out a hideaway, some 200 feet off and below the Nepenthe, easy to spot by the long iron chain on roadway, and by its air of mystery too; maybe with Dobermans on the loose in the bargain: "Esalen is the hot number up here, they push the swankiest property in Sur, stuck away in that cove. And no peeking or poaching, except for 'joiners' at forty dollars a day or more, if you're into that sort of thing." Call it the ultimate in Californ' raffled chic, at the end of a long line of same.

On the trip back to Asilomar, we all rapped about Big Sur. Sadly, I said, the poetry has gone. Never never never never, to paraphrase King Lear, can you repeat the magic of a Miller, the Beats or the mythic Jeffers in the same place twice. The hot real-estate deal—yes! The phoenix rising from ashes of past creativity—nada! As for the Esalen thing, the

"You-me" feelie movement: How strange that they're always looking inward, always peeling the ego onion, when all around them are eyebogglers of god's own acres, if they would only reach out (no cost at all) and do a feelie on that! And if they would only come off the Big Sur mountain, and try walking their egos through the lettuce fields and on the picket line, maybe they would find a therapy for the "unfulfilled" beyond even the Esalen's reigning guru.

3/At convention's end the next day, the four of us joined for the ride back to San Francisco. Though both women lived in Sacramento, they said they'd be glad to drop Bob and me off, and have a round of drinks too, if they could drive—one of them put it—in and out of the freeway mess "short of a migraine send up." (It seems the "Jewel City" can't be passed up lightly, given any excuse for a quickie visit.) On the scenic route that afternoon, the sky was one long canopy of mottled washy blue, the sun was a steady bronze fire pouring down in diaphanous orbs, and the whole tingling eyeful much like at Big Sur the day before. We moved along at a 50-55 clip, all remarking how inviting the surf looked, but noticing too how *disinviting* the big breakers, as the watery tonnage pounded up against the sheared cliffs for miles around. At one point, the sudden change in terrain, and the four of us responding, practically all at once, to the notion of a swim. What tempted us was a stretch of copper-colored beach that loomed just ahead—no more than a quarter-mile long and with blaze of sunshine as if in sheets. The beach positioned snugly between a sliced cliff at one end, and long capelike turn of hills topped by a lighthouse at the other.

We came off the roadway and parked nearby. The four of us were in the surf soon enough, not so much *in* as wading up to our knees. (Clothes rolled up to thighs, shoes and stockings left on beach.) There were eight or ten other visitors, none of whom ventured beyond waistline depth. It was obvious that when you were in it—as opposed to merely gazing at it from a moving car—the Pacific was by no means a placid pool; but more like a roiling, bouncing body of water with an undertow that could as easily take you fathoms deep, as ride you playfully out and back again as if saddled to a friendly dolphin. It's all a matter of aquatic know-how. And we four weren't so much riding as kicking up some froth, or pouncing on half-buried sea shells for souvenirs.

As we headed back to the car, after a half-hour or so refresher, a rheumatic old 1940s bus kicked up some wheelskidding sand in our path as it came to a jerking halt on a level side of the beach. On the body of the vehicle was a cloth rectangular pennant: STATE OF CALIFORNIA FARM REHABILITATION PROGRAM. The instant the bus stopped, out rushed a crew of 15 or 20 young men. They were stripping off their denim work clothes, and discarding each piece on the fly, till they were down to bathing trunks or their jockey shorts. Several Chicanos, eight or ten whites, about half a dozen blacks. It was not so much the lean, hungry look of their bodies as the scarred look of the ghetto-barrio and the deprived look of the reformatory that caught your eye. They all made a beeline, and then a shouting rush, out over their heads into the bracing surf. We four stopped to watch as they bobbed around as if on pogos, four or five of them swimming further out yet, the swimmers then closing back on the beach on the incoming rollers. The incident had a John Steinbeck "feel," with flash out of mind from *The Grapes of Wrath*. A tableau of some captured moments of play, some coltish and watery high-jinks, then back to the sweaty belly of the land.

4/The approaches to San Francisco, as you move along the ribbony highway, call for a Hemingway brush stroke. Hill after lonely hill, chained together like brown elephants; as you close on the city, more chained hills, these dotted with colonies of ranchlike houses in pastels of blue, green, yellow or ivory; and more than a few jutting outward, cantilever style, from the topmost reaches of hill; so that you had the impression, during the frequent cloud forays that scud by the city, that house and hill are on a collision course. We came off the freeway at a point not far from the Golden Gate Bridge, and we parked moments later for a seventh inning stretch and closeup view of the bridge and the bay. For the two women probably a routine look, but for Bob and myself our very first.

Though we had some blockage at first, standing in a thick copse of trees and underbrush, our eyes could still pick out highlights. Ruth, owner and driver of the car, led the way to an abandoned gun emplacement that looked like a relic out of World War II with the Big Bertha guns stripped away clean. The four of us, with a robust wind blowing from the bay, then climbed onto the cement parapets. A short distance beyond them rose the immensely stark and dominating golden-orange arches. Extraordinary both in their symmetry and crosshatched power. The arches lofting skyward like a pair of Jacob's ladders, American steel biblical. And the glints of sun coloring the two like fretted sheaths of

Man Here Says He's Been To Californ'   129

fire. You could, and I did, make comparisons. The Golden Gate "modern" is essence-esthetics of overwater roadway at the midcentury; the Brooklyn Bridge "gothic" a bridge roadway threaded through the needles of four cathedral-like portals, last and best of breed at century's end. (There's the jumper comparison too: Over 500 death leaps off the Golden Gate; no more than a handful off the Brooklyn Bridge.)

With the wind biting at us, the euphoria of the view, the cheerful three or four hours up from Asilomar—what better than a parting round of drinks? Ruth and her friend, Connie, both agreed readily enough, though they still had a two-hour trip to Sacramento on tap. They suggested Fisherman's Wharf; Ruth, meantime, took us on leisurely tour of the Presidio, which she described, not undeservedly at that, as the "home of west coast military princelings." Picture a gridlike enclave of about twenty square blocks, the Presidio itself a richly endowed mini city, with building after building of scrubbed, mansion-like headquarters for the brass; the headquarters, and the GI spit-and-polish barracks too, all laid out like a country club; with extravagent floral doodlings, lined up as if by the numbers, along the walks and buildings alike. The only thing missing was a polo field, and that little item may have been tucked away on the outer reaches, so grandiose a parsel of real estate was this west coast military haven.

If the Presidio is the arcadian boondocks, call Fisherman's Wharf the Coney Island West. We got to the Wharf around six, and found the streets jammed with slow-moving cars and fast-stepping jaywalkers. It was a risky though amiable crunch, hip-to-fender encounters all down the line. Many in the crowd were on the prowl for *the* restaurant, the name-fame eateries being just about the only wheel on the Wharf. (St. Francis, on his home turf, comes in many personas, the gourmet not least.) Ruth made two-dozen twists and turns, finally lucking into a parking spot a hundred feet or so from a tall, four-master schooner, a display piece tied to the dock like a trophy of nostalgia. We got out of the car and joined the parade, finally choosing the double-decker Franciscan, with its picture-window access on the bay, for our farewell drinks.

After we ordered a round, Bob hurried off to make a phonecall. *His* particular wheel was "shelter in," as they called it at the religious orders, and he was playing it via three or four contacts at the SF orders. Soon he was back at the table, two fingers raised in a V. Breezily he announced, "We're all set for tonight, at the least." And to the girls, "I'm introducing Mr. Bernard to the monastic life. Can you picture him at prayer, counting beads with the Maryknoll fathers?" If they were amused, they were mystified as well. Until I mentioned the Pugsley, Bernard arrangement. Which I called, "Our slightly less than Faustian deal."

I revealed that three or four weeks back, Bob had suggested (nay, he implored!) that we book flight together to San Francisco, telling me: "I want to hold your hand at the takeoff; I hate that part of the flight." I told the girls that I mulled it over (after all whose hand would *I* be holding, the pilot's?) and that we did get together finally. And that Bob had survived, gritting his teeth and all, the TWA 747's roaring whoosh off the apron. And that he survived too the emergency landing at O'Hare; the starboard engine conking out an hour or two out of Kennedy. And the two-hour delay to repair the engine, during which he sloshed drinks (compliments of TWA) like a trooper. And the smooth takeoff and flight the rest of the way. Now, I concluded, Bob would be making good the deal. I was looking forward to sharing the mysteries ("Did you say Maryknoll?") of the order.

They knew the Maryknoll residence, and they picked up freshly on the "arrangement." Ruth said the Webster Street manse was "As posh as they come, with the Italian consulate squatted like a Renaissance villa just across the street." Upon our return to the car, they offered to drop us off at Maryknoll, good companions to the wire. Getting out of the clogged-up Wharf caused Ruth to lose her direction for a time. She zipped past several intersections trying to avoid the big, swinging cliffhangers that bisect the town like a runaway ride out of the film *Bullitt*. Then over to Webster, and to the Maryknoll residence, first look of which gave a pleasant jolt. It was indeed a posh, 5- or 6-story chiseled darkstone beauty that spelled riches in *this* world. They helped us with the luggage, the four of us embraced, we all promised we'd keep in touch by mail. As they headed for the freeway, I yelled over to them, "All good vigils on Reagan turf." (Both women were in their mid-30s. Both married, but not working at it. Both with kids on the home range. They had vigils, and more, to cope with.)

5/Our Maryknoll visit was a short one, but time enough to sample its charms. In the mahogany-paneled vestibule we were greeted by a Fr. Daley (Bob's Maryknoll contact), a tall brusque man in pressed business suit who instructed us: "You'll share the double just off the stairway on fifth-floor. The beds are made—they ought to be!—towels and soap are in the water closet." We ran into a Maryknoll priest later that evening, a 30-ish man with a kind of Mephisto play of smile under his pointed beard. He was lodged on the same floor, and seemed to know his way around (right off, he ushered us into the whiskey-TV room for a "pre-dinner belt") not only at the residence, but in pretty near all of Frisco. When Bob asked about restaurants, Maryknoller ran off several in North Beach, playing each in a round robin as regards "Quality but expensive," "Ordinary but reasonable," "Cheap but gut-filling," and so on. He added, "For the after-dinner menu, just roam through North Beach, where they let it all hang out like the wash." A hint of kinky doings lurking on street corners, the way Maryknoller winked and stroked his beard.

The next two nights, I discovered the North Beach scene, only a mile or two from the residence. The famed strip-joint glitter; the equally famed though more highbrow City Lights Book Shop; the porn-corn poster emporiums, and tourist parlors stocked with plastic gimmicks; the coffee-houses and pubs, trafficking in backroom poetry readings. All told a lurching, freewheeling marathon. Loudest, the jabberwocky of the hawkers, outside the strips. One of whom offered in buttonholing lunges at passerbys, "The first topless off a college campus, stunning, dark-eyed, eighteen-year-old Nellie Ann. If you pass her by, it's your own *big big loss!*"

Other strips, other spiels. At the subterranian hungri i, Mort Sahl's old show case: "Ain't offerin' politics cabaret these days, but we're sure heavy into the NEW topless and bottomless." And the big mommy of them all, Ms. Carol Doda's former digs, with gleaming brass plaque out front: ON THIS SPOT, IN 1964, THE FIRST SILICONE TOPLESS WAS BORN. And the oddly triangular City Lights, where Frisco poets and writers make standup browsing a casual art form. And the coffee-house readings: often hard to tell where mediocrity ends and the poetry begins, but there's charged up energy to spare. That's the North Beach, in its nightly meanderings, and while not 100% joyride, it has the Frisco *au go go* mood. Put by one partisan, matching the east and west coasts: "New York City is the original hassle; San Francisco is the non-hassle, period." Hassle or no hassle, I kept the "Hang in there, Gotham!" faith.

2d night Maryknoll closing. We got back from North Beach after midnight, only to find our luggage in the vestibule. Bob, more in anger than surprise, whistled the single word: "Evicted!" Attached to one of the bags was a note: "Robert: Several of our Maryknoll padres flew in from Uruguay. I had to make room for them. I'm sure you understand. Fr. Daley." We both stood there wondering: Was it the round with the bearded padre (Bob and I had a shot each of California brandy; the bearded one had two shots of Bourbon)? Was it the eight or nine local calls we made between us? Or was it actually the Uruguay padres, *in the flesh*? However we sliced it, there would be no counting beads, or continuing our freebie stay, at the Maryknoll manse. As for Pugsley's other contacts, that would have to wait till morning. Meantime, we cabbed over the the Tenderloin Y, made it under the wire for "last available double."

I spent the last part of my trip, seven days or thereabouts, at the Franciscan College residence, narrow three-story pink stucco at Army and Folsom. Using no small expertise, Bob contacted a Fr. Matthew at Franciscan, who cheerfully flagged us on. We checked out of Tenderloin Y, and taxied over to the residence, both feeling "upwardly mobile" at the change. Fr. "Matt," as he wanted to be called, met us at the gate entrance. He settled us in a room each on the 2d floor; part of a clean, well-lighted setup of twelve or fourteen all told. While not up to Maryknoll's mahogany tone, the Franciscan digs had advantages of its own. First was Fr. Matt himself, 30-ish and originally from New Jersey, as chatty as Fr. Daley was offish. He gave us carte blanche on kitchen, TV and library. He said, "Nothing fancy; buy make yourselves at home." And there was no threat of eviction, Matt assuring us, "Bookings are down this time of year, the odds are you won't be bumped."

And the informal raps with several Franciscans, most times in the tiny library, talk and bottle of wine flowing equally free. ("Don't buy the Gallo's," I was cautioned, "that bunch is anti-Chávez!") Much of what they said convinced me, beyond my own idea of what orders "were all about," of the Franciscans' deep involvement with the farmworkers. And the succoring of prisoners, in the California and other prisons. And the all-around tension, quite aside from counting of beads, in pursuing these missions "Without blessings from the bishop; he does his thing, we do ours." (As one Franciscan put it.)

During one particular rap, the local bishop got a long-distance phone call from Fresno, asking support for the UFW picketers, two of whom had been gunned down only days earlier. (An echo of the Asilomar call, but now it was Joan Baez doing the calling.) When the news filtered to the residence, two of the Franciscans, with no more than a nod between them, made ready to go the Fresno within the hour.

One was a young Arizonian, dressed in blazing Indian poncho, who'd described himself as "Half Chicano, half gringo." The other, a tough-talking, muscular New Yorker, "landsman from the East Village," he exclaimed in a street growl. Earlier, the Arizona priest had dropped a statistic, which he developed as he went along: "The per annum California agribusiness is a sixteen to seventeen billion dollar pyramidal giant. While the farmworkers are a landless, homeless army at the bottom of the pyramid, with average per annum earning of less than two thousand dollars . . ."

What made the image all the more vivid, as I toured around Frisco later that week, was the sight of what could easily be more banks per square foot than anywhere in the US. There was no hill, no neighborhood, but that it wasn't studded with them. The Bank Americas, the Wells Fargos, the TransAmericas, the Crockers. To name only the western banking houses. Clustered by the tens, on several Frisco streets. And by the hundreds, in the financial district. And talking of pyramids, there was the TransAmerica headquarters, a cream-colored Junior Cheops of a building, rising some 30-stories on North Beach's skyline. To, literally, a garishly pyramidal apex. And with all the banks—apropos the Franciscan's image—crowded together at the top layer; Del Monte and the other packing combines, hogging the next layer down; the ranchers and middlemen, just below the Del Montes; and finally the 80 or 90 thousand that pick the fruit and lettuce and grapes, who are of course at the bottom of the pyramid. And if San Francisco, as natives are quick to tell you, is indeed the "Jewel City," it remains for the farmworkers to buff the jewel to a high sheen—whatever the role of the higher-ups.

6/The 2d leg of my journey. Looking for Bill Childress's "very live writing scene"; I chased through Berkeley; took in several North Beach readings; ferried over to Sausalito (for the highly touted "houseboat action"); snooped in on the Rolling Stone-Straight Arrow Books operation; all by way of a handle on the poets, writers and small-press people; the indigenous Cal' voice, I told myself, perhaps romantically, that *had to be there.* My hunch was that the extravaganza of space; the wildly free ocean; the richness of chained hill, and sunsetty valley; add to which, the complexity of *Californias* himself; and the totem of his anxiety, the San Andreas Fault . . . my hunch was that all these had to inspire, and lend themselves to, the making of the muse. And all of which wooly-haired man, about 35 but no face creases, sharply mod dressed, calf boots gleaming to a high polish. He confided as how "Straight Arrow is an upfront California enterprise; who needs the east coast hustle . . ." The co-publisher leaned down from his desk, to pat the head of a large shaggy French poodle; Rinzler's smartly furnished office, and the open spaces of Straight's floorthrough, being the home away from home for doggie. Rinzler, an easy talker, went a couple of notes nostalgic, eyes misting a little behind the biker wraparound shades: "I'm a New Jersey boy, myself. I got to love New York for a while, there. The East Village, the West Village. But now, the wife and I, we have the beaches; we have all the scenery to chew on. And of course, we have a real gone publishing winner. And we don't need, want to know about, or envy that *other* city!" What prospects for the future? Rinzler reared back in his chair, "The sky's the limit, believe it!" Shaggy hound paddled off, then returned in a slow-circling lope. All was cool, near noiseless. Broken by a groupie shout, from the adjoining doorless office. "Phone call for you, Alan; give it the old pizzazz." A study in nonchalence, Rinzler's boots flopped over on his desk, as he pursued the unlimited skies of altogether now Cal' publisher.

One early afternoon, Bill Childress comes a'calling. From his Mountain View home some 20-miles inland. He barrels out of his station wagon, races up the stairs of the Franciscan residence, and looks me (and the two padres in the office) over with quizzical glint of eye. He says, "I see you made it to Calipiggery at last! With a St. Francis due bill in the bargain!" We chat for a while, and then drive off for lunch. Childress is explosively run-on, hot as firecrackers, on California writers, and related matters. He says he's making "the necessary buck— for the wife, three kids and bread on the table" as travel writer for *Argosy, Westways, Smithsonian* and other mags. We stop at a pub just off Haight-Ashbury, owned by a former Hell's Kitchen Irishman. The pubman wants to know, after his twenty years or more in Frisco, if the Kitchen is still the same; and I tell him, "Neither you nor James Cagney would recognize the place." After a round and light lunch, Childress bounces up from table, goes out to the wagon, and then returns with tape recorder and camera. He shuffles the equipment around, leans forward with a pencil mike, and instructs me: "Man, we gotta get a full tape down. Tell it good—what strikes you out here, the writing and the schlock, lay it on the line!" Yeah, I assure Childress, right on the line! And we do an hour or more. From my end, short takes only, on the Cal' trip. But with Childress's jumping, cueing and leading; a good deal more, on the New York scene. What's your buddy Seymour Krim up to? What's the Jack of Spades at Times Books (John Leonard) done for small presses lately, if at all? The tape rolls twice around, and out. Driving back to the residence, Childress pours it on: "It's a damn good tape; gonna parlay you, Ferlinghetti, Bill Saroyan and Charlie Bukowski—when I catch up with Buk. There's a Doubleday editor, she wants to do the project. It'll be a helluva book . . ." The bantamly rugged, Daniel Boone jacketed, tawny bearded Chilly. Only a day or two later, he was off and jetting to Ceylon, on an *Argosy* assignment.

7/There were other trips around town, between times. Quarter-mile walks from residence to Army and Mission intersection, where I'd catch the bumpy rides for short hops. They threw in a San Francisco Transportation transfer, good at almost any stop on the spokewheel. A great buy at 25 cents, even with the occasional foul-up of overhead lines. Hops to the marmoreal Civic Center; those acres-wide stretches of marble, gushing fountains and knee-high pools of water; or San Francisco's in-scale answer to Washington, D.C.'s marble saturation. And to the grandly appointed SF Public Library; with its plentiful stacks of little mags, chapbooks and the like; probably more of those than anywhere west of U of Wisconsin's famed collection. And to City Lights Book Shop, seven or eight visits on my prowls through North Beach, sort of bookman's version of drunken sailor who comes roaming back to his favorite ginmill for another elbow-bending round.

Twelve-thirteen days in another town, in another country. The long-delayed virgin tour, the long-delayed Balboa journey, achieved at last! And when I got off the Frisco merry-go-round my last time, I had a flashback twinge of regret; but also a flashforward to my hour of arrival back home, when I would once again hop aboard New York's own merry-go-round. With its wide circle of rings up for the grabbing, even some gold ones among them.

Five Beekman Street

FLASHBACK FLASHFORWARD Christmas Day, 1973. Here, in the cubbyhole office at Five Beekman, a relative silence with phone in added up, as I touched the various bases, if not to out-and-out illusion, at least to an illusive search.

It could be I was focusing on trees; thus missing the deepranging forests. There's no question but that, up and down the long Cal' coast, strong pockets of original poetry and other writing, and supportive alternative publishing, do exist with more bang than whimper. (The whimper vis-à-vis—who else?—the New York establishment. A longtime west coast mood that may be fading in Cal's own press of business, in both senses of the word "press.") Partly from what I heard, and partly from eye-level witness, I'd list such hot centers as Bolinas; Venice West in the Los Angeles area; the Carmel and Monterey peninsula; the surprising Sacramento turf; those, as well as the Bay Area hot spots, are variously alive and working, if edgily at times, at the hectic game of lit. And that it's the "indie" entrepreneur mainly, who gets the California writing launched; said indie who beats through the bushes for foundation grants; and who searches out the printshops—usually oddball shops—that just happen to have "an idle press handy"; and who stubbornly lucks past the other arcane problems—such as the vagaries of distribution—that stand in the way of the discovery role.

Typical of the breed is one Paul Foreman; Texan transplant and himself a sort of triple-threat; he's a poet, fiction writer and small-press publisher all in one. Paul is a lanky, energetic man, pushing to mid-30s; he's snugly housed (with his wife, Foster; who's also a transplant; in her case, from the Old Dominion) in the lower half of a two-family red shingled about a mile from the sprawling Berkeley campus. Between them, the Foremans know pretty near all the lines, the scuttlebutt, the new and not-so-new writers afloat, with target in the Bay Area. Their seven-day schedule includes, besides the fingerprinted grit of over-transom submissions, the arranging of readings for whatever "real new talent" they've found for their stable. The next stage, luck and available bread riding on it, is publication for the artist; in one or more of their several formats; such as *Hyperion*, a little mag; or Headstone Press, and Touch Press, both of which Foreman co-publishes. There's usually a quickness to put forth energy and bread to match the touting. It may be the quintessential "California thing," more indeed than anywhere in the spectrum of littles.

I tracked the Foremans down, the afternoon I went over to Berkeley. They were having a vendetta with Ma Bell, and crotchety Ma had offed their phone. Paul picked me up in his wheezing Volks, outside the main campus gate. Then back to their house, for tasty samplings of Foster's yogurt recipe. Then over to a family-style Berkeley restaurant, for a really filling and pennies-cheap Cantonese, all you could down for two bucks per person. During which they primed me for the nighttime gig in North Beach by one of the Foremans' new discoveries, a young New Mexico poet named Paula Allen. From the restaurant we drove over to the reading—at the Coffee House on Grant Avenue—and during the ride (and indeed from the moment I'd met the couple) I was awash in the high-octane repartee of the Bay Area mover and shaker. (You take the couple out of the south, but you can't take the magnolia drawl out of the couple.) As for the poetry, and the 50 cent mugs of beer, they had the tang of freshness. The lines had a knife-sharp imagery, fleshed with "tale-telling" from the plains Indian experience. (The poet was half Lebanese, half Indian.) Only the cold light of time, and hit-miss frivolity of muse, will confirm the "discovery."

The choppy ferry ride to Sausalito, Mediterranean-like rock that juts up from the bay, 100-thou' homes perched high in leafy isolation. It turned out to be a rock-candy downer; at least the Pier 5 tangle of houseboats I ventured after; trying to locate former Manhattanite and longtime friend LM, a sometime filmmaker-cinematographer. The long march to his rickety houseboat; and, when I strode down the gangway, he was so very stoned on grass and booze that it took him several glazed moments to recognize me. And who then, upon collecting himself with an effort, boasted, "We've gotta heavy scene on Pier 5"; but what hit my eye like a buzzing wasp were the derelict houseboats, the ancient and hollowed out ferries, the busted World War II landing craft; with pretty near all of Pier 5 trailing dog dung underfoot; and the roaming canine packs not a little menacing. A kind of hip version of Maxim Gorky's depths, grafted onto the showy Sausalito playpen of wealth, doubledecker yachts and glad-handing under the western sunset.

I visited with *Rolling Stone*'s Charles Perry; and Straight Arrow Books' Alan Rinzler; both holed in a 100-year-old darkstone fortress on Third; call it Bay Area Stonehenge, on the cubed skyline of the "new" Frisco. *Rolling Stone*'s fourth-floor offices, chockfull of Eames-chic furniture, secretaries in hotpants toting coffee and Coke from the machines. Editor Perry showed off the wall gallery of Ralph Steadman originals; those political cartoons of the primal scream; or return of George Grosz, loosed on the Prussianized Nixon era. Two floors down I met, and talked with, the Straight's co-publisher Alan Rinzler. A suspension, a steady wave of calm outside the big 7th-floor window facing pompously handsome Woolworth Building. Broken, on the instant of four P.M., by the four percussive bellrings of St. Paul's down the street. Lower Broadway, the Park Row strip, the narrow gorge of Nassau, City Hall Park itself—all mantled in the sunless gray of an afternoon where people-cars are also in relative state of suspension. The tall New England pine—with hundreds of holiday ornaments topped by five-pointed star inching to and fro on upper-30s wind—looking a little the sadder for the no-lights policy of austerity decreed by the prez, the mayor; and yet, the tree on a lofty highrise, planted firmly in the sod of the City Hall green, is more than "when you've seen one you've seen them all" quip of that passing expert on our politics and our lifestyle, veep who copped the plea. The bigness, the dark ambience surrounding the decorations, are both witness to a contrariness in our US hopes, illusions; Christmas 1973 is an amalgam of greatness that eludes us and darkening thoughts, actions and evasions that worry the better image-deed (of what we could be!) almost to extinction.

Back to this office, these surroundings, on the 10th anniversary of "the most general" magazine. To my own slicing back and forward in time, from the day some five or six years ago when I "associated" with the operation; and even quite further back in time; say the late forties, early fifties; when I had previous "physical" connectedness; by virtue of cutting journalist teeth on the late Standard News Association, located in the old Herald Tribune building on Park Row, hard by the still remaining bronze visage of Ben Franklin (who peers out on City Hall—now as then—with craggy, crinkled look of man with the lamp); my job in those days was lobster-tour reporter, three nights a week, at the Bergen Street news shack across from Brooklyn Police Headquarters; and "instant" rewrite man, at the receiving end of the district man's telephone calls, in Standard's teletype rooms on the other two nights. And when Tony Anastasia had a rumble—usually some hotlead flying around in the dark of night on the Brooklyn piers—the order was "Drop whatever you're doing, grab a cab over there!"

Gone, of course, the turreted Herald Trib building, replaced by the Vermont stone husk of Pace College (pardon, Pace University, they've recently upped the "complex," in both senses, by acquiring more real-estate; and perhaps even more of a corner on Universals); but there are other landmarks—the lowslung, spare graystone beauty of City Hall; the lovely, if increasingly enroached upon, cathedral-like towers of

Brooklyn Bridge; and a late-arrival, not more than a brick's throw from BB—the squatted, boxlike, as-if-by-computer, new police headquarters; and downstreet by 200 yards or so, the brooding dun simplicity of needle-spired St. Paul's Chapel, alive on each hour, with the pealing of bell; and steeped in the cobwebby memory of one George Washington, back in the 1790s, kneeling at prayer in silken breeches, in the tiny mid-sanctuary box; and several paces north of St. Paul's, that paragon Woolworth birthday cake of (let's call it) the "New Protestantism"; or stone by carved stone, spire by lacy gothic spire, of 1920s American-biz upward mobility (*always* upward!); and dominant over all, our 20th century replica of Egyptology totemism; the runways-long Twin Towers built with speculative, bullish "scrip" of the Street and sweaty palms-muscle of hardhats.

And, speaking of hardhats, memory of running battles. Hardhats versus "Get out of Nam" college youth. Battles through Wall Street, City Hall Park, Pace College. Both sides torn—and "tearing up the pavement"—over the furies of Moratorium; the passions of "Bomb 'em back to the stone age." With "Lindsley's" City Hall flag the big trophy. Hardhats infiltrate to City Hall roof; run flag back up to full-mast. Pace students jeer, toss rocks. The hats attack, beer churning inside guts like hot liquid metal, rampage through Pace's new building; they shred the furniture apart; bounce hard knuckles off heads, noses of students. With roving—on midafternoon arrivals—usually missing the brawls; but getting those cold stares, more than was healthy, from hats who wanna know "You one of those aging hippies?" So wadda you say to that?

The Five Beekman pile is a 100-year-old, 10 story redbrick, graybrick with vaulting rooftop gingerbread (no doubt avant back then); building wedged on Nassau, and street-through Theatre Alley (the On Broadway of its time?); nearby plaque under foot honoring HENRY JARVIS RAYMOND 1820-1869 FIRST EDITOR AND COFOUNDER OF THE NEW YORK TIMES HE NOT ONLY PREACHED BUT PRACTICED TO SUBSTITUTE REASON FOR PREJUDICE . . .; and a building that once boasted, if that's not too strong, the Norman Thomas wing of the Socialist Party as tenant; and more recently, had the rag-taggle War Resisters League (along with the journals *Liberation* and *Win*) on entire 10th floor; years of uneasy landlord-WRL flak ("Yes, you pay da rent, but . . ."); till one day all the hairy, bouncy comings & goings of peace freeks—up the slow elevators to the 10th digs and down—got the building agents itchy;

they wouldn't renew the lease after fifteen years of, well, bouncy comings & goings. As to *The Smith* hutch at Five Beekman, really two shoebox rooms, walls plastered with posters-letters-knocks-boosts detritis of the ten-year operation; us'n folks—the Smither, the roving editor & rest of the ongoing mob of writers, poets, journalist hustlers and obsessives—no doubt shaping up more & more as Five's resident weirdos; now that WRL's gone over to Lafayette Street; but the bills & rent get paid; so the most they (agents, lawyer-tenants, Wackenhut security boys) can fault us on is the "weirdo" chatter; on Cosmep problems, on poets who are up-poets who are down, and the like; which they might be overhearing on the fly, from elevator to elevator ride.

The question: What might this Five Beekman transom be doing, over that five year period, to the head of a former overgrounder, pastmaster (and part-time) flackcopy writer for Restaurant Associates and others, contributor to raunch mags like *Dude, Gent, Nugget* and *Rogue*? Five's transom being the line of connection with the world of the littles, the unknown writing freaks, the poets in all the US Mudvilles raking their own gardens of the WORD? Well, it did joggle his head, change it more than notches in direction of surprise, hope for—indeed—the WORD that had practically no traffic with overground SUCCESS. From manuscript pile to manuscript pile he had window-openings on a whole spectrum of writers who—in the boozy tart phrase of Bukowski—wouldn't "blow an 8 cent stamp submitting to *The New Yorker*." (The Buk lesson, sad to say, not entirely learned by roving himself, not to this day.) He got the over-transom picture, all through these past five, of talented tummlers like Ray Puechner out of Milwaukee; writer-small publisher on boots Len Fulton out of Paradise, Calif; strong feminist poesy voices like Tarheel State's Judith Hogan and Nola's Kate Rose; occasional thin-envelope gems from Bob Sward up Canada way; littlemag movers & fine writers like Art and Glee Knight, who, besides, are into the American Lit "teach," at small Pennsylvania college; those are only a sampling of the tens, hundreds that have helped—and been helped by—*The Smith* and other littles in the by-now vast, state by state, wall to wall conspiracy to resurrect the WORD from the dollar drones, by and large, of New York's "One mil' for 3 books in the oven" kind of writing career that's the bane—and the banality—of big, conglommy publishing at this end of year of our Lord, 1973.

Yes, he's kited his surprises on the jetstream of those mss; flooding over the Five Beekman transom; five years of that gone by; and looking for more, and playing typewriter keys of his own.

1974

Walter Lowenfels

BOOKS & BERETS & OTHER WINDFALLS Walter Lowenfels' wide, bridgework smile is affable as ever, as he stands just inside the Cobble Hill mini townhouse entrance. It's a wintry Saturday evening, tailend hour of a book party, honored author Lowenfels greets you with hurrahing, hugging grasp around the shoulders. Then, with a bearish growl, "Where've you been; the party started at five o'clock." You run it down: "Blame it on the cabbie; lucky I made it out here, across the bridge from Manhattan . . . to this dense forest of Cobble Hill." On the way over, in the wettish and chilling mist, with the cabbie losing his compass; as between Warren Street and Warren Place; it struck you Cobble Hill is a winner; especially, the row on row enclave of 1870s houses, next door to Brooklyn Heights; the townies hidden, and huddled together, among the vines, trees and narrow hedges.

So to the party, it's in celebration of Lowenfels' short, new work called *Reality Prime, pages from a journal*; published by the hosts, Kirby Congdon and Ralph Simmons, under their Cycle Press imprint. The crowd is tightly impacted, up and down the duplex's winding stairs, in and out of the wood-paneled rooms and hallways. You notice the across-generations aspect; eight or ten young poets and artists; Michael Andre, Roger Gaess and Charles Haseloff, among them; and a couple of others, Layle Silbert and Roberto Faber, maybe a lap-around-older; and finally, three or four from Walt's own generation, keeping memory and fires alive with reminiscences. But remember—though Walt Lowenfels is in his mid-70s, don't test him with a hammerlock, or with your ad-hoc party humor, likely he'll ace you at both.

Now he's at center of the swirl, the drinking and chattering crowd, all sort of chained around him, like at a Maypole soiree; the guests "dancing" the hour away; Walt calling tunes in that high-pitched, slightly nasal rush of conversation; with the by-now-trademarked—and rakishly positioned—black beret on his head; the curlicues of white locks, spilling over to back of his neck. The image of course is immediate; the black beret (if not this one, some other) of his Paris days. Foremost of which, the thirties, when he and Henry Miller and Michael Fraenkel formed the "Death School"; a writers-artists group that, as Walt now describes it to you, reflected "a hopeless time, in a pooped out era." Miller, more than any, riding "the waves of decadence," riding them "gleefully," according to Lowenfels.

You last ran into Lowenfels, the night of the Cambodian blitz, at Eighth Avenue and Twentieth, just up the street from Saint Peter's Church; charged and outgoing as ever, the beret at jaunty angle, he was on his way to a poetry reading; Walt and Robert Bly and several others; and the warming flash of his words bouyed you up; something like, *The poetry always speaks louder than the bombs.* Many books and battles, later; here's Walter Lowenfels, still the active agent, of poetry-life-politics; a tall, knotted, treelike persona; rings of years attesting to good passions well spent. Now he says he must leave; back to Peekskill, an hour or so away; the "careful ride on the skidding road"; but not before his parting few words, about his new project, the anthology of poems called *For Neruda For Chile.* And after he's gone, Kirby and Ralph, tipping drinks to "the longevity of all of us."

Yes, live as long as Longfellow, and you have it made.

Lindsay Anderson

GETTING BACK ON THE MOVIE VAN We'd all nerve the four-story hike up the open, iron fire exit of the RKO Fordham, in the north Bronx, and by huddled prearrangement—after one of the gang paid his way in—we kids would hold breath for the big, topstairs door to be pried open from inside; and then four of us, or maybe even six, would pour through to the top balcony seats. We'd be home free, in the high, mile-away-from-screen, black void of the moviehouse; where, we'd tell each other, "They fly the mail to Pittsburgh." Now of late—and nearly a

Getting Back On The Movie Van

half-century since—I've fallen off the movie van; recoiled, as it were, from too much rotgut; too much of the bottled violence of the *Magnum Force* type flick; and the saccharine-soapy juvenilia, posing as daring political nostalgia, of the Streisanded *The Way We Were*'s. But I got back on recently, and it's good to report, at least for this one trip, the highs I felt, the sheer exuberance that ran over me, while sitting through the epic, two and a half hour odyssey of a film: *Oh Lucky Man!*

First some broad strokes. To say that director Lindsay Anderson has borrowed from a wide pantheon (Godard of *Weekend* and *Pierre la fou*, Kubrick of *Clockwork Orange*, and even Fellini of *8½*) is to accent the craft, and crafty brilliance, of a filmmaker who has absorbed the best, and has transmuted it into his own fine vision and achievement. Nor does the magic ring of suggestion end there; for along with the filmic transmutations, there are the literary ones; *Lucky Man*'s young everyman naif touching bases with, going back in time, Fielding's Tom Jones; and forward, with Bellow's Augie March. The breadth of detail, the richness of vignette, add up to, finally, the largeness of a *Canterbury Tales*; let loose on a 20th century terrain that's endlessly labyrinthian, both in joys and sorrows.

Conceived almost like opera, more say *Magic Flute* than *Don Giovanni*, and with big chunks of libretto (plot) spliced by way of the filmic blackout; plus a rock score that's as spare as it is poignant, in a gutsy post-Beatles vein—*Lucky Man* moves along at near breathless clip. Each scene has a stunning, bravura impact, measured no less by an insight that's coolly macabre, as by the calm innocence of a "hero" to whom everything in life is both promise and threat, at one and the same time. *Item*. Mick Travis, blue-eyed bumpkin in white uniform, on the way up in a coffee beans enterprise. He is chosen—and is seduced in the bargain—for sales stardom in the North English provinces. His sponsor is starchy Rachel Roberts, an aging Circe of the black bubbly, who swaps coffee-tasting (and sexual) spits with Mick, then heads him to the floor, for *real* sex. *Item*. In the Scottish provinces—and in rapid takes—there are all kinds of pleasures and dangers! Strip show at a porno den with Mick the guest of a pair of seedy local pols—who get *their* rocks off by ogling stag movies and live bouts of fucking, by turn. *Item*. Later Mick is a witness to a deadly road crackup; he's told to "Get lost, if you don't want trubble!" by two constables; who then proceed to ransack the loot from the crackup; later still he's kidnapped by some secret, quasi-fascist org; he's held captive, beaten up, and made to "confess." *Item*. Upon his escape, after an explosion in what seems like the org's mystery nuclear plant, he wanders the lush Scots countryside; hurt, depleted and near to starving, he then chances upon a tiny, bombed-out church where a ceremony—sort of Easter Offertory of "bread" of life—is in progress; and as Travis makes to devour a chalah-like loaf, he's intercepted by a handsome, earthmother type who offers her capacious breast for feeding. (Yes, it's sort of *Grapes of Wrath*, over again; but with its own permutation of newness, epiphany.) *Item*. Nursed back to health, and taking leave of the earthmother Eden, Mick then rises-falls into the now world of London; through rescue by a traveling rock group; during which rescue, seduction once again, this time by a cooky-beautiful dropout rocker; herself the daughter of the "richest man in England." With the help of the daughter, and his own connivance added, Mick Travis meets the Moneybags (call him a J. Paul Getty persona, oleaginous and scheming by turns, played with great panache by Ralph Richardson). Very soon—and of course innocently—Mick becomes involved in the politics of bullion smuggling. *Item*: He winds up in gaol; but upon gaining his freedom, he goes through a Tolstoyan change; descends to the lower depths—in the human quagmire of East London—and for his transformation holy pains, he's near lynched by the very tagended mob he wants (oh so desperately!) to offer the gift of hope.

And what a hero Mick Travis is—as Malcolm McDowell portrays the marathon role! Scapegrace youth whirling on the wheel of chance; whirling in that labyrinth of English "Commerce," porkie country politics, international bullion smuggling; and bedded down, on several turns of the wheel, by all manner of hyperactive Ms's (proving that in the latter doings, too, innocence is surer foil than mere worldliness); and finally, the sly intelligence overwhelming the traces of Cockney blur, that still clings to him. McDowell's sendups, as he builds nuance upon nuance of surprise, mood upon mood of pained-pleasured discovery, are nothing short of Mozartian, in their range and naturalness.

As for *Lucky Man*'s clout, staying power. There is no way, at least to this viewer, you can fault its impact, in terms of landing a high perch in the 70s pantheon. Anyway, not with the charge, as was put to me by one doubter, that *Lucky Man* was more "forced than tour de force." For it's not merely "numbers," or the sheer narrative splash, that Anderson has going for him; beyond all that, there's the surgical probing, the layering on layering, aimed at the jugular; probing of a cultural milieu that is, well, just about terminally sick. Nor is Anderson a director who can't, so to speak, come in out of his own gloom; much in the way that, say, Ingmar Bergman can't. *Item.* There's *Lucky Man*'s concluding scene, a kind of masked ball for the entire company, a freeform ceremony of work completed, or Fellini with body English. You meet them all, once over again, but now with a breakout of joy, erasing the grotesquery of their film personas; as the lot of them do a bouncy, crowded London-style rock sashaying; all daisy-chained, as it were, in a tacky but very "danceable" casting studio. The scene lingers in time, and in the head of the moviegoer, as the cast, the director, the grips, and others all but wink out at us.

That's what "Flying the mail to Pittsburgh," to us Bronx kids, was all about.

*

To the Roving Editor
The Newsletter
5 Beekman St.
New York, N.Y. 10038
USA

57 Greencroft Gdns.
London NW6
England

May 24, 1974

DEAR ROVING EDITOR,

When I was passing through New York recently some friend gave me a copy of The Newsletter for March 30th, 1974 in which you wrote about seeing O LUCKY MAN! I didn't read it immediately, I must admit, because I have been belabored by so many reviews in the last year, most of them picky and most of them failing totally to understand (even seeming wilfully to misunderstand) what the whole thing was about. But the other day I did read your account of seeing the film, and was so delighted by it that I can't resist writing to thank you.

It is not just that you understood so much of what the film was hoping to say, but also that you actually enjoyed it as an entertainment in the way that I hoped a lot of people—and particularly young people—would enjoy it. But American youth seems to have become much more conformist in the last few years, and is certainly more naively self-satisfied than I had imagined. We had a rather dismal preview weekend of the film at Yale, to which Warner Brothers had enterprisingly invited editors and film critics of College magazines. Of course instead of enthusiasm and discernment we encountered befuddlement and a good deal of defensive scorn. The whole thing was very unfortunate, because I think the top brass of Warner Brothers were expecting the picture to get a sort of "Graduate" reception, and when they got much less than that they began to get frightened, want cuts etc. etc.

I don't really know that O LUCKY MAN! does borrow from Godard and Kubrick. Don't you think perhaps that it is more a question of certain affinities? I do admire Godard, though I haven't seen very many of his pictures, and they always irritate me exceedingly. Of course he is influenced by Brecht, and so, I suppose, am I. I certainly don't think that I am influenced by Stanley Kubrick (certainly no more than "Clockwork Orange" is influenced by "If. . . ."—a fact which is very seldom pointed out). The Clinic sequence in O LUCKY MAN! wasn't inspired by "Clockwork Orange," at least I don't think so. There is one "inside" joke in it, where one doctor says to the other before starting their experimental investigation of Mick: "Ready when you are, Stanley." This was Malcolm's idea (I mean the Christian name)—and so unaware was I of the parallel with "Clockwork Orange" that I never noticed it. But you know people do get very over-aware of these things. For instance I have had it cleverly pointed out to me that the name on Alan Price's electronic gear is "Orange." This happens to be the trade name of the particular kind of gear Alan has always used, and again so far was I of even thinking about Kubrick's film that it never even occurred to me to have it painted out . . .

There are of course references in the film—mostly jokey—to the style of the Russian silent masters, and the long tracking shot when Mick is escaping from the Atomic Establishment is really a quotation from the first shot of the Czech film by Nemec, "Diamonds of the Night." I thought of the last sequence as being more in the nature of a theatrical curtain call than a homage to Fellini. (Honestly, I have never seen "8½" all the way through.) I hope all this doesn't sound too defensive. I am really pleased and flattered by the kind of parallels you draw—such as the *Magic Flute,* or *Tom Jones.* When David Sherwin and Malcolm began working on the idea, I suggested that they should get inspiration from Kafka's "America", from Voltaire's "Candide" and from Thornton Wilder's "Heaven's my Destination". Epic satire in fact.

The people who didn't like the film were chiefly liberal intellectuals I think. I.e., people fundamentally committed to "the way things are," but occupying a safe, politely protesting position. A deep and ruthless scepticism is something people like this find too disturbing to tolerate. However, your response to the film and your understanding of it have really cheered me up and made me feel that the work will survive, however much it is currently misunderstood or played down.

Thank you for the encouragement.

With all best wishes,
Yours sincerely,
LINDSAY ANDERSON

Off Off Broadway

JESTER'S DAY AT LINCOLN CENTER Broadway's yellow and black street signs, from 72nd down to Lincoln Center, had been changed to read OFF OFF BROADWAY. The Off Off Festival, a fortnight's celebration of NYC theater events, opened with a parade the first Saturday in May of double-off acting fraternity, who traipsed down from 77th and Central Park West to Lincoln Center in all their po' folks costume splendor to perform in dozens of live outdoor shows.

As the paraders moved in on the plaza fountain, the stone concourses, and other spaces of travertine LC, they stopped at their open booths that were assembled overnight and decked brightly in crepe streamers, with each group hawking its theater wares. Later there were dozens of back-to-back performances, by the various groups, held under three or four huge geodesic domes all wrapped halfway down from the top with transparent wind-whipped plastic.

At the full tilt of this sunny, streamer-filled day so lavish was the display by so enthusiastic a bunch of terpsichoreans, actors, clowns, etc., and so warm the reception by the thousands of spectators, that one had the impression of a visitation by the Wizard of Oz.

For the starchy, opera-cloaked Lincoln Center precincts, it was a case of the King vacating his throne for the Jester to allow the latter his one afternoon of japing under the sun; and then back to the shadows and "Mind your manners!" And indeed the total absence of LC's private fuzz (those walkie-talkie boys in blue who guard the temples and who give one Westsider the Kafkaesque willies) put into even bolder relief the strange sight of open cheer and released fun on LC turf one Saturday afternoon in May.

Among the groups that performed—all more or less in fifteen minute spots—were the Nuestro Theatre, who offered what sounded like classic Calderon, pure Castillian mime and speech, that had anglo and spanglish audience, both, hanging on for the bell-like tones; and Viveca Lindfors, doing several takes with passion, strong commitment, from her "I Am a Women" format; the Ontological-Hysteric Theatre, which sounds like hospital-ward therapy, but is actually "visual orientation," in the Richard Foreman bag; and 2 or 3 gay acting groups, one of which put on a dazzling display of see-through costume schlock, or transvestism striving mightily to gussy-up as art. These were only 4 dollops in an urban rainstorm of alfresco theater, seen by thousands from noon to near nightfall. And the backdrops of course lending their own aura of theatricality, with Alexander Calder's giant darkened praying-mantis sculpture at the Library entrance, Henry Moore's elegant and poignantly mysterious man-woman grouping rising from the shallow pool, the gigantic Chagall frescoes visible through the Met Opera's skyhigh lobby windows, the long stone walks and concourses, all blending in what could be labeled "De Mille—Rockefeller Modern." (The Rockefellers deal in Kultural Komplexes.)

The Off Off event engendered good vibes, maybe even beyond what the most fargone city-buff would have guessed. And with one acting company, just off ending a revival of Clifford Odets's *Waiting for Lefty*, filling the bill to a "T." Jester, plus a little extra, in the form of a marching chorus. The five young troupers, wheeling in and out of the crowds, singing away loudly and lustfully. Some vintage "Lefty" tunes. The ballsy "I'm Stickin' with the Union," the glinting nostalgia of "Shenandoah," the perky and jesterly "Brother Can You Spare a Dime!" and more in the Depression genre. Spare-a-dime spirit yodelers letting it all hang out, on flinty give-a-dime turf.

Four radical poets

HEY, POET, WADDAYU READING! The West End is Columbia U's new watering hole for poets, at one end of the Manhattan reading spectrum. St. Marks in-the-Bouwerie, where Peter Stuyvesant is buried, is at the other end. The first has been offering, after a lukewarm shakedown period, some Sunday afternoon gigs that're catching on. In one such recent gig, we heard an unlikely duo, which offered a mesh of styles that had the roomful of about 100 clapping loud: Jackson MacLow and Ed Sanders. In the soft, Tiffany-lamp glow, with the crowd easily and informally wedged into rough wooden tables-stools, warming down their beers, wines and coffees—Jack MacLow opened the set, doing his thing. An ensemble happening, his two young children and musical girl Friday assisting, of "Vocabulary" pieces that included bells, triangles, recorders and other catchpenny instruments. Jack and company stood before the bank of mikes, and for close on to an hour delighted with cantata-like rendition of hissed words, random musical phrasings, a cappella nonsense soundings, pyramidings—running words and scales together, in endless patterns. The group would pile up, stack by stack, such repeating words as "emanation," "noise," "bells"; and such phrases as, "see the bells shine"; and so on. Building it, always building, for the tasty lipsmacking pleasure. Their own, and the crowd's. Or he'd come off the floor podium, toot his way through the audience, a graying bushy-bearded gnome, whose tootings and word-plays had a birdlike blitheness. Was it poetry? you ask. Well, call it poetry in tongues.

Next came Ed Sanders, former Fug rocker, and Pentagon-levitation monger. If Jack MacLow's thing was piquant, Ed's was poker-faced outrage. Wrapped to the nines in yards-long shawl, he read from an unpublished work called "Tales of Beestruck Glory"; some fictional takes out of the early 60s, or the in-between years of late Beats and early, east side dropout-dope eras. Broad funny strokes, involving a collation of Mad Ave types, archly straight-jacketed publishing honchos, rampantly uptight academicians, gurgling pie-thrower dudes, and nascent political freakeries. It was vintage Sanders all the way, with poker face and voice about as dry as William S. Burroughs's, next to both of whom Carrie Nation's was mere slobbering! Later on, at the bar TV orgy of watching "the baskets," Ed was wetting his whistle on beers, and trying hard to levitate the Knicks to overtime win, against the Celtics. And if he didn't cause the Pengaton to rise; he sure lofted Bill Bradley and team, during some very tight playing, high and wide enough to sink those winning baskets!

At the other end of town, several nights later, a St. Marks reading by Allen Ginsberg and Michael McClure. Picture St. Marks, with Chicano ¡LIBERTAD! banner down front left, velvety purple-gold Episcopal pennant at center, gleaming coneshaped spots from top of ceiling, graceful and pockmarked 150-year-old columns holding up narrow balcony and choir loft. And a tightly packed audience—500 or more—of poetry juicers who want their lines, couplets and quatrains hot off the pages, loud and clear! Angry lines, daring, funny, insulting! (If the poet votes with language/metaphor; the audience votes with its ears!) An upbeat, punchy mood comes across quickly; east side homeboy Allen, and Californ's Mike McClure, swapping poem-for-poem at the mike. Allen knuckles out his anger, a long Swiftian piece on the Middle East, curling wrath targed at self-righteous, millennial *jihad!* on all sides. "... BEN GURION SENT ME HERE!/NASSER AND SADAT SENT ME HERE!/ARAFAT SENT ME HERE! MESSIAH SENT ME HERE! ..." Blood reddens the desert; longhair students, baker's dozen of poets, east side streetpeople, go numb at the prickly anger of lines. Suddenly—a rakish happening—flash of nude body jumping through the crowd! Is it, can it be, Corso in the torso! Cheers, groans, whistles! It's Gregory Corso, black cowl of hair shading moonstruck eyes, bare flesh going to middleage flabby, bellyfat surrounds dimpled halfmasted cock. He lands up front in seconds flat; U-turns back through the crowd, for last-row pew. Allen announces, "New York's first poetry streaker!" And Mike McClure, "How do you top that act!" McClure's own lines, elegant, and misty, a little bit sudsy sad. (The il pensoroso side, of the author of the Beard.) A grandly mix for juicers, who go out into the night, on wheels of daring poesy.

Reprise. St. Lukes Chapel, the West Village, 48 hours later. Potluck dinner of War Resisters League, honoring Daniel Berrigan, who'll receive WRL's Fourteenth Annual Peace Award, presented by Allen Ginsberg. About 300 activists, youthful longhairs, scattering of children, polish off trayfuls of home goodies. They loosen bodies from tables, hunch down lotus-style on wooden basketball court. Allen reads Middle East poem, prior to award ceremony. Eye penetrating as Horus, voice softer than at St. Marks, the numbing accusation remains. When

My Week On A Bed Of Nails   153

two kids scoot through the seated crowd, he ad-libs a two-liner into his poem, "Children booting pink Spaldeen/on St. Lukes gymnasium floor . . ." The poem over, Allen introduces Dan Berrigan, who is dressed informally mod, his sharp features cleft with tension of jet lag. (He'd flown in from Paris, that same afternoon.) Allen hands over award parchment, the two embrace warmly, audience rises and cheers Father Dan. And poet-priest-witnesser, with hardly a trace of controversy in word or manner, speaks some thoughts on the pain-isolation of being "wrong." And the irony has flavor, like salt on the tongue.

Protest rounds

MY WEEK ON A BED OF NAILS The Monday, April 15 week begins with heavy pedestrian traffic at the Church Street offices of Internal Revenue, crowds with heads still bent from pouring over the tax forms, bodies almost buffeted into the lowerfloor IRS dungeon by April wind coming off the Hudson River. And lunch-hour antitax demo, behind the long line of police barriers, on the side street nearest 130 Church. More than a few of the tax supplicants buffeted by War Resisters in the bargain, as taxers stop to catch WRL's pitch: SOME FORTY PER CENT OF YOUR TAXES GOES INTO THE BOTTOMLESS PENTAGON BUDGET! And twained in protest, despite their differences in politics, ten or twelve YAFers in tricorn hats (the Bill Buckley Jr. Federalist syndrome), who likewise are pissed at the Feds' octopus reach into the taxpayer's pocket. And a third group doing street theater, fifteen or more from Le Living, they form a circle and stomp on the ground then do a pirouette in 360 degree turns, while clapping hands to the beat of a solo bongo drum, all topped by a cadenced chant like jungle-rhythm on the April wind: "Stop the killing/Be-fore it's too late!/Organize resistance/Be-fore it's too late!/Feed the people/Be-fore it's too late! . . ." The Church—Murray Street canyon, triangulated by City Hall Park, old St. Paul's Chapel, and the World Trade Twin Towers, could be one of the baddest, Mid-Americanist, walking angry scenes for demos anywhere. And yet even here, on this "No-tomorrow!" tax day, there's more than a hint the chants and slogans reflect the boil of Mr. and Mrs. Taxpayer, as the latter make their annual, lastmile journey to pay tribute at the shrine of IRS.

One block farther west, at postage-stamp City Hall Park, marathon five-borough demos of poverty, youth center, community action, and other groups. Now going into the eighth day, and termination date left open, hundreds troop along the flattened grassy quadrangle, for daytime tours of placarding, sloganing, marching in the round, taped speeches. All through the long nights, the rainy nights evoking Eliot's "April is the cruelest month," and with cold drafts coming in off the Hudson, they hunker inside the slick and yellowed camping tepees. And when the midnight skies clear, they continue with the vigil, four in the lead holding up a blackened wooden coffin, the whole scene ghostly-lit by giant glassined candles on top the coffin, and the coffin bearing the placarded message: HERE LIES BILL H.R. 12464. Groups from the Bronx River area: parading housewives, young high school dudes, children in strollers, poverty workers with street smarts. Round and round they go, to their own chorus of shouts: *"What do we want?"/ "Bill H.R. 12464!"/"When do we want it?"/"Yesterday!"* . . . Hour after hour, they come into the park, they do their own thing, they depart, and others arrive. An accordian movement, on legs, on bikes, on strollers. Now a group from Bed-Stuy, now from lower east side, now from Jackson Heights, in Queens. Blacks, poor white, and Spanglish, using marching power. For jobs, daycare centers, housing, education. Call it, for not a few of them, a kind of political teething. Taking that first bite, at the hide of bureaucratic apathy. And the familiar, rolling, musical voice, coming from the loud speaker: "I have a dream . . ." Clarion out of the past, flooding the memory, it still has the chill of truth! "I have a dream . . ." Gettysburg Address, of the poverty movement! Flooding in over City Hall Park, the purling-strong voice drowns out lower Broadway rubberoid traffic. That Monday afternoon, and Tuesday, and the day after.

On Wednesday, tripping the National Book Award light fantastic. Leaving the 5 Beekman office, and heading for NBA press room at the Biltmore, I catch the park chanting in diminishing waves, as I duck into the Brooklyn Bridge IRT station. The sullen hot subway cars, the beginning itch of anticipation, what else will be new at NBA? (It's the 25th Annual, publishers' p-r party at six, the grand ballroom with the faded carpenting.) At the press room, I meet a quartet of NBA receptionists, one of whom smiles a vague smile of recognition: "The Newsletter, sure, just lay them down on the press table." A pause, and then: "Of course, we're never sure *what* you'll say about us." Later, at the p-r party, I look around for the authors, the NBA winners, but pickings are thin. (They'll blossom tomorrow, at the Tully Hall awards ceremony, and the party at the Americana afterward.) So I hit the steam tables, the booze lines, and I try juicing some book gossip. Youngish promo girl from name pub house: "I've seen you around; *who are you?*" And the photographer, from a booktrade mag, stacked handsomely, *her* picture should be taken! She snaps her Rolliflex at me: "It doesn't matter if I don't know you; but I think I do." Pretty soon, the meegrims threaten, so I slide into a chair. Bolts of pain, around the eyes. It eases for a while, then book columnist Bill Cole comes by. "I'm doing conversation items," he tells you; "for the *Times* (Book Review) Guest Word." Taking that as open-ended invite, I say to him: "I'm sorry Kael got the Arts and Letters; no stopping the film reviewers, now that they have NBA legitimacy." And Cole says, "I might just quote you, at that." A couple of belts of booze, and so home by route of a rocky bus ride, and swiftly into bed, as the full meegrims hit the fan.

Next day, Thursday, I'm at Tully Hall. To catch the NBA winners, in the flesh. Murray Kempton (Contemporary Affairs) praises Izzy Stone's muckraking journalism; Adrienne Rich (Poetry co-winner with Ginsberg) "splits" her prize—which NBA had already split by half—with two other women poets, also-rans, and denounces "patriarchal" NBA operation; and Pauline Kael, whose acceptance "reel" I'll never know, I got there too late. And the other winners—for Fiction, for Biography, the Sciences, Childrens Books, etc. The no-shows are Thomas Pynchon and I.B. Singer (Fiction co-winners) and Ginsberg and one or two others. The writers on stage, suited and gowned smartly, are hard to pick out from the NBA apparats, the event all slick-as-velvet, and the walking-it-straight posture. And the packed audience is a hightide of velvet, 1000 or more bobbing their heads for the bon mot here, the witty acceptance word there. Near two hours of ritual—the intros, handing over the thou' checks, the authors' speeches. Right down to the last winner, Tom Pynchon, with an unannounced ringer standing in for Pyn: Comic Irwin Corey, who can ham Hamlet, among other of his shtick, to the consistency of an overturned bowl of porridge. He looms up short, in all his 5-5 elegance, dressed Vegas style informal, and fingering his "acceptance" notes like a swarm of attacking bees. Corey-Pynchon has the crowd baffled, maybe even *violated!* Some remarks,

"He *could* be Pynchon! His fracturings, and the *Gravity's Rainbow* text, are so very near alike!" The Americana ballroom later that night. The bookpub world, on shoulder-to-shoulder display, the buzzings and greetings on the fly, the homings to piled-high steam tables, and watering cubicles. Everybody "working the room." Very big room, lots of work. "Eh, not to cut you off, but must say hello to a hot editor!" Zoom zoom zoom! I hold out, till meegrims close in. And send me walking, cabbing on eggshells to my bed of nails.

Friday's calendar: ANARCHIST CONFERENCE—LIVE AND LET LIVE FESTIVAL. At Hunter College, block-square city gothic on Park Avenue, surrounded by royal mansions like Spanish House, the elegance of which—put mildly—is more Carlist than Syndicalist. Where but in New York: One gathering of, say, the grandchildren of fiery Emma Goldman! The other, just 50 feet north, the well-heeled roomful, under the rosy light of huge crystal chandelier, of partisans (I'd guess) of the Caudillo! Opening-night agenda at Hunter: "ABC of Anarchism," "Anarcho Feminism," "Film: *1984*" and more. About 250 show up, at lowceiling dungeon of a room. Several take turns at the standup mike: "ten-minute limit—can be waived by majority vote." A mix of campus kids, commune people, street activists, freewheeling radicals. And a handful of movement vets, including a man from the I.W.W. who shouts into the mike: "The Left has exploited campus radicalism *far too long*; students are the most repressed group of all!" And, the matching non sequitur, from way out in rightfield, beefy suit-&-tie loner winging it for "radical capitalism." He pleads, "Don't pass us by; we want freedom too!" and he gets funny-money support, "Yeah, end fluoridation, give pure water back to the people!" And one lanky, longhaired youth from "Cambridge's off-campus scene": "We're testing the turf in the nabes, and in our private lives. Checking it out for communitarian change, without political hype." And several mentions of Symbionese—all keenly wary of "violence as end in itself." As the night moves along, I'm on a Coney Island loop da loop. Rooting for the kids—the dandy clean communitarians!—on the one hand. Measuring the Blakean "flights," in context of the City Hall demos, the bread-&-butter politicking, on the other. Not, *which is better?* But rather, *how meld the two, in the charnel house of Nixxon-Exxon Ethics?* And so home sometime past midnight, with no sign of the meegrims on this night.

How To Get To Gem's Spa . . .

On the first Monday in May, people in the City Hall area, who'd seen the comings & goings for six or seven weeks on end, now couldn't help but notice the sudden change: the park quadrangle was empty of marchers. At some moment on that weekend, the marchers had folded their tents and collected their placards, and they went back to their nabes. Ending, in the city-wide spokewheel, what was easily the biggest, and the longest, and the most varied demo of its kind since, say, the Great Depression. And, in sharp contrast to the latter, with the most upbeat of vibes. Lots of singing; jive dancing, easy rapping, and bongo-ing. Along with the serious side, the appeals to passersby to "Check out what we're saying." And causing, one would say, a mutual ruboff of effects. The marchers, getting the glint of "speaking truth to power." The onlooking whitecollar, and the City Hall pols, cocking *their* ears for "the message." The latter may even have learned something.

Cosmep Baedeker

HOW TO GET TO GEM'S SPA FROM THE COLUMBIA CAMPUS WITHOUT BEING MUGGED, RIPPED OFF, MOLESTED OR BAD-MOUTHED ON THE WAY DOWN Natives in their better moments like to think of New York as Fun City. Others more often than not see it as kind of Paranoia on the Subway. However it lays with you personally as Cosmep out-of-towner, a few notes of orientation should be of value on your stay here.

For starters there's the Columbia campus, site for meetings and lodging during the '74 Conference. Columbia is sort of double-exposure image, one part ivy prestige and one part urban sprawl with its tension and challenge. The vast Harlem community breathes on Columbia's neck at the Morningside Heights juncture, a neighbor whose needs and wants often are in push-come-to-shove dichotomy with the 90% white middle-class transient campus population. But bypassing extended comment on town-gown hassling, we'll push on with your trip to Gem's Spa for New York's numero uno egg-cream.

It's likely you'll be on tight budget, hence travel by subway is logical. Also educational, the rolling, graffiti-splashed cars allow for quick study of *genus gothamus*. At Columbia's own station at 116 Street take the Broadway Local going downtown to Sheridan Square.

Observe the glassy-eyed look of riders, each locked into own closed-circuit of daydreaming. The ritual of anonymity is broken, it's an IRT non-sched happening, by the pop music of a tuned-up radio, loud keenings that drown even the subway's screech, radio belonging to a legless alms-collector, who trundles from car to subway car on his self-propelled buggycart, his dexterity on wheels matched only by the elan ("Look folks, it's really easy!") of his wide, toothy smiles. The response is sudden and upbeat, as the carful of riders outdo each other in competition to bounce coins in the alms box. After cart and man disappear into the next car, back go the riders to their closed-circuit.

When you exit at Sheridan Square, you'll be at the geographic heart of Greenwich Village. Observe the iron statue of General Phil Sheridan in crusty stance on the tiny park green, and try to imagine whether his look is benign or censorial as he gazes down on the nightly flotsam of winos and "Got a subway token?" hustlers who roam by. Next a visit to famed Lion's Head Bar just across from the green, where on very short notice you'll be hot in the middle of some quick-fuse political, journalistic and related chatter. At the Head's three-deep bar rail you'll be privy to tougher impeachment ground-plans, deeper and more lasting novels, shrewder sports tips and predictions, wiser opinions on who should be next mayor, or even dog-catcher (the Village's turd problem is hotly polemical), than are bruited about in any other bar in town. Lion's Head, the sozzled talkathon on Christopher Street.

After your stop at Lion's Head, walk east to Eighth Street and Sixth Avenue, where you'll spot the Nathan's corner, a good bet for a quick culinary dip: Coney Island franks, burgers and clams are still Coney Island at Nathan's! The corner itself is like a cement wedge of London's Hyde Park, with all manner of politics exotica, from early Mao to middle Muslim to late Symbionese to future JDL, up for grabs in two styles: jive and super-jive. The whole scene infiltrated once again by the subway-token hustler, more than likely the same cat who "hit" you earlier at Sheridan Square.

From the Nathan's scene, visit the Eighth Street Book Shop, about a block further east, where little mags and small-press books are, sort of, a *dedication*: if not sales-wise, surely browsing-wise. Take a moment to ask about your chapbook of poems, or any other small-press title, it's s.o.p. to "case" Eighth for far-out imprints. And if they're not stocking your book, you'll want to inform them of its "importance," and where they can order it. And if they are stocking it, but have it buried somewhere in the stacks, you'll want to suggest a "more visible" exposure. And if your book is *already* visible, like the ones on Eighth's dozen or so handy merry-go-rounds, you'll want to escalate to: "Is there any chance for a window display?" As we say, it's s.o.p. at Eighth.

A walk of five or six blocks more, still going east, and you'll be at St. Mark's Place and Third Avenue, entranceway to "where it all started." Which is to say, the roaring 1960s counter culture. St. Mark's is the imaginary line, or call it "climate," that seperates West from East Village, or middleclass from prole territory, with some blurring here and there such as Bowl and Board and two or three chic boutiques along St. Mark's. Take note of historic Cooper Union, somber pile of Vermont umber granite, with hallowed memory of A. Lincoln giving a key speech (he said later it won him the election) in CU's long, many-columned Great Hall. And just up the street, the spot where James Fenimore Cooper's home once stood, which now houses the St. Mark's Baths, popular meeting place for the boys in the band, who like to come by of an evening to work on their body tone.

Now you've one short block to go for Gem's, located at St. Mark's and Second Avenue, but you might want to visit—100 feet or so this side of Gem's—the East Side Book Shop, a smaller but hipper version of Eighth. And East Side does freebies, so don't leave without a supply of polit tracts, ecology pamphlets, and the like. And while you're at it, there are some good buys, from Lit to Third World to Occult to Zen, so take a little naches, leave a little bread.

Okay, it's the last 100 feet or so, and you've arrived. The famed Gem's Spa with its narrow barricaded look, 24-hour traffic feeding in from cobblestone Second and blacktop St. Mark's, nighttime clatches of heads and poets and activists doing their corner raps, and others zinging by for their *Times*, *SoHo News* or *Daily World* from Gem's Spa's way-open-ended news and periodical racks. And of course join the line, for the house special, the Gem's Spa's own secret-ingredient egg-cream. And you don't want to know "how" they do it, or "what's in it." You simply reach for chocolate coated glass, draw glass to lips while the froth's still frothing, and you gulp it down and enjoy! It's all "very heavy," as they say. It's been the Gem's Spa's thing for years, decades.

You may still be primed, after your back-to-back Village tour, for one last sweep down Second Avenue, for a quick look at two or three former and present in spots. At Second Avenue and Sixth Street, you'll notice the dead marquee, sticking out over the street like a mausoleum slab, of the former Fillmore East rock shrine; and just next door to Fillmore, the big darkened windows of Ratner's, where until very recently, you could parlay—for a winner nosh double—the Gem Spa's egg-cream with Ratner's own deluxe cheese cake. Sadly, both the Fillmore and the Ratner's noshery now are but black holes on Second Avenue's never-static firmament. Then make for Phebe's, two south and one east, at the Bowery and Fourth Street, the whitewashed brick facade, tarry for a while over a mug of beer, and listen in (Phebe's is the Off Off Sardi's) on "the great play I'm writing," and "the super funky part I'm reading for," and "the really smash director bit I'm considering." A good deal of which may indeed be true, but then again, it could be in the nature of central casting "optimism." And that's show biz, whether at Phebe's or Sardi's.

Now, as to "not getting mugged," etc., there's little point in holding your breath, as there's no sure Rx for your itinerary. However, there are two cardinal rules, observe them and trust to luck for the rest. 1/Walk at all times at a brisk, close-to-curb pace, and do affect if you must—in your encounters with token hustlers and others of that ilk—a kind of "I'm a stranger here, myself!" persona. And 2/be sure you have a good supply of NYC subway tokens, at the ready, in case all else fails.

On your trip back to Columbia, stick with the Broadway Local, a misstep here to either of two other trains (express) will land you in Harlem. That won't be exactly a crisis, but you should nonetheless know the geography, not to mention the sociology, before you wander off to 116 Street and Lenox Avenue. And while you're at it get off at the Columbus Circle stop, for the "Alternatives in Print" bash (Sunday through Tuesday of Cosmep week from 10 to 10) at the New York Cultural Center, not more than a block or two from the station. Alternatives is also a New York first, and you'll be swimming in and out of near 250 booths, with books and periodicals from small-press operations around the country, all under the roof of the former Huntington Hartford modern art museum, the $20-million bomb with the brown-lollypop columns up front, which once housed not a small number of "Hunts's" extravagant collection of Dalis. (Or Dali's Delicatessen.)

Once back on the campus, stroll across the College Walk on 116 Street, stop at the Sun Dial and look around. You'll be facing Alma Mater, the Low Memorial and the Mathematics building. The trio was the Winter Palace complex laid siege by students—junior faculty back in

1967, with Mark Rudd playing Trotsky to president Grayson Kirk's Kerensky. It will be recalled that Rudd and his red-banner proles captured Kirk's top-floor offices, ransacked the inner sanctum for plans-papers showing Columbia's bent for "elitist expansion," and broke into Kirk's private humidor of expensive cigars, which they lit up and enjoyed with feet-on-desks panache of your most exclusive, trustee-style gathering. And that the bold guerrilla thrust came to bloody end after seven or eight tension-filled days and nights when (in the spookiness of the 3 A.M. hour and while most Harlem Columbia-watchers were asleep) the NYC fuzz suddenly bulled through with billies-on-skulls' attack. The ferocity of which resounded clear over to Gracie Mansion, where the then Mayor Lindsay (who claimed he personally never ordered the attack) was himself presumably in a fitful sleep that night.

Now six or seven years later, when streakers rove by in the pale moonlight, don't discount their revolutionary fervor. It's really a case of Mark Rudd's children going umbilical, baring souls in penance (they've read their Veblen, you know!) for the consumer ridden, boutique ridden US economy. Going the route of Mao, with a touch of Pan thrown in for classic effect.

Before heading for the Residence Hall, you'll want to idle by the West End Bar for a nightcap, it's the watering hole for Columbia's and Barnard's lions and lionesses. In West End's mahogany walled, Tiffany lamped ambience, shouldered together in the narrow booths, Columbians and friends rapped out their epics, their poems, their rebellion, and of course they still do. It was the once-only time of promise. Let the next day's challenge, gloom or whatever come as it will.

Thus sat Ginsberg-Corso-Kerouac, to recall one such trio, so polish down a glass for them, and for the Cosmep future.

First New York Book Fair

THE PUSH-AND-SHOVE BOOK FAIR It's a humid, mid-90s Sunday afternoon in July, and hundreds are pouring into Columbus Circle, some taking a quick siesta at the splashy, centerpiece fountain. They're heading for the "Alternatives in Print" book fair, at the New York Cultural Center, on the south island of Columbus Circle. The three-day event, several months in the planning, has the buzzing excitement of a "First." And a Left Bank touch, books and metal tables outside the entrance, big peppermint beach umbrellas overhead. From out of the Midtown cornucopia, including Central Park happenings, Lincoln Center matinees, and several museums in the area, they choose this particular event, which involves several hundred small-press operations from as far apart as Portland, Oregon, and Portland, Maine. The relatively homeless and undernourished small-pressers have the welcome mat out on this day.

At the 4 P.M. hour the crowd is five-deep, snaking clear around the brown-lollypop columns, and hugging the harsh whitestone facade of the Center. Slowly, they get the signal from the two guards, and they go through the glass circular door, as others are leaving. Once inside they work their way to eighth-floor stop and then down; a helter-skelter crowd "glomming each other," as one visitor puts it, and with vibes that spell "the place to be, don't miss it."

It's 90% a New York book-buying, book-browsing crowd, most of whom can "hack Brentanos and Doubleday, but this kind of far-out display I never did see anywhere!" The young man who made the remark, and the girl he was with, both walked a tightrope across the parqueted floors; going from booth to booth for still more giveaways; such as poetry printouts, bookflyers and catalogs; their bosoms distended with the weight of their loot. Others are likewise weighted down, but not all the items are freebie, as witness the small-pressers doing a brisk business behind their individual booths.

Up for sale are hundreds of titles, including slim poetry chapbooks, ecology and Third World studies, books from the feminist presses, how-to's on farming and communitarian living, Chicano and Indian, prison writings, Tarot and other phases of the occult, peace and rad-politics mags, and more in the genre. All part of the flotilla of little formats that Auden rhapsodized over in an early poem (if memory serves), a flotilla that sails from island to island of our culture, and unloads its own unique literary wares. And a movement that has since burgeoned widely, in each of the 50 states, sparked of course by increasing programs of grants; but a movement that's essentially self-starting, and that tries (often with mixed results) for a lifestyle and expression that's invariably at odds with the received signal of overground publishing. It's as if the Oregon small-presser, from his neck of geography at one end, and the Maine small-presser from his at the other, are too busy

The Push-And-Shove Book Fair 163

vibing to their own signal to catch the big holler of names and sales and deals that originate in publishing powerhouses like New York City.

Librarians had their own big convention at three Midtown hotels that same week. And while hopes ran high among small-press people for some kind of winking courtship, if not out-and-out marriage (saleswise), the relatively small number of shows from the librarian encampments was cause for disappointment. Likewise disappointing were the no-shows, except for driblets from such houses as Avon and Warner's Paperback, from the publishing overground; though one conceivably might have missed, because of their air of anonymity behind their dark shades, some who *were* in fact from the big houses; and who seemed in any case to be floating from booth to booth, asking little and buying less, but whose studied concentration bespoke more than browser's interest. The media people, on the other hand, swooped down on the book fair eagerly, with local and out-of-town press, and TVers from two or three big networks, coming by at all hours, the latter adding their own Kilowatt (and crowd-pulling) power to the Center's already brightly lit mahogany galleries.

Near ten o'clock on closing night, with energies depleted and spirits high, they all folded their tables, but not before dealing off, in the one-for-one exchange traditional among littles, their remaining stocks of books and other material. One small-press operator, active for some years on both east and west coasts, put it: "We made a big score in public awareness of what we're all about." With an estimated crowd of eight or nine thousand for the three-day event, and with practically all carrying off their share of the tonnage of material on display, the case for increasing visibility, distribution, sales and reviews (for small-press titles) would seem to have been made. And even the symbology was on target, the storming of one citadel of spoiled-rich sensibility, the former Huntington Hartford museum with its overstock of Dalis (or Dali's Deli), by the alternative presses from the two Portlands and all points in between.

Thanks to the several individuals who sweated out the nuts and bolts over months of planning; and to the Cosmep network over-all; and to New York State Council on the Arts, who bankrolled about half the expense with a $6,800 grant. But no thanks to the Center's management, the mahouts who run the white elephant on the south corner of Columbus Circle; and who, after pocketing $6,000 for use of the three floors, broke the rule of free-admission when (on the last day) they posted a sign which read: "Pay what you want, but you must pay something." Whereupon Brooklyn College librarian Jackie Eubanks, a pro with no-nonsense style, planted herself in front of the sign and told visitors: "You don't have to pay anything."

Puppets, dancers and baseball

THE FREEBIE ARTS First a Saturday evening in tree-shaded, klieg-lit Museum of Modern Art sculpture garden, crowd of 500 or more midtowners in neat cottons, spectrum-colored sports clothes, lots of tanned and barebacked flesh on the hoof. They're comfortably seated or standing around the massive Rodin Balzac, the sprawled Maillol earth-lady (flowing like a river) in the tiny pool, the goatish Picasso bronze, and dozens more such pieces lying in shadow as if ready to spring at you, or throw tantrum-like leer as dappled patterns of light-dark hit them. For its air of relaxation, nonpushy nods and winks and exchanges, few places on the cement grid can equal the one-acre reserve lost between fortress-like St. Thomas Church, dun-colored Dorset Hotel and Fifth Avenue highrise office cubes.

It's as if many in the crowd, somewhere along the hot Saturday routine, opted to pass up the Long Island (or some other) invite, and decided to stick around instead and get the feel of walking down Fifth, taking in bookshops and boutiques, with eyes-wide-open freshness of the tourist. Now they're seated and waiting, on Eames-style metal chairs that give like wicker, for the evening's special. MOMA's Summergarden Punch and Judy show, with a difference. Light barbs off the headlines sprinkled among the ragamuffin pratfalls, the falsetto screech and holler of P & J and the rest. Children in the audience, wise to the one-liner jape like all good TV watchers, including even the women's-lib thrusts, shout their approval or disdain as the spirit moves them.

The puppetman is Steven Hansen, six-feet-plus and he moves like a ballet, as he performs inside the almost-human yellow bag with clown's legs, a kind of walking stage that conceals (says the program) a wide variety of sound effects: bicycle horns between legs, bells and tambourine on his hips, a slide whistle around his neck, and air hoses enabl-

The Freebie Arts

ing him to blow sirens, kazoos, bird calls, and emit puffs of smoke for the devil. His show is classic Punch and Judy, loaded with topical gags. And he's clicking them off, with Palace-like timing and exuberance all leading to that, eh, point in time when he introduces the "What's My Line?" mystery guest.

After a pregnant ten-second pause, the audience huddled in silence, up comes the new puppet in town. A puppet with a ski-launch proboscis, heavy-lidded eyes that almost burst from sockets, and honeyed alligator smiles. It's dressed in a stickly dark formal suit, the top-of-the-cake matrimonial display kind. For openers the wriggly puppet announces: "Now let's make one thing very clear!" The unctious tone signals quick howls of recognition. One youngster of about five plays interlocutor with glee: "Look at that, mommy, it's the man from the Watergate!" Puppetman Hansen sours back: "Okay, sonny, *this is my gig!*" So to the windup, with some breezy ad-libs on the impeachment.

Hansen sheds his walking stage, gathers together his props and instruments. He banters with the kids and informs others he'll be performing in Central Park and elsewhere through the summer. The full battery of kliegs come up, the two fountains bubble forth once again. (Now the sculptures lose their leering, pouncing menace.) Another Friday-through-Sunday program, from six P.M. to eleven, in MOMA's Summergarden series through September.

Central Park's Belvedere tower and lake, with rocky inclines and moatlike appearance, is the nearest thing we have to New World Graustarkian on the Manhattan skyline. Thousands know the spot from visits to Shakespeare Festival playhouse, itself no mean replica of the medieval, with its Tudor and Plantagenet flags snapping away on the bowlshaped rooftops. And just 100 feet or so north of the lake, on level turf surrounded by thick stands of shade-trees, there are marathon rounds of folk dancing, from two to five, on Sunday afternoons. And here again the European style holds sway.

Hundreds stop by to watch, more than a few joining in at some point, as groups of as many as 50 or 60 for some dances, go swirling around in circles or earthy jigs, mazurkas or polkas, as the music crackles on the tape machine. It's come as you are, break in when you're ready. The dress of course is Manhattan backyardsy: jeans, cottons, tablecloth hankies, sneakers, And for the hardcore folkies, there's never enough, each dance handled (or "footed") with gliding ease, whether difficult ones like the Hungarian Czardas, or the simpler, bouncing-along kind such as the Virginia Reel.

The caller hardly waits for the end of one, when he's setting his tape machine for the next, announcing loudly as he trips the button, "All join in for an Israeli Mazurka!" His call mingling with the center-fielder's, "I got it; it's all mine!" As fielder moves back fast, Latin Bombers emblazened on uniform, to haul in a long flyball. Just 50 feet or so short of the dancing crowd. Runners, joggers in the softball dance at one end of the field. Reelers, waltzers and foot-tappers doing their own dance at the other.

London

RETRIPPING September '74 trip opens with several mishaps, while still on New York side of pond. After 40-minute wait for Carey bus at East Side Terminal (they should close it down, if that's their best!), I get to Kennedy and find myself shutout 20 minutes before 7 P.M. flight time on Pan Am reservation. The cool, vaguely Eurasian ticket clerk: "It's impossible to get you on, plane's been full up as of six-fifteen." I raise a row: "Liberty Travel booked my ticket and Pan Am must honor it!" Clerk, silkenly: "Liberty Travel doesn't know what it's doing!" The long and short of it: Put me on alternate flight, Pan Am or any other, and as afterthought, "Get me on BOAC, they're the London home team and they aim to satisfy." And sure enough, after he makes quick phonecall, BOAC tells him yes for their 8 P.M. flight. Silken hands back my Pan Am ticket and throws in a bus pass, "Take yellow airport bus just outside, British Airways terminal." He adds, smiling a little meanly, "The pass will save you fifty cents."

STARTERS My first night in town, flopped at New York ex-patriate filmmaker Steve Dwoskin's pad on Ladbroke Grove. When I phoned from Heathrow that morning, I was flagged on by Steve's associate, darkly bearded, slightly nervous young Spaniard named Paco; who told me he wasn't sure, but thought I could stay that night and maybe the next, Steve was on Continent (for West German flick deal) and wasn't due back for 48-72 hours. (I need the vigorish of one or two days at a friend's place, then I stride on my own for hotel. Otherwise, I tend to unravel a bit.) That first evening, like tourist fish on spawning ritual, I wend over to Piccadilly. Eros statue, the kidney-shaped island, the cement reserve for wetbacker freaks from five corners of the globe. The bumper-to-bumper traffic, the Esperanto hustle, the circling parade, as you and hundreds guppy about inside the waist-high rail. Then, my first downer: They've cut a halfmoon swath, like a deep abdominal wound, right through the 150-foot island! For, would you believe, queue-up of London sightseeing buses! And that's only the opening shiv, I'm told, in a ground plan of more surgeries. Result, the Dilly goes Disney. One big commercial wheel for the dollar/pound/mark/franc. Other London areas—Bloomsbury is prime!—are in for the wrecking ball treatment. On Great Russell Street, famed for its graceful homes, oldstyle publishing houses (Andre Deutsch, Hamish Hamilton, others) and general livability—right in the quiet eye of Bloomsbury—they're skyrocketing a 20-25 story YMCA, the rockribbed waffled coarseness of which portends breakup of Victorian continuity. Today, it's the YMCA. Tomorrow, it's the U of London, with their own sprawl on the boards. Both are in on the Bloomsbury kill. (And can the British Museum be far behind?) Summed up by one Londoner, "They'll [U of London] rip apart Gordon Street houses, and build a College of Environmental Studies." The wry on his breath was very English.

THE LEVANTINE MAZE OF SUSSEX GARDENS   I pushed my luck at Steve's, had to vacate when he showed earlier than expected. (Though trussed from waist down, the Brooklyn boy is a demon behind wheels. He beat his own, his girlfriend's and Paco's timeclocks—all had Steve arriving some 12 hours later.) But I was assured: "You'll find a room in Sussex Gardens, couple miles from Ladbroke, any hour of day or night." Well, I have news, getting a hotel daytime is no big deal. London's a tourist wholesaler, can absorb beehives at pockets as various as 20-30 pounds a day at American traps like Hilton and 3 pounds and up with breakfast thrown in at seedy-elegant 3-story hotels in Bloomsbury. And you get help from cabbie or bowlerhat. Nighttime, it's a different ballgame. The shadows fall, 98% of London is asleep, the streets are in captivity to low-scudding clouds. I call for a taxi (the hour's 01:00) and I'm picked up outside Ladbroke address. "Take me to Sussex Gardens," I tell the cabbie. Expecting, of course, that he'll drop me at a hotel by that name. But I soon realize as he zigs and zags through gloom-shrouded streets, that Sussex Gardens is a jungle of 4-story cheapie, cheerless tourist warrens: have your pick. I get out, pay the cabbie, start my search—lugging my three bags with the nonchalance of a 2d-story man about to be caught "fleeing the scene." And, the unnerving repetition of signs, NO ROOMS. Baggage and 2d-story complex gets heavier, block by deserted block. At one point, a Bobbie looms out of the murky-orange of street lamp. He tosses me a casual salute, "Are you lost or something?" I reach for my passport, explain I need a room. Sympathetic, though hardly reassuring, he directs me to a row of hotels deeper into the maze. About 100 no-no's later, I finally bounce to one hotel that *may* have a room. Call it the No Name, scruffy narrow entrance, shoebox lobby, yawning Indian chap: "Lucky you caught me, we don't usually book at this hour." (It's past 2 A.M.) Waves of relief—I'll be sacked in at last! Plus, a sudden twinge of panic: "You didn't put me in the register! I don't wanna be swallowed in this fine hotel, anonymous and unknown to the entire city of London!" Ah yes, he pencils my name on a dogeared pad. Next, a night of sleepless shudders, up and out of bed every half hour, can't get a handle—sense of location—in weblike, walled over No Name. Next morning, late hour of 11, dress quickly and down to phone, my migraine tick the only sure thing I know. Call to Jay Landesman, member of the expatriate roster, I tell him I'm about to take cab to Heathrow for a flight home. Jay counters, "Don't make a move; I'll be right over!" Arrives in a dented, high-roofed autobus. We lurch around town, and he finally drops me off at small hotel in Blooms—they have a room, I'll take it. I begin to get the handle, "Hard by British Museum, U of London; Dilly and West End ten-minutes by cab, bus." But please, no more talk of Sussex Gardens.

ACCIDENT PRONE   Travel 3000 miles, you crack your finger in doorjamb. The left middle-finger, turns purple-and-blue from nail down. Not too much pain, but hotelier advises I go over—four or five blocks up Bloomsbury—to London U accident ward. Well, back home I do obstacle courses before I get myself to a dispensary. Here, on Bloomsbury turf, I figure: "Go check it out; see how they do it, the London way." First surprise: Yes, we'll certainly have a look. No, there are no forms to fill, just your name and date of birth, please. The accident ward, large and brightly-decored waiting room, 15 or 20 patients sitting around on midweek morning. Minor cases, for the most, like my own cracked finger. 2d surprise: Passing the time, I get me a cup of tea, in the convenient hospital cafe (staff *and* patients) on the same ground floor. 3d surprise: Soon—less than half hour wait—I'm called and young English medico has a look. Asks, can you flex finger ("Yes.") and how'd it happen ("No, I'm not accident prone, except when discombobulated with worry"). Doctor, on first glance, says it doesn't look serious, but he sends me to X-ray room for pics, after writing up simple one-sheet form. Another 20 minutes, and I have the X-ray shots—two of them—I go back with them to medico's desk. And that's the 4th surprise: The technician handing *me* the X-rays, this never happened in any New York emergency ward or clinic that I can remember. (Top secret, all that folderol!) Medico looks X-rays over in another room, and 10-minutes later, he's back at desk: "A slight bone-chip under the nail, not to worry, it will self-heal inside two or three weeks." All leading to 5th surprise: I come full circle, back to registress, London girl with creamy-pink complexion, half-notes of melody in voice (Londoners don't speak *flat*, if you just listen and catch the music). And, I'm expecting, waiting for, ask about, some indication of: "How much will that be?" A smile, and she bids me "Have a good day." Nothing else, not a tuppence charge. If that's welfare medicine, I want a dosage when I next visit Downtown Beekman.

WAXWORKS CANDIDATE ON BBC   His name is Jeremy Thorpe (on TV box it's always "Jeremy"), his face and warbly voice unrelentingly cold and bloodless. Thorpe is the Liberal Party panjandrum, and BBC is having a Jeremy-&-the-Libs carnival in the fortnight I'm in London. First I see him and party in convention at Brighton. Youngish politicos in starchy mod dress, they're into a kind of lip-reading sincerity as they reprise the Liberal "platform": catechism of *one single issue*, which I read as "Co-illish!" E.g. *Coalition*, they knead it, roll it firm on the board, stretch it out by the yard,. And there's Jeremy himself, equine-longish features, gray pallored image flooding the box at all hours. A kind of nonstop, non-personality blob of punishment inflicted on millions compliments of BBC. Take one particular airing. Thorpe's in the TV dock, facing two very tough political journalists: (1) tart-tongued Irishman from *The Observer*, and (2) the man from *The Guardian*, call him the scalpel from the Left, who's outfitted in a flaring, footwide kerchief-tie that—on the US box—might alone get him 86d for indecent dress. The two have at Jeremy, between the buzzsaw of *Observer* and scalpel of *Guardian*, Thorpe can't cope except to repeat—with sincerity—the Liberal catechism. So twists the political weathervane in the UK. Slowly, slowly on the wind of rhetoric. Hunch: Labor Party, in a clear-majority in House of Commons, with Jeremy and Ted Heath co-illishing in retirement.

BBC TAKE TWO   I'm visiting with Clancy Sigal and Margaret Walters—at their fifth-floor atelier pad on Wigmore—when BBC rings Clancy (about 8 P.M.) and asks would he come on the late news special, but two hours hence, and comment on President Ford's amnesty for draft resisters, deserters. Clancy—active in the London Nam protest movement—makes several phone calls in effort to get couple of GIs and resisters to give their own rap on BBC program. He draws a blank, calls news director, is asked would he appear himself. Later—after BBC-arranged taxi drops us there—the three of us are in a large studio, and with barely a 5-minute warm-up, between BBC guy and Clancy, the latter is next seated in studio telecast chair, facing what can only be described as plaster-of-Paris BBC news specialist. Margaret and I ensconced in tiny gallery darkroom, catching the action on several mini studio boxes. Plaster—in no small snit over Clancy's openers—pushes his theme on amnesty: "Well, they did break the law, after all." CS: "The government and Pentagon broke the law in the first place—with far greater consequence than the personal act of refusing to fight in an illegal war." Plaster then wields his big club: "How will the folks who lost their loved ones in Vietnam feel about amnesty?" Expatriate author Sigal—himself a World War II veteran—offers a cool "Hear, hear!" but he insists that President Ford (who has been clanking like an Edsel, at that) will have to do better than penalties of 2 years' service if he wants to get the resisters back to the states. All in all, a lightning-like BBC number. No studio back home would've come up with this kind of ad-hoc controversy short of, say a 24-hour think tank of preparation, chain-of-editorial-command and the lot. Clancy: "It's classic BBC casting of left-winger vs. right-winger in exact, by the ounce, balance."

THE KEATSIAN SLEEP   I take the 28 bus to Hampstead, a sunny Wednesday afternoon, and I'm at the wrong end of Hampstead Heath for what I had in mind. Another go at what's easily the most dramatic view of London from terra firma: the long scanning from the

Heath's high ground to the misty towers, spires of the inner city below and away—in a linear perspective that calls up a Turner or an El Greco picture. Yet once there at the last stop I get off and wander around—and I then discover what turns out a "find" all its own. The modestly-scaled, greening mews inside which stands the whitewashed, 2-story house where John Keats lived, for 2 or 3 years of his short 26. And composed—among other of his later poems—the "Ode to a Nightingale." Nightingale, or so the plaque says, was completed one morning, right there on the grounds, in a 2- or 3-hour rush of inspiration. The plaque itself stands reveted under a 7-foot plum tree, the tree a replica of the very one Keats sat under (to quote from the plaque again) as he recalled—and shaped in verse—the Hampstead nightingale song. Later I moved from room to room, sampling the Keatsian relics, original manuscripts, letters and other memorabilia. The trove included several lockets of hair—Keats's, Fanny Brawne's and one or two more. Proving, I'd guess, that the magico was in it (the hair) long before the Beatles. Then I came upon a large, mounted printout of the Ode, which hangs from the sitting room wall. I stood there and read it, line by magical line, and I began to feel a kind of transport, an astral sensation, a chill in the bones—coming from 80 lines or so overall, and it struck me, no lines I'd read, no word-music I'd heard, could be so packed with genius. Keats, caught in the upbeat of Nightingale song, which he transposes into the life-force; and then, in counterpoint lines, he's caught in the profoundly equal downdrift of his death-premonition, his death-wish; the two polar moods twained, one with the other, in a seamless and brilliantly musical lament. With "throwaways" like "Tender is the night"; and "the alien corn"; and what dozens more; begged, borrowed or culled—taken possession of—by such as F. Scott Fitzgerald and others. Lastly there's the Joseph Severn sketch of Keats, the deathbed sketch, with Severn's annotation: "28 Janr, 3 o'clock, morng. Drawn to keep me awake—a deadly sweat was on him all this night." The poet's flirtation, his very yearning, made real at last. A sort of drowning, on river of his own fading body.

SHOOTING A FLICK   I meet Lindsay Anderson on set at Elstree Studio, the London suburbs. He's shooting David Storey's play *In Celebration* for the American Film Theatre, and he invited me out for a look and chat. It took several days, half dozen phonecalls to get through, but now that I meet him, Anderson (one of the hottest tickets in London film and stage) turns out to be friendly, easy interview. No flaming temperament, no outbursts. (An actress tells me, "Everyone wants to work with Lindsay, he's a groove, the best.") He introduces me to the cast—Alan Bates among others. I mention to Bates—it's fresh on my tongue—that he's a sort of "found" star (like found poem) with one of the hippest of New York audiences; the all-night and mostly young movie honchos who flop into the Elgin on 19th Street for midnight runs of *King of Hearts*; and that it's one long night of howls, *Hearts* sort of the anchor, in the triple-header movie orgy. ("Lindsay," the actor yells, turning a shade pink, "did you hear that." And Anderson, "Well, Alan, you might just make cruddy stardom, yet.") Anderson, as I take it in, comes over as lowkeyed study. He's fiftyish, slightly rumped in fawn-colored corduroy work clothes, hawkish sharp features, and graying Brechtian crew cut. He looks like he's ready to swoop, talons bared, right down on the cast when they flub their lines. Yet in take after take, the spareness of method, the almost benign director-actor noodling, comes over with little of the expected "ulcers." And, if there's a hint, now and then, of outburst just below the surface, in practice he's left most of it in the wings. At the lunch break, taken in the Elstree dining room, we get into rap about Thorpe—this and that on the UK, US fronts. And I'm soon trapped in Straits of Apathy, hard by the Sea of Cynicism, that's how much of a downer UK politics is. I mention the Social Contract (far-out radical, next to *our* politics) and hunch that Labor's got a big-win coming up; and like tolling of bells the reaction is "Bullshit promises." Anderson: The politics is burned-out; no change will come from duffers at the top. Well, what about the youth, nothing hot-angry-hopeful, coming from below? Lindsay Anderson: The youth—they're more out of it than the duffers. I rear up, "Well, I guess the a-k's will have to do it, won't they?" He's baffled, till I explain, "Alte Kokers, like you and me." A waspish grin, and then, "Agreed, cheers, for all us a-k's in the arts."

LEND LEAST THEATRE   Regent Street is elegant and commercial, sort of gradually turning and lowrise Fifth Avenue, gateway to Piccadilly at one end, handsome Regents Park at the other. Almost smack in the middle, and a good cricket-shot's distance from Cavendish Square, you come upon the Regent Theatre, with toney black-white marquee offering: LET MY PEOPLE COME. On display in the lobby, and on the street, are the porn-corn blurbs from *Come's* New York Village

Gate run. In the immediate vicinity, are window displays of Aeroflot office (holidaying peasants in spirited folk-dancing, handsome posters of Leningrad); and similar displays in windows of Polish Airlines (holidaying peasants in spirited folk-dancing, handsome posters of Warsaw). Picture the people's democracies' bluecollar office workers at Aeroflot and Polish Airlines out for a lunchtime stroll—stopping by the Regent Theatre and copping a look at the *Come* blurbs: "Kapitalistski kultural decadence; what else can you expect!"

Independent Democrats

THE VID CROUPIERS COUNT THE VOTE Election night at the VID (Village Independent Democrats) is a kind of fishbowl of counting votes in an atmosphere of Saturday night beer-and-pretzels comraderie—more so when the count is going their way. The upstairs loft just west of Sheridan Square is itself a nabe club giving off almost around-the-clock signals in one of the highest-density political areas in NYC. (Clout, you might say, different from the sauna-and-muscle emporium next door.) And, in terms of the local effort, a little touch of the French arrondissement Fourteenth of July celebration sans the wearing of the tricolor sash.

I got there around ten, still time to see VID's croupiers chalking the votes up and down the wall blackboard, with its narrow columns indicating candidates, the district web, and maybe even (at least to VID's X-ray eyes) the blocks and very apartment houses themselves. The tattoo of erasures and chalkings of new totals, as the party watchers would arrive from the polling places and hand over their figures, lent its own tension over and above the kind of "CBS projects this" and "NBC projects that" tallying that was flashing on the loft's tiny TV box.

As I looked the crowd over for a clue, I got the *real* projection on the fly, the happy faces and upbeat chatter indicating "big victory" in the making. And never mind the computer "input" of the nets which supposedly gives Cronkite the Anchor and his various lesser Ankies the end result of a contest after, say, a mere 100 votes—out of say a potential 10,000—has been accounted for.

Of course the thrush-throated sounds of victory, to the sitting and standing klatch of about twenty of us around the box, was a lot more tuneful than the cawlike drone of the TV messengers in 1972. The switch for so partisan a bunch as the VID, who can sense voter rhythms with the ear of bird-dogs in the brush, was like the notice of a not inconsiderable bounty in the morning mail from a long-forgotten uncle. In this case from an uncle (Mr. Sam) whom VIDers and others had reason to suppose would not be getting in touch *that* soon after the '72 debacle. Which too made the beer and wine and No Cal, already flowing in freebie round this one night of the year, the more potable in the gulping.

For an election that one Ankie called "lethargic," there were more than a few surprising areas of interest. Take just the western pair of Colorado and South Dakota, linked directly by unhappy memory of 1972. In the former, the McGovern stalwart, Gary Hart, was making the kind of voting sounds; against of course the Nixon stalwart, Peter Dominick; that eluded Hart's team, to put the case mildly, in the overrun of "Four more years" votes.

But perhaps even more crucially, if the Colorado race looked good at about the 11 o'clock hour, the South Dakota returns at the same hour were like the sounding of brass, the roll of the tympani, ushering one political Lazarus right back into the limelight. And when CBS flashed to the South Dakotan's headquarters, all of us at the box drew in closer. One watcher vaguely wishing that, in the flush of his victory, said South Dakotan would speak out against the false gods of Creep, dirty tricks and laundered campaign bucks. But not a line, not a syllable, did he utter of past injury. Instead, to Cronkite's worry that "perhaps a mandate for your party might be a mixed blessing," the South Dakota senator offered, as coolly as in a Politics One lesson: "Well, Walter, I don't see the vote as a party mandate, so much as a demand from the American voter for action...." And he listed, among other targets, "the case of the oil monopoly ..." And no surprise if, as the saying goes, *his* (Senator McGovern's) future has just begun.

Back to the local scene, with VID's co-leader planting herself at midfloor, and shouting above the din for attention. Tall, red-headed, energetic, and in her late-20s. And just a bit nervous, before giving her own run-down. She spoke of "whopping majorities for the entire VID slate." Then she introduced, in a kind of change-of-guard ritual, one past VID co-leader, Councilperson Carol Greitzer: "In Carol's contest we show a big, four and a half to one lead over *both* opposition candidates combined. . . ." A good round of cheers, each one of the VIDers grasping as it were some part of the Greitzer landslide as his or her own contribution to the team effort.

One VID member from Argentina, and before, that, an escapee from Nazi Germany, picked up on the Cronkite-McGovern exchange about "party mandate"; saying, "It's an important distinction, putting people before party, and now *our work* has only just begun." And that, she concluded, is what "voting is all about."

1975

SoHo

THE 24-HOUR FLOATING PARTY GAME *Artists and writers are the loneliest people in the world.—A SoHo party host* After the Lil Picard post-Christmas happening—at whitewalled basement gallery on Greene in the SoHo desert. Several of us waiting around on street, listening and passing on the word about "parties," loose groupings of 2s and 3s and 4s hanging by among the loft buildings of mazelike number, layered shoulder to shoulder—the buildings that is—on cobblestone streets like canyons. The whole night scene lit up sharper than daylight, under punishing glare of the high-intensity sodium lamps. Earlier, the venerable Lil, 70-plus and white-haired and bouncy, doing her thing in black leotards, energizing the audience of 100 or more, as she mimes her way round and through the displays of steeltubing sculpture. It's a neo-Dada masque, rite of passage back to classic Greek posturing gods-goddesses, and forward to anarchic free-form body-is-beautiful polymorphous sex dance/celebration. It's Saturday night winter-solstice interlude, get-together of Lil's friends, artists and dancers, SoHo inner circlers, and walkins off the street.

After the Picard, after the sendoff cups of white and red grape, some of us still palming the pastic cups out on street—experimental video gathering/party only a block or two away. The word leaps from person to person, and it's out of the first gallery, then off caravaning south on Greene, in the 2s and 3s—headed for the second gallery called Kitchen. The never-ending daisy chain of parties behind walls. (SoHo is the black hole in the city constellation: No neighborhood blade of grass, no supermarketed ambience, not even a Laundromat, to call their own. So they make the social time of day, the convivial hour of night, with the 24-hour floating party game.)

We're now at 95 Wooster, the Kitchen two flights up, and someone cautions, "Better walk it; can't trust the elevators." (Rumor has it they're checking Missing Persons reports, in some of those shaftways, going back to Judge Crater's disappearance.) So we hike the creaky wooden stairs, come upon good-size crowd of video freaks, the off off Madison video, most sitting yoga around two TV boxes—boxes going ape with peppermint-stick designs in black and white. And if you ask "When does the program begin?" you don't know peppermint-sticks' worth about farout experimental video.

More grape in plastic cups, the TV boxes now doing Larry Poons gray-dots-on-grayer-ground motifs. Soon the party word again, this one's at 195 Grand, and the 2s and 3s rise from the Kitchen floor. Go out into street caravaning down Wooster—where's *Grand*? where's *195*? We head block or two south, then east over to Broadway and beyond. It's past midnight, tourist hour for Italian coffee-and at Ferrara's, marquee house sign lit up in 1920s style orange frosted bulbs. One of us curious to know, put almost *sotto voce* soft, "That's where Joey Gallo met the hit man, right?" (Wrong, Joey was gunned down at Umberto's clam House just nearby.) Well, he didn't have to *sotto voce* it, the crowd's waiting the line at Ferrara's, and the streets are deserted that hour of night, as befits the family life style.

The six of us, still making tracks on Grand, numbers 175-177 coming up. Deeper into the east side, to old Eldridge Street, and someone pops the question.

"The Sunday pushcart scene, right?"

"Wrong, not Eldridge, maybe Orchard and Mulberry."

Eldridge, Orchard, Mulberry—so eerily quiet now, you could shoot off a cannon. But only a few hours hence, at five or six in the morning, the bivouac of pushcarts at curbstones, the army of Mother Courages shouting their wares ("It costs *me* more, believe it!"), to background chimes of Little Italy's churchbells.

We arrive at 195 Grand. All gather round the entrance, look up at the arched windows for sign of party, sign of *life*. A gloomy 6-story rawboned hybrid, part warehouse, part tenement, the hulk awash in city nightshadows. Dusky phantoms on field of 3-click traffic lights, and liquid misty orange street lamps. One of us rings an apartment bell, another tries forcing knob on double-locked hallway door. If there's anybody home, partying or whatever, they're not home to *our* caravan of six.

Two from our group, teacher–student dancer couple, peel off for a taxi; while the other four head in direction of Phebe's, located at Bowery and Fourth. We go north on Eldridge, holding breath a little, as we walk past "murderer's row" landscape—the rotting buildings, the glowing smoky red garbage fires, the sudden movement of slickly gray rat on the prowl. And two derelicts in contour—like two gray bundles of rags hunched over the fires—or was that last an apparition? On the same street, a neighborhood social club, jukebox sounds wafting past barricaded sheetmetal entrance. Do we nose in on *that* scene? Well, the Christmas spirit is abroad, so why not?

But one of us cautions "*That's* a no-no; Christmas cheer or not!"

And so on to Phebe's, where 60c gets you mug of dark/light beer. We head west toward Bowery, past big yawning cement schoolyard, couple of 12-year-olds jumping one-on-one baskets (miming it, with no ball) inside wafflelike steel fence, *at that crazy hour and under the pouring-down globes*! On the other side of street, an open Sanitation Department motor pool, the brute curbstone sweepers bedded down for night before resuming the garbage wars.

We all split around two, after quick round at Phebe's bar, swapping the word on SoHo circuit come New Year's Eve.

The waning, rain-soaked hours, like 1974's mood itself: The deep soggy melancholy, the bottom-line worry over this, that and the other. And the highup sodium lights, the carrot-colored shafts brighter than daytime, cutting through the mixing wetly with the sheets of rain. But SoHo does its number—the nabe game on this last night of year the one barrier against prevailing gloom. On tap a literary happening, and "Everybody's list" party.

I head for Wooster, can't find the street, grab a skidding taxi, cabby puts me right at 195—just four short blocks from where I hailed him! (He didn't pull the flag, asks "Whatever yu wanna give." I hand over four bits, he throws me a mock cheery "Happy New Year, if you can believe it.") Walk two flights up, I'm in the Artists Space gallery, 100-by-100 whitewalled—the marathon reading of Gertrude Stein's *The Making of Americans* in progress. It began that afternoon, the various readers coming by at prearranged hours. They sit down at open table, top bare except for the Stein book, the small recorder turning noiselessly, the glass pitcher of water. At the moment it's avantist Jackson MacLow, he's hunched over the thick volume and reads the lines with Hasidic intensity.

Around the big room, 10 or 12 are sprawled out on faded foam-rubber mats, or stuck off in corner where two are flexing in silent calisthenics. And one other couple, each in his-her early 20s, down on the floor in a yogic squat, they're facing each other, and carefully braiding each other's longish hanks of hair. I stay an hour or two, waving in on the monotone of the Stein-line, the artful prolixity of repetition, the cataracts of sound, the Gertrude voodoo.

So it's out of the Artists Space, and walk two blocks south, to 95 Wooster party. The "everybody's list" year-end blowout, and it's exactly that. The hosts, a bearded artist, his Mama Cass girted old lady, neither keeping book on who's invited, who's crashing. A whirling mix of SoHo regulars, student artists, name and non-name poets and writers, sprinkle of uptown galleryites, and the grapevine walkins. The clothes from denims, to homemade caftans, to kicky leathers, to glitter chic. And the 3-piece-suit man, professor off a Long Island campus, with Broadway gowned wife on arm. They announce, "We just saw the Neil Simon play—it's a howler!" (Their best line of the night, and nobody listening.) Huge cutglass bowl of sangria, outsize wheel of cheese, stone-oven loaves of brown bread, brought bottles of hardstuff by the dozen. At 12 midnight sharp, the whirl slows down, everybody hugging in the new, embracing and laughing, and even some tears.

"Ever heard of Henry Wallace's ever-normal granary?"

"No, what's that?"

"Anyway, this is the ever-normal SoHo party."

The pounding rock music, heard clear down to the street. The two-way traffic, up and down the shadowy stairwell, like subway escalator at five quitting time. It's past two when I leave, and they're stil trooping the stairs. Out on Wooster, as I head back to Stein reading, a trio of parked Lincoln Conti's, chauffeurs idling at wheels, after dropping uptown passengers at still another SoHo party—"formal" dress jazz bash that has aura of slumming.

Back at Artists Space. More reading, drone of Stein-line cutting the 3 A.M. slumbers. Anna Lockwood, one of the planners, taking catnaps, curled into sleeping bag at walled-off corner. *The Making of Americans*

... *The Making of* ... *The Making* ... *The* ... Some 50 readers or more, over 900 pages of text, upwards of 48 hours (through noon of January 2) before it's over. All caught on the turning acetate decks, all of it in the record book.

At the Elgin

"EASY RIDER" REVISITED Six years after its premiere, and it still touches a raw nerve of what the 1960s counterculture cum drug experience was all about. Fact is that on the recent and "cooler" viewing of a spring, 1975, night at Chelsea's Elgin Cinema, one pardoned one's self and then gasped out the words "mod masterpiece," although a failed masterpiece. Main ingredients of which—a deep and ongoing mood of searching and lostness, a visceral humor laced with random playfulness, the near and far dangers-delights of on-the-road odyssey, and ebbing-flowing of our "native" violence and equally native pastoral yearning. All adding up to the revelatory worm of defeat inside the apple of the "dream."

But first some words of recall—to the summer of 1970, when one could witness, by virtue of practically around-the-clock showings at the smallish Piccadilly cinema, the deep impress *Rider* had on London and European moviegoers. They were taking a hard look—almost in a spooky silence—at the flashing technicolored images, lonely encounters and out-of-doors nocturnal "trippings," they saw-toothed dangers and interludes of hope, and they seemed to be grasping for that larger image of America in generational, and of course other, turmoil of the 1960s. And if Vietnam was the dominant political (not to say "imperialist") experience of that decade, it should be added that *Rider*, for the same European audience, appeared to offer more than a glinting clue to the deep fissures (call it the experience of "backlash") that were the social-cultural side of the Nam coin.

Rider's main theme or "spine"—so richly American in its ambiguity—is stated almost immediately, even while the film credits are flashed on screen, through the metaphor of "dealing." The variants of which, of course, are well-nigh limitless: the deal, the hit, the fix, the score, the connection. The All-American concepts, whether in politics, at the local supermarket, in the financial community, or the high and low precincts of crime. In the same opener scene, we see the two biker heroes—Billy and Captain America—hopping about hither and yon, just this side of the US-Mex border airport Tarmac, with the 747s and DC-10s, like a swarm of mod pterodactyls, zooming in low overhead for landings. The dealing pair, themselves a species of mod Bedouins of hip, are the hinge of the three-part deal: They receive, and then pay for, a good stash of powdery white dope; they then deal back the stash, presumably at twice or more what they paid, to the third party—an Orson Wellesian, behind-dark-shades, out of the limousine character; bikers all the while savoring the stake that'll get them wheeling off to Mardi Gras. And get them wheeling off, at the farther side of the "dream," to some remote paradisal layover in Florida . . . maybe the end-of-the-road Keys.

The entire scene—no more than 10-minutes' or so duration—is a model of economy, good pacing, and lowkeyed tension. But more than all these together, there's the metaphoric "planting" (the way Captain America sausages the bankroll deep inside the bike's gas tank) of that worm of defeat, even as you find yourself suspending, at least for the moment, all moral "judgment" over the deal. Such as, "Bad money leads to a bad end." You're not merely suspending judgment; you're indeed *rooting for them all the way.*

Call it the Americanus Q.E.D.: The successful deal equals freedom. Or at least it would seem that way. In the on-the-road encounters, handsomely caught by Laszlo Kovacs's cameras, the weave of metaphor is rarely lost. The bikers have made their score, and they're *enjoying it to the full.* Through the long, praying-mantis-like strides of jut-wheeled bikes; through the beauty and density of terrain (Arizona, New Mexico badlands, etc.); through the four or five "hits" of grass under open skies; through the chow-down with the rancher and family; and the stopover at the farming commune in the hills; where one lifestyle rubs off momentarily (and pleasurably) on the other—through all these fast-paced travels, the bikers are enjoying themselves. But—and here's the "monkey" on their backs—the darker side keeps breaking through. The slow tease that maybe *their* freedom, when compared with rancher-and-family's, and with the commune people's, is little more than a *scattered* freedom, at best. And somewhat later, of course, the explosive larger truth hits home. The truth that the bikers, so far from being the "easy riders," in our open-spaces America, are indeed more like clay ducks at some Coney Island shooting gallery—in the eyes of certain volatile redneck types. The latter of whom the third rider—the pickup cum piggy-back rider—sums up in his lemon-bitter musing: *They believe in freedom, all right. The freedom to beat on you, if they don't like your hairstyle.*

Now if that doesn't exactly ring bells, in terms of the "revealed truth", *Rider's* main theme (i.e., sudden bouts of violence interrupting, and at the last stages, killing off, the paradisal search) is nonetheless deeply rooted in the 1960s turmoil. And it's the very *shock* of the violence, comparable in its gut immediacy, its *primordial* immediacy, to that of lightning chopping down a tree—that finally transforms *Rider* from not altogether unpredictable genre film, to paradigm of an entire era. One test of this is to ask, as I've done in some eight or ten instances recently: "What's the main sense of the film?" And to get back the answer, almost the same in every case, whether respondent liked or bad-mouthed the film, that they all felt the explosive shock, the visceral impact. Call it a nerve-ends violence, next to the workaday, and the conditioned, and the pushbutton kind—of the average Hollywood flick.

On yet another point. Some have called *Rider*, one way or another, a "commercial hype." And while the lingo may be on target, the observation itself would seem considerably less so. The fact is that hardly anybody, least of all the money men, expected *Rider* to be a boxoffice success. And further that Dennis Hopper—the blackballed archangel of Hollywood and Vine—was having his usual troubles raising the money. So that when the boxoffice lightning struck, you'd have to call that a happy accident, rather than a "commercial hype." As for Peter Fonda, he was at the time coming off, pretty near, the same wave of "success" as Hopper—meaning, little more than a *ripple*. And Jack Nicholson and his role, which was offered first to Rip Torn, who was not available: Call that a casebook example, in other words, of accident and genius, or the genius of accident, winning out over the pre-tested—or "out of the computer"—Hollywood casting. And cinematographer Laszlo Kovacs, of whom it can be guessed, that not *talent*, but previous boxoffice record, was the gamble. So much for the notion of "hype."

And to round it out. Hopper-Fonda-Nicholson, both for the gutsy story line (with an assist of course from Terry Southern), and more than a few viscerally punchy acting moments; those, plus a certain naturalness and tone, without which (and at the very least) no film can be called "classic." The late Warren Finnerty, in the cameo role of the rancher. The commune people and turf, practically a "virgin" territory for Hollywood, and hence a breakthrough for the dropout scene. The Nola bordello pair, certainly creditable enough as pill-popping freakouts go. The rednecks doing their thing in the southern diner: the honchos stare the bikers down in a high sizzle, even as the clutch of younguns Dixie belles stare them "up" (from an opposite booth) in equally high sizzle. (Has anyone commented that Dennis Hopper, in the diner encounter, has caught—at least to this eye—what seems like an overtone from the work of another Hopper, the painter, Edward Hopper: vide, the "triangular" involvement, the tart subtlety of detail, the smolder of tension?) And there's Laszlo Kovacs—his cameras are not only athletic, they sort of drink in the near and far terrain with extraordinary fluidity, lyric feel. And finally the background rock, most by Steppenwolf and The Byrds, the takes are rarely intrusive, or groupie-smarmy.

It's more than six years after, and the shock is still in it.

Books and journalism

OF BOOK AWARDS & MEDIA TALKATHONS The National Book Awards, the 26th annual, is an old show in town. More awards than ever, yet a kind of pall of *déjà vu* that has everyone blinking. The very ground-rules have that *très predictable* look: What makes *this* poet, *this* novelist, *this* historian—better than the others. Lots of pairs of eyes, scanning thousands of lines of type, burning the midnight wattage night after night, wherewith the honored judges, in each category, to come up with the best author of the lot—by their lites. And if no individual stir was made—none that provoked the lobby talk of past NBA winners like the Mailers and the Berrymans—let it be said the experts were conceded their expertise all the way. Well, *almost* all the way, the exception being in Fiction. Why, it was bruited softly, did Joseph Heller get passed by, honors given to the likes of split-decision winners, Robert Stone and Thomas Williams. (The latter, especially, getting the goose from the Hellerites: "Thomas *who?*")

Actually the award ceremonies—at Lincoln Center's Philharmonic

Hall, lately called "Avery Fisher Hall," and an acoustic loser of a barn by any name—did surface with mild echo of past NBA "surprise": When the youthful academic, Theodore Rosengarten, was handed his thousand prize, for the Nat Turner–Nate Shaw "memory" book, he gave a crisp, short talk and then announced that he'd donate one-half his prize to Attica defense. All to a good round of applause, but here again, it was barely ripples, next to the waves—and walkouts by some—that greeted past Poetry winner Robert Bly, when Bly donated his prize money to Vietnam resistance.

At the Americana Hotel finale that evening—bowls of iced shrimp and other goodies up for the chomping in the Grand Ballroom—there was indeed what you'd call a riffle of controversy: On the very same hotel floor, in another and much smaller room, called (and the irony wasn't lost on most) the Versailles Room, a competing award ceremony named "Rational Book Awards," with honors to the "industry's own"—the middle & lower echelon office, editorial and other workers from big publishing. Sponsored by such activists as Kitty Krupat, District 65 Publishing Division organizer, and Linda Faulhaber, President, Association of Harper & Row Employees—the Rational loosed some mild shafts, including "Humanitarian of the Year" award to Raymond C. Hagel, executive biggie over at Macmillan. (Feminist Party's Florynce Kennedy, black lawyer with acid-blue tongue, called for ". . . boycott, girlcott, Africott and apricott [of] the books of publishing houses that mistreat their employees.") The Rational ran it down, with some old-time Union chanting by Pete Seeger, even while the Grand Ballroom crowd was doing its own in the old-time palace manner.

All told the whiff of rebel grapeshot, and cry of the cultural streetfighter, were not so punishing as to upset the rather staid boozing, the continuous chomping, going on in the Grand Ballroom. Still, there were some few among the ballroom crowd, who did cock an ear for the "bulletins" coming from the anti-NBA bash. But here agin—from opposite side of barricade—no expression so ridden with angst as to upset the air of *bon-homie*, self-congratulation, word-of-mouth on *who's climbing the ladder at what house*. (Call it moral skinnydipping, or the baring of souls, a kind of split-loyalty syndrome that's endemic to publishing.) This reporter, even so, grew a bit weary of the kind of openers, barely the "Hello's, how you doing" were over with, that went: "You know, I myself came up through the ranks, and I know how they [the working stiffs] feel." Openers from the Warner Paperback editor, and the Avon exec biggie, put with that right-on sincerity, almost Chekhovian in pitch, or "good will" offertory to soften the economic time of day.

Hot organizing licks ("Stickin' with the union") in the Versailles Room; cool bookish chatter (sounds of burbling brook) in the Grand Ballroom. And flashforward to fortnight or so later, when roving runs into the same Warner editor, who unbends with his *own* bulletin: "I'm no longer at Warner; I've been fired." Said with no sweat at all, it's simply the economic time of day, after all.

And the annual cliffhanger: Will there be an NBA—the 27th—in 1976? Tall and bald-domed Roger Stevens, Mr. Money conduit for the Arts, was hard-pressed for an answer. It seems the publishers have gone "sour," they won't bankroll the event (upwards of 70-thousand) any longer, but they're not against outside help. Foundations, private money, or whatever. And Stevens—who weaved his own skein of mumbling "Maybe's"—tried on several occasions to unravel the tangle of possible sources. He kept repeating—like the umpire waiting out the rain for the "Play Ball!"—that he felt confident the money would be "forthcoming from an outside source." One strong rumor of which, the American Academy of Arts and Letters. But wait—the Academy would be "sponsor," if the bankrolling, from such as Ford Foundation, would in the meantime be (as they say) "forthcoming." All in all, the prospects looked dim.

And a flashback add. I get an invite from McGraw-Hill, luncheon and talk by W. W. Rostow, for the Monday of NBA opening. They're launching Rostow's book (*How It All Began: Origins of the Modern Economy*) and they want press to come by the 50th-floor M-H dining room. For cocktails, roast-beef lunch, informal chat with author.

I take jet-elevator to fiftieth, find *several* dining rooms, get sidetracked to the wrong one. Me, picking my way, past 40 or more lookalikes. Sales and editorial dressed to the nines, business-suit-wise. It's sort of peptalk luncheon meeting, maybe the *Business Week* bunch. Almost all forty of them, in the meantime, suspending their drinking, between the cup and the lip, as they look me over—longhair graylocks in unpressed suit, *no way does he have the right dining room!* I keep a "newsie's" posture, walking soft on eggshells of pastel carpeting, as I retreat back to the hallway. (The *Easy Rider* syndrome, like bikers vacating the southern diner.)

Of Book Awards & Media Talkathons 187

Minutes later, I find the room. The McGraw-Hill lady p-r whispers me to a table, and I join twenty or more from press. White linen tablecloths and napkins, handsome silver service, roast-beef to a pinkish-brown turn. All but Rostow are dipping in, as author makes his pitch. Some Rostowisms:

The story of these past twenty years . . . It's a very fragile world we live in . . . I mention Aristotle in the book . . . In a piece I did in *Newsweek* . . . Paul [Samuelson?] wants *this*; Arthur [Burns?] wants *that* . . . The kind of stuff we teach our children is inadequate. . . .

As he stands beside the table, the avuncular delivery, the owlish eyes behind pink glasses, the ring-a-ling of "norms" and statistics, betrays no hint of Rostow's former role, Harvard prof in land of "domino" theories. Nor, to bring the persona up to date, is this Rostow of the "Hearts and Minds" film. Where he blows his academic cool, while trying to parry a question on Nam, like a harpooned whale. Not even when the press has at him, re the priorities of "civilian over military" needs, does Rostow drop the image of Father Benign spelling out economic facts of life to kiddies.

After the NBA week, (MORE)'s Fourth A.J. Liebling Counter-Convention, held at big-boostering Commodore Hotel. The (MORE) indeed had more than usual, of panels, and big-name byliners, the latter mostly from the New York–Washington newspaper and TV axis. The 4-day journalistic talkathon, which drew some 1400 at the topper $20 registration, was tiered in kind of seperate-but-equal rounds, to accommodate strong Women's Lib undertow.

Roving, this time around, opted against registering. Hence, he didn't feel compelled, as in a Chinese menu, to taste a little of "A," and a little of "B," and a little of "C." The menu at full course—some 25 panels and lesser exchanges—brought on more than a few cases of media overload or journalistic "cramps." And if consciousness-raising is the name of the game, in the fragmented and loser-weeper 1970s, you can be sure (MORE)'s was a 4-day airing—from glittering to nitpicking—of all the "Wadda we doin' wrong?" confessionals in the print, and other media, business.

And speaking of the "business," it was embarrassing to hear Gene Roberts (former New York Timesman and currently editor of the

Philadelphia *Inquirer*) use the locution, during the star-studded Saturday night panel ("Self-Censorship: Journalism's Dirty Little Secret"), the "newspaper business" at least a dozen times, in response to one solitary question. The usage kept popping into his rap, like some echo of papal faith in the High Calling, and one wanted to yell out, even over the stiffly structured operandi ("Questions on paper only—no discussion from the floor!"), that did he (Roberts) believe that all the young journalists in the crowded hall—and there were more of those than any other category—saw *their* work in the context of the "newspaper business"? The price of and captivity to rhetoric, the higher up you go on the "newspaper business" ladder! But then again, what do you do with panels that go by name, "Dirty Little Secret"? More of those in four days than you'll find in a dozen leaves out of your average shrink's daybook.

Other than that we caught, on the same Saturday night panel, the "switched role" irony of Sidney (*SoHo News*) Zion's overwrought attack on the "mirage" of press freedom; even while from the extreme other end—both in ideology and podium seat—came the syrupy appeals for "Understanding—I know I'm not in frinedly company," from the Nixon press operative Bruce Herschensohn. All said and done, the (MORE) Fourth Counter-Convention did pose, like an overriding motif, the dilemma: "Counter to *what*?"

Walt Whitman's New York

WALK ON THE WHITMAN SIDE Picture an oblong of, roughly, four downtown streets by two, with Nassau the central mall, and the St. Paul's street (Vesey) and City Hall Plaza, the southern and northern boundaries respectively. Looming high over which, just a little to the west, the remarkable generation-gap duo, gothic Woolworth Building and cubelike Twin Towers "skychasers." Picture that and you'd have, on the occasion of a recent Walt Whitman walk, the kind of literary "dig" that matched—at least for the 200 or more who showed up—the rarest find of the most confirmed pyramid-watcher in all the valley of the Nile.

In the packed oblong of gray, grime-coated buildings, several of which are 100 years old and more, the crowd touring the traffic-empty streets, on a cloudy, warm summer Sunday afternoon, stopped at various points, as the tour leaders—Whitman biographer Gay Wilson Allen, and Majorie Pearson of Landmarks Preservation, among others— gave short capsule talks relating to WW's newspaper "experiences," his prowls along the narrow, single-block Theatre Alley (which housed the Broadway "hits" of that day), his "coverage" of the then "uptown and super chic" Astor Hotel, which stood just across from St. Paul's graveyard. There were more such incidents from out of a short three-year span—1840—1842—in Whitman's newspaper writing and editing days.

Whitman came alive—the sense of echoing footsteps and tapping cane was both spooky and "real"—in biographer Allen's short, crisp rundown of anecdotes over a hand-held bullhorn. There was the time Whitman visited, in a building just off Nassau, fellow poet and newspaper editor Edgar Allan Poe, who had bought some of Whitman's pieces for use in his Broadway Journal. Whitman had come by—and how familiar it all sounds for then or now—to pick up a check for the work, only to be told by the journal's editor that he'd have to wait "just a little while longer." Poe, Allen said, was fond of Whitman and must have been "pained and embarrassed" to have had to dismiss him empty-handed.

And then there was Whitman's visit to Fowler's Phrenological Center, publishers of the popular (and quick-selling) "head charts," with offices at 131 Nassau, where proprietor Fowler—according to Allen—upon giving Whitman a routine "reading" for unusual headbumps and the like, declared the poet "an unmistakable genius." The two became friends, Fowler putting up the money for the second edition of *Leaves of Grass*. But, added Allen, Fowler did the good deed anonymously: for "business reasons" he didn't want to associate himself with Whitman's "barbaric yawp" reputation.

The main points of the itinerary over, the tour next gathered at City Hall Plaza, where the walkers eased down on the first four or five rows of stone steps leading to the hall's sweeping portico. Dress in the main was jeans or summer cottons, and there were a couple of prams standing empty for the moment on the periphery of the crowd. A lectern with gooseneck mike was placed 20 feet or so back from the steps, and two flags, one national, the other city, billowed out now and then in the intermittent breeze. Two policemen stood at the open doors of their prowl car, parked another 20 feet back. They seemed, with the others, to be waiting for the readings to begin. Marjorie Pearson of Landmarks gave some background on City Hall—started in 1802, completed in 1811—and then pointed in the direction of what she called the "Boss Tweed Court House just north of the hall, an expensive boondoggle and a beautiful building even with the over-charges."

The first reader—doing several of Whitman's shorter poems—was poet Paul Zweig, a slim-bodied man in his mid-30s, medium height, dark thinning hair, wearing an open-neck shirt and rough-textured tan cord trousers. The poems, read mostly in unaccented tone, were trademark Whitman: on brotherhood, on familial love, one or two "nature" pieces. Not much "yawp" in these.

Next was, again, biographer Allen, 60-ish, with tufts of gray hair sticking over his ears and out from the back of his head, jacketless and almost stringbean tall, six-two or so. His manner and locution was an odd mixture of harrumphing academese and off-the-cuff, Yankee-inflected, homey detail. Allen spoke about and then read from what he called "Whitman's 'Speciman Days' genre." Allen is extremely knowledgeable on the subject of WW; one wasn't always sure where comment ended and text began. And when it finally became clear, there was the realization that the Whitman extract, with its aura of random violence and assassination threat, spoke sharply to our own time. At any rate, Whitman describes Abe Lincoln's afternoon stop at the Astor, en route to Washington for the 1861 inaugural ceremony. It is a vividly detailed portrait: Lincoln, tall and stovepipe-hatted, sandwiched out of one of the three barouches of the presidential party, stopped for a moment or two as he surveyed the huge crowd—estimated at "10,000 or more"—and, looking over their heads, greeted them casually with a slightly raised hand, before disappearing into the Astor lobby. And there's the brevity of Whitman's description: the tense, ominously speechless crowd, at least half of which is "anti-Abolitionist," and Whitman speculating on how many—and who among them—might be secreting an assassination weapon, a knife ready to flash and thrust, a pistol to pump.

A kind of radar chill from another time. The City Hall audience listening raptly to the all-too-familiar "overtone" of this Whitman text, this very early-on new journalism. Which indeed fleshed out Allen's earlier comment, or reminder, that Whitman was as much the working journalist as ever he was the journeyman poet.

The last reader was poet Galway Kinnell, looking not so much lean and hungry as country squire down for an afternoon visit to the city, in woodsy jacket. Kinnell has sharp features and hazel-blue eyes, and a cowlick of thinning brown hair, which he kept brushing back with his hand. He offered, in modulated middle-register, and the more pointed for that, Whitman's great Lincoln ode—not the complete text, but random stanzas that built powerfully as he moved along. A sort of chanting, painterly mosaic—soft touch of bright color in hermit thrush lines, the "lustrous and drooping" star in western sky, the iridescent purple of lilac incantation, the "rich green" of heart-shaped leaves, and, finally, the mournful gray-black of the Lincoln cortege.

The mood of the crowd was somber as Kinnell ended his read. Some few on the top steps weaved their heads and shoulders—like the moving surface of a lake—to the ode's cadences. "When lilacs last in the dooryard bloom'd . . ." He's not so much the national poet, as bardic singer of universal, hence deathless, love lines.

It was over. On the way back to my office I stopped for a short exchange with the two cops by their prowl car.

Me: "What did you think of the reading?"

First Cop: "Sure thing, that Whitman guy said it all."

Second Cop: "Better the poetry than the crazy demos we've been getting down here lately."

2nd New York Book Fair

BOOKING IN AT CUSTOMS Over 300 small independent publishers and little-magazine buffs showed up for the second New York Book Fair. The three day event was, as they say, "something else again." The scene was Cass Gilbert's Customs House, in itself *the* surprise for many. This was no small coup: the Beaux Arts beauty—at least its spacious rotunda—had been dark for some 15 years. The small-pressers displayed their books, poetry chapbooks, graphics, political tracts on two floors, all under the handsome dome (with its early Reginald Marsh frescoes) of the mottled gray Customs.

It took some visitors longer than others to discover the "find," but sooner or later they all would search out the space, heads craned upward as they scanned the dome, and remark on the "familiar" look of the frescoes. (Sort of "commercial" Marsh and not up to the boisterous signature of his best work but unmistakable for its energy and tone.) And if Marsh made his speciall impress on memory, other features, like the wide circular marble stairway, the ornate mahogany-and-gilt second-floor office, where poets gave readings, the vast oval marble "bookstand" (dubbed by someone "Nightmare Jean Arp"), where about half the presses had their displays, made for added curiosity and pleasure to the eye. The sum total of these effects—leaving aside nearby Battery Park for the moment—assured the Book Fair its own footnote of "unusual," in the never-ending volume of Gotham events.

There was of course the practical side: the vast, growing network of small presses—long in need of some kind of distribution to get their books before a wide public—had for those three days the "bookstore" visibility and sales potential denied them for the most part in the everyday world of big-publishing books and magazines. As for getting Customs House, this in itself was an epic battle of sorts. Starting back in February and continuing to barely one month before opening, the fair committee had to "outtalk the talkers": politicos in Washington, and some at City Hall, who kept passing the buck, the building's very "lease" being in no small jurisdictional tangle.

The magic word, finally, was money; enough, that is, to clean up the debris, repair two elevators, replace broken windows, hire guards, etc. It took something over $9,000 to "put the key in the door"—pretty near all the grant money from New York State Council, with additional help from National Endowment. Other expenses—publicity flyers and posters, freebies like catalogs and balloons for the kids—were absorbed by the registration fee of $25. (Not all the exhibitors could afford the fee, but they were flagged on anyway, fee or not.) No small persuasion was the fact that the book people said they wanted to involve the entire lower Manhattan area, from Wall Street brokers to Twin Towers white collars. And the clincher: When was the last time lower Manhattan had an important literary event?

Customs House, even so, was a calcualted risk, reflected in the tight vote, at the last of several meetings, of five-to-four *not* to go back to the scene of last year's book fair, the Cultural Center at Columbus Circle. The majority felt that, for all the good turnout of 10,000, during the humid mid-90s three days in July, the midtown scene was full of "downers," not to speak of the Center's crabbed footage; and that in any case, the name of *this* game was not simply numbers but rather the

Booking In At Customs 193

venture for new space, add to which the challenge, and rare opportunity, of cracking a not small architectural gem. Also, the site meant easier travel for Brooklyn and Staten Island visitors, and the special ambience of wide lawns and harbor view, readings in Battery Park and on the ferries.

The displays were as varied in look as in content. The design and printing know-how went a good deal beyond—recession or not—the learning-by-doing stage that characterized the movement in the pre-foundation-grants period. Magazines like *Fiction* (Boston), feminist tabloids like *Off Our Backs* (Washington), poetry softback-hardback operations like the Crossing Press's (Trumansburg, N.Y.), the Black Box poetry magazine-cassette format (Washington), the wide assortment of mimeographed sheets and broadsides, showed not only the professionalism, but the kind of experimentation, that fuels the movement at its best.

Did the Customs risk pay off? Consensus of he small-pressers, after they packed crates and departed, was affirmative. *Item.* The crowd, although smaller than last year's, was more at ease, more inclined to browse and ask questions and, in some cases, to buy books. (Gil and Deborah Williams's Bellevue Press, with their graphics-poetry line out Binghamton, N.Y., chalked up more on Memorial Day alone, the opening day, than in the three full days at midtown last year.) *Item.* When thousands of catalog sheets arrived at Customs, uncollated, the feeling of panic was quickly overcome when visitors pitched in and did their own collating. *Item.* Expatriate writer Clancy Sigal, in from London with the manuscript of his new novel, all but filled a spiral notebook with impressions on the fair, for a New York roundup he's doing for the B.B.C. Now and then he'd repeat, like a chirper starling rooting for worms, the one-word comment: "Smashing!" *Item.* On the minus side, a lack of sizable crowds. With some 200,000 to draw from, in the City Hall–Battery Park enclave, it could hardly be denied that the brokers and white collars—except for lunchtime spurts—made themselves conspicuous by their absence. *Item.* The "unfinished" state of Customs, mostly the rather bad lighting; the opaque (dirty) windows; the inaccessible areas.

But one point was sure: The caravan of small presses, if only for those 72 hours, had made an instructive breakthrough, both in terms of their own product, and in showing the way to use of valuable space like Customs. (It was news to many that Landmarks never put the "seal" on

One Battery Place. And that without it Customs could easily be bulldozed, for one more of those spunglass highrise cubes.) And who'd have thought, a couple of years ago, that a pickup team of obscure pamphleteers, poetry publishers, women's groups and the like could mount a major cultural event, play host to some 8,000 or 9,000, satisfy new reader-listener curiosity.

Galileo on screen

TOPOL FIDDLES WITH UNIVERSE Of the Bertolt Brecht *Galileo*, the rule can be stated: Short of sinking the play by way of miscasting in the main role, all other mishaps can be more or less comfortably absorbed in the matrix of a wry, abundantly intelligent, and always fresh playscript.

In this first of a series of six new films for 1975 from the Ely Landau American Film Theatre, director Joseph Losey has plunged ahead to create a good if sometimes breezy equilibrium of forces, the camera lending presence and excitement to the individual set-pieces and to the larger compass of street spectacle, high church meetings, and those poignant (and sometimes chilling) dialogs of Galileoan challenge to fixed ideas. The latter drama of course is the heart of the play, and Losey has captured several tense scenes.

Item. Galileo comes to Rome, to explain his earth-around-sun discovery to a jittery papal court. The surface is all polish, red-robed cardinals acting out a pantomine of mother church firmness, leavened with antique faith in the wisdom of the gospel. Through the maze of church/state power and threat, Galileo moves with the cautious playfulness (or is it craftiness) of a kind of child of science who must pursue *his* games to the end.

Item. A saturnalia, a black masque, hundreds of townfolk gathered round a troup of traveling players, all celebrating the "doomsday" of G's discoveries. Drunks, lechers, whores, peasants—they imbibe, fornicate, and clown away their demons in a bacchanalian orgy. The scene gives offhand echo of Peter Brook's lacerating *Marat/Sade*; but Losey can't quite reach the heights (or depths) of *M/S*'s inspired madness.

Item. Galileo's recantation scene is muffed by Losey to the extent that it happens off-screen. But he's created in its place a stunning mime-like lament acted out on near-barren set that gives off giant shadows, and endless vista of space. Picture a vast backdrop of purest white, in front of which two groupings of figures: 1) Galileo's loving daughter, offering up incantation of prayer that G *will* recant, the "Benedictus" hymn coming from her throat like frantic flutings of birds; and 2) the trio of Galileo's helpers, off in an opposite corner of the huge set, uttering equally passionate mumblings that he *won't* recant. The set-piece is pure theater of the eye, but somewhat less effective as theater of "text."

Hence the spine of the film is reasonably effective and, here and there, even inspired. Losey manages to impart trauma of deep change, all the earth-centered in the early seventeenth century looking as it were through the Galileo glass, and holding breath at what they see. As for the cast other than Galileo, it's all sort of Old-hat Bravura, but with ensemble panache that's trademarked "pure Royal Shakespeare." John Gielgud as the Old Cardinal; Patrick Magee (with that fiery Dublin/UK rasp) as Cardinal Bellarmin; Michael Lonsdale as "enlightened" Cardinal/Pope Berberini; Edward Fox (butter *would* melt in his mouth) sending the shivers up and down spines as the Cardinal Inquisitor; Clive Revill and Georgia Brown winging it wantonly, as Ballad Singer and Ballad Singer's wife; they all indeed act up their various storms on the eve.

As for the Galileo, the Israeli actor Topol all but upends the film. He's trapped in a vaudeville that can't distinguish the nuances, the minor black from major white keys, the very differences in persona, between hell-rake fiddler-on-roof on one hand, and "star-tossed" discoverer on the other. Charles Laughton, in no way a *better* physiognomy than Topol's, still managed to look/act the part like he owned it. Nor is it a case of englished or jewished Galileo, simply one of acting on target. Topol can't get off the vaudeville trolley, except fleetingly in the last scene where he catches glimmerings of G's remorse while in "exile" in Florence. And this suggests not so much Topol's latent talents as the large promise of a role he can't deliver on.

All in all maybe the paradox should be restated, turned around at least some 180 degrees: Even with the disaster of miscasting in the main role, the Brecht script has that larger-than-life brio that can be enjoyed on its own stagey terms.

Item. I get an okay for press coverage of New Yorker, the *Walter Reade* New Yorker if you plasse. The Landau publicity lady, "There will be two tickets at the boxoffice; screening at eight."

Only to be told at boxoffice, "We have no record of the call." The no-no coming from a battling, frilly-lace-shirted Reade man. Roving: "Well, sir, I'm writing up this filmgig. It's *their* [Landau org] property, *they* okayed me for the seat." Frilly-lace: "I don't question your credentials [after I show him palmful of bona fides] but I'm not permitted [etc. etc.]." And a pause, and then: "Why don't you purchase a ticket [a fiver] and American Film Theatre will reimburse you."

Roving, ignoring the suggestion, "You better make a call, to your Walter Reade night man, the Reade chain *must* have a night man." He nods me a nod, goes back inside, comes out again in quick time, smiles me a halfsmile. He tells me, "Well, I'll do it this time, even though I've turned back several others, who claimed *they're* 'bona fides.' Better go in now, the film's been on fifteen minutes or so."

No recanting for your Galileo of the press.

West coast syndrome

CALIFORNIA TAKE TWO Go west, middle-age man, try a hunk of the grand turf! The Horace Greeley call, wrenched a bit in this case, was partly what sent you to California; and once there, you saw things that shake an easterner's bones, seduce his eyes, hone him to what's ticking-best in the land. It was only your 2d trip out there, an added spur being the 3-day San Francisco Book Fair, back-to-back with a 4-day small-press conference at UC-Davis campus. And the ride down to the Venice—Los Angeles area, for your first visit. All told, a zooming 10-day package; the time, early in July. (And the far continent trinity—ocean-girted space, new horizons, primeval risk—taking hold even as you sighted, on the flight across from Kennedy, the trackless, dirt-brown and lichen-carpeted Sierras. The jumbo vaulting along, all those jetstreamed miles, in parallel sweep to the serrated humpbacked peaks. The cushion between belly of plane, and the vast Sierras below, no more than what appeared to be 1,000 feet or so. The captain piping, "We'll soon be over San Joaquin Valley, and make our approach to SFO." And you musing, "Easy does it by the 747 Pegasus route. But how pray did they get across the Big Brownie, in the homesteader '49 days?")

California Take Two 197

You arrive at San Francisco on a midweek night, in time for a late party given by the 200-odd book fair exhibitors (the latter a bad word for this diverse group of alternative publishers and little-mag fantasists who'd as soon give the stuff away as "beg" the sale), and they wheel out an outsize cake of gooey chocolate, the three tiny candles (it's the 3d SF book fair) making a dancing trio of flames in the drafy basement complex, down in the bowels of Veterans Memorial Building, just across from elegant SF city hall. Several of the local book people doing their own dance of joy-celebration; the freewheeling style telling you that you're 3,000 miles from the apple in more ways than the geographic.

In the many-roomed basement, everybody legging this way or that, through the maze of book bins and long tables stacked high with assorted formats, the beer and wine flowing easy, and the local SF rock group of 4, blaring out the ragas (and the whatevers), while the mostly younger press-mag people loosen their limbs and their bodies, to shake off the stiffness of 10-hours of standing around, the hawking of wares, meeting other displayers from out-of-town and out-of-state, and talking up "alternative" to visitors and the book-curious. Ten-hours of all that, but now they're loosening the jams, piling up anecdote on anecdote, very hot off the carousel of small press doings.

You're off the plane barely an hour, and settled into the nearby YMCA Hotel; you dump baggage and take a quick wash, then walk over to Veterans and lose yourself on this cross-continent scene. But you soon run into past book fair and Cosmep (the small press org) buffs, like the bluff-talky poet Al Winans, who then takes you in hand and introduces you to a clutch of west coast tummlers: John Bennett and New York—Frisco router Jack Micheline and several others. And Winans runs it down coolly: "Meet the roving guy himself, he's in from New York . . ." All the while the SFers are doing a kind of Marxian (the 4 Marx Brothers, not Karl) parody number, they're pumping each other with flailing fists, working off some of the bumpy nervousness and chatter, the *books-poets-books-readings-books-NEA-grants-upbeat-downbeat routine*, outriders of the word shooting the breeze on their own proud turf. (At midnight on that first night, they're all scattering out to the street and gone. Some for the North Beach nightcap, others for home or hotel for the old beddy-bye. Micheline, rougue poet of coffee house and pub, shouts over: "C'mon, we got wheels, goin' to Vesuvius for a round." *That Jack! Don't know whether he's gonna kiss you or spit!* You decide no, head for the nearby Doggie Burger. Depressing, jerkwater scene. But good for the hunger pangs, triple-stacked burger and Coke, the works.)

After the 3-day book fair, you're off to the small-press conference. An hour and a half from SF to Davis, maybe less. Winans souping his much used wheels to 65 on endless strip of freeway, elongated slate-gray Bay Area on one side, impacted hills with boxlike houses perched this way and that on the other. A while later we exit the freeway this side of Sacramento, circling around till we hit Davis's sprawling green belt campus, whose buildings are an odd combination of Bauhaus slick and cow campus wooden sheds that bespeak Davis's beginnings as California's most prestigious agricollege. Al and you and several others have arrived a little early; we're greeted by main planner of the Cosmep gig; the small press editor-publisher and Davis librarian eminence, garrulous and articulate punster, the lean and jumpy Noel Peattie. He tags each of us with laminated name card, hands over the keys and explains the lodging setup. He cracks open the beer and wine, describes several eating places in town (one named "Sambo's," if you can believe), and makes apology for the campus dining hall: "The service is hardly normal, what with July Fourth Weekend and all, but even the normal ain't normal." (Noel walks you over to his car, he wants you to see the license plate. It reads SIPAPOU, name of a Cal' Indian tribe and title of his lit'ry quarterly. He must have clout, at Sacramento license bureau.)

Saturday morning, up and around at 10. The blinking-eyed adjustment to aquablue skies, the smell of eucalyptus and cow dung. During early-afternoon agenda break, you hitch a ride to campus's outsize swimming pool. A relaxed crowd of some 150 students, faculty, service people, the kids. They're sunning themselves or romping about on the greens, or doing running jumps in the mirrorlike pool. Real-life advertisement for suburbia west with college education, at play. All the bronzed lean bodies, with the beechnut California look. All so neatly "environmental," they bite into the ruby-red cherry, they don't have to spit out the pit. (It's been pitted for them.)

Noel, and several of the faculty, play host to 60 or 70 Cosmepers at early-evening alfresco feed. A sunken patio, two or three giant shade trees, hard by the main campus library. Globs of fried chicken, the beers and the soda pop. The good chomping, laced with the chatter-chatter of poets, local academics, and six or seven visiting librarians. And what's a "Cosmep?" someone asks. But for sure it's a medley of accents, from Jim Cody's lowkeyed southwest, to Al Winans's let-it-hang-out

California Take Two 199

Berkeley, to Judy Hogan's drawled Carolina, to Hugh Fox's sprung East Lansing (Michigan State U), to Jackie Eubanks's go-go Brooklyn Heights, to Daine Kruchkow's flat-a's Newburyport, Mass ... A medley of spiels and motifs, up and down the scale of alternative writing, the nerve-ends publishing (with a little help from the mutha-culture budget) ... All the non-names, the experimentals, the freakers and shouters; they're turning to the new voice, deep inside the sometimes loony, sometimes inspiring, sometimes bitchy and despairing, US lit-polit-cultural space ... And that's Cosmep, the org and network, with some 900 members in practically all 50 states. (Canada, Australia, and New Zealand, too.)

After the feedbag, the poetry reading. In the pile-carpeted, frosty-lighted, and overly humid lounge, a short walk from the library. The first of two sets is all-Davis lineup—three or four women poets, Noel with quartet of short ones, and resident star Karl Shapiro, neatly green-shirted, with graying groomed hair, ending the set. From Noel and the two women, good craftsy stuff, lines that move with soft-shoe finesse, like steps in a ballet. (Sure, they've sold to *The New Yorker*, and to *Harper's*, no knock in that.) But the ear, this easterner's ear, is too easily beguiled. Poem after well-shaped poem. And it all sounded so *distant*. As for Shapiro's—his was a long, pulsating, torment-filled epitaph, the death-throes of Ludwig van Beethoven, all the pretty and epical chapters of musical genius run together in fevered memory, during the last hours of his life. (Hardly distant; more like shards of glass that draw blood.) Then the 2d set, the all-Cosmep reading. And it's a turbulent sea-change, your ear suddenly goes *roaring*. As graybeard, pipe-smoking poet John Harris—who's from the Venice, Calif., boondocks—tenses the whole roomful as if with hooks, as he reads his long Hemingwayesque poem: Two climbers in tandem who're caught in, then doubling over into, the failed ecstasy, the rushing death, of a botched mountain climb. And Paul Foreman, with some angry lines on Yevtushenko; and, in another poem, some images that go homing back, songlike, to his East Texas childhood. And James Krusoe, who offers three or four "quieter" but likewise bracing poems. (Krusoe is from same boondocks as Harris.)

You're holed in later that night, the good roomy pocket with Swedish modern, picture window looking out on the pancaked lawns, the accommodation a look-alike to twenty or thirty others, in the double-leveled quad of lodgings. It's about 11 or so, and most have bedded down for the night, but you cop a restless walk looking for others, you hope to bump into stragglers for a Coke klatch or something. And the aloneness of standing on lawn, under endless dark sky with blue needles of stars, and the low pastel-shaded buildings lined with hedges, the big white-painted tower with the UCD letters in black. Lots of activity that long day, small squabbles and inspired feedbacks too, the evening poetry reading the topper, but nobody around at the now 11 hour; and the feeling of lostness, on a vast stretching ground of the mid-Cal' map, the man-made showers turning up-down on manicured campus green; and the 3,000 mile drift from home (a full continent away); the aloneness accented by moonlit contour of girl in pedal-pushers, moving briskly across the road on bicycle in flat open country; a kind of 3-dimensional rendering, an apparition of Andrew Wyeth painting come alive; as the stillness, the flatness, the vastness of turf, holds you captive.

Through Saturday and Sunday, and most of Monday, the Cosmep agenda choo-choos onward. Sparked by hardnosed challenges, passionate appeals, rhetorical flourishes (dotting those "i" 's), and bouts of humor. The small-pressers, stopping only for lunchroom breaks, and nighttime beer breathers and parties, walk the long campus to Roessler Hall, flop into the steeply banked rows of seats, and do an eyeball-to-eyeball number with panelists: *Show me!* Close-to-vest topics. Such as women's rights—and the lack of them—in the small-press network. (No illusions re the big publishers, hardly. It's just that at Davis, you had to keep your *friends* honest. Make the extra push in consciousness raising.) The absence of minority voices: you could shoot off a cannon for all the Black, Latino and Indian no-shows in the hall. This, face it, is a quilting-bee of almost *all-white* cultural voices. And the perennial how-to's: better production of books, wider distribution, savings on mailings, etc. And the ever-lively topic of funding, no less than National Endowment Mr. Moneybags, himself, Leonard Randolph, flying in for the panel. And the roving editor, who's also on the panel, putting it: "Nine hundred of anything spells votes. And nine hundred of *us*—small potatoes or not—*has* to spell more clout than we know. We claim funding for *our* national resource, much as the oil depletion crowd claims funding for theirs . . ." Also, the "Writers in Prison" panel, which you had missed, and which moved one Cosmeper to say, "Tremendous . . . greater than anything we have ever had."

After the Cosmep, the ride back to San Francisco, with George

Drury Smith of *Beyond Baroque* mag-foundation in Venice. George invites you to "a whole different scene," meaning the Venice–Los Angeles areas, and you're very "up" for the trip (your first), especially the "LA plastic Babylon," as it's been called. But first the stopover, through early Tuesday morning, at the same "Y" hotel in SF. That night you take cable car for North Beach, a rattley-ho people-shaker of a ride, then you walk over to City Lights Book Shop. It's still there, dwarfed by the Carol Doda style nudie emporiums, lost among the garish marquee lights and the horny spiels rampant on the night air. And still there, in all its triangular grayness, with the world's most conscientious book browsers, down in the basement minefield picking over the explosive stuff—the Jack Spicer chapbooks, the Harold Norse's, the Charlie Plymell's, the early Bukowski. Then you look in on Vesuvius bistro, next door door to City Lights. Whence a 20-ish young lady, slim and playful and black, grabs you by the wrist, demands "Where you from; where you going." You tell her New York, heading for Los Angeles. She squeezes your wrist tighter, and croons, "My uncle is a numbers man, up there in Harlem . . ." More squeezes, and then, "San Francisco, and old New York, they're both real groovy. But pass up Los Angeles, it's nowhere."

An early start, about 8 on Tuesday, for ride down to Venice. George Drury Smith, strapped in comfortably, behind the wheel of his new Toyota. You pass up the harness, telling Smith, "Good center of gravity to this seat, wanna enjoy the ride to the full." The long, long push on the freeways. Now straight, now gradually turning, the smooth macadam cushion. Past the Santa Claras, the San Joses, the Paso Robleses, the San Luis Obispos. There we stop for lunch, immaculate San Luis Obispo, all tucked in neatly, houses sun-splashed and washed in pastel, tucked in among the densely greening hills. Lunch—best dipped-pastrami west of Carnegie Deli—taken in outside patio with beach umbrellas cutting the heat for shade. And a short visit, nearby, to old, pre-Revolutionary church, named San Luis Obispo, the dark narrow peaked nave, the reliquary and memento rooms, with walls of hard stucco, wooden beams worn but caulked firm. All musty on the inside, and platformed, with surrounding lush foliage, and shade trees, on solid rock foundation, in the open—lending an American western classic look. Then both of us "pricing" the main-drag shops, including the grottoed strip with leather-goods stalls, men's and women's boutiques, handtooled jewelry displays. And finding the stuff—in town of Obispo that, surely, has no other side of tracks—not just wellcrafted but price that's "right." And stopping by—one of last fillip for the road—at what must be the ultimate in ice cream parlordom, the mahogany-walled Swensen's where, as well as being waited on by suntanned, Lolita-like counter help, we get double-dippers (for 4-bits) that satisfy all the way back to the car.

Going south past Obispo, backdrops of rugged hills, the chugging oil wells, the endless green carpet of agriproducts, and later, the sudden presence of ocean, driving through Santa Barbara and beyond—the long coastline, the metal glint of sea under orangeburnt sky. And farther out to sea, as Smith holds the Toyota to an easy 55, you spot the towering oil rigs, twins rising from the briny deep like mastadons on steel stilts, they're back in operation, and gulping up the black liquid gold. With mocked-up "island" in the stream—ribbon of sand topped by some palm trees—that's actually the sea-to-shore conduit for the oil. All the stealthy watery chug-chugging—until the next spill blows out of control and pisses the dirty stuff right up to the shoreline. (All the saintly ones, discovering the Santa Barbaras, the nuevo Edens, one-two-and-more centuries ago. Now come the saintly, garbed in the white frocks of laboratory, doing the missionary work with computers, with cost-analysis abracadabras, for the Exxon-Mobil-Richfield Church, the holy oil substituted for holy water, at all the founts of, eh, Mother Progress.)

"We're almost there," George announces. Greater Los Angeles, the famed San Andreas sprawler you've heard about, car-happy and miles-marching. Along the Malibu strip, the oceanfront houses, the horizontal pile-up of boxlike units. (You live in one of those, you're facing the slate sea, permanently, 24 hours round the clock. And you can go crinkled bananas, take on the dry look of a stuffed bird.) He points to a deserted, gone-to-seed mansion: "The former Hearst—Marion Davis love nest. Most of the estate has been broken up, for grab-'em-cheap cabanas, but the mansion is still Hearst property." And on the land side of narrow freeway, the sheared cliffs of Santa Monica, dotted with glass wraparound houses. And the lone rancho notorious, perched high on a ledge: "That one's J. Paul Getty's digs," George says. And the blond-stone condominiums, just off the serpentine roadway, lurking King Kongs some 40-stories high: The elevator up, elevator down, living by the sea. And further along, the hotel-like Synanon complex, and the blocklong Nichirin Shoshu academy, both of them hard by the beach. (Call the first the therapy way for the strung-out, and the second, the

California Take Two

Zen way for the TMs, all by the numbers. All in the Los Angeles oceanic style.)

Moments later we're in Venice; and you've heard about that place, too. The late flowering of Beats, the canals megilla, the Charlie Bukowski freakout thing. Touch of the poet, wave of the black flag of anarchism, rumble of the avant-garde maven, holler of the anti-Nam activist. All the hairy doings just next door to—and in "Up Yours!" opposition to—the permanent floating Rose Bowl of Los Angeles kitsch. (And most of it caught, George tells you, in Lawrence Lipton's *Holy Barbarians*.) And driving by oceanside Venice, the low-profiled shacks, the touristy hotels. A mini Coney Island aspect, the body-beautiful surfer dudes, rather than escapees from ghetto, setting the pace. And further inland, Venice of the diminishing, and the drying out, canals. Only four or five remain, where once—in post World War II heyday—there were dozens. The missing ones filled over with concrete, you're told, to make room for more colonies of stuccoed homes. And the Venice of boutiques, accent mostly on seaside tacky; and bistros like the Brandywine—bloodred hamburgers and vegetarian carrot pie on same menu; and bossy antique shops like "The Merchant of Venice," prices ranging from high to spectacularly high. (Call it "the pound of flesh.") And the smallish-crowded Venice Library, looking seedy-elegant on slight rise of velvety lawn; the librarian owning, proudly but worried, the day you visited: "We're open six days a week; but that may be changed, *soon*."

Speeding it up, getting the camera-eye flashes, the last 72 hours of the trip. And you're anxious, gotta get the Venice and LA "handle," before return to New York. . . . George parks in *Beyond Baroque* alleyway, on West Washington in Venice. Bushed—after 8-hour, 400-plus miles turn of wheels—he lets out a hoarse groan of used-up energy. We gather our baggage, and walk to his top-floor apartment, one of four in a 3-story oddity, the building in near-link with two other oddities: *Baroque*'s orange-green pagoda offices, entrance through same alleyway; and just behind that, the small-craft repair yard, packed with beached boats. (The yard has you mezmerized, seeing it from George's living room windows. *Raise anchor, cleave to the wind* . . . and all that jazz!) His three-roomer, including tiny office and desk, in a chaos of piled-up mail, tape-recorders and cassettes, mounds of little mags. The phone buzzing away, no more than we arrive, and he's heating up a pot of coffee.

One of the calls—this for starters on that last leg—from a young man named Randy (not his real name), going through hoops of heavy boozing, who blurts out that he's "desperate," and that only George can help. (Besides his involvement with BB, and his two-day-a-week tour as printer in outside shop "for the bread," George Drury Smith is sort of elder-guide—he's mid-40s or so—to several youthful boozers in the Venice chapter of AA.) Randy arrives shortly thereafter, flushed, and wearing a flowered tank-top. (The California look, the bleach-blond hair, the breezy "Not to worry" manner.) Goerge suggests dinner, and while Randy's out of the room, he tells you: "He's not slept nor eaten in three days. It's curtains, if I don't turn him around, now." Before we leave the apartment, you chat a while with Randy. If he's boozed to the gills, he doesn't really show it, not through that Cal' scrim of self-assurance, anyway. He says he's 26; he looks more like 20. You chide him, "I take you for a surfer, bet you're into that, right?" Randy, cooly: "Well, wrong, but thanks. The only surfing I do is under the tables at gay bars." The three of us hop over to the Brandywine, and Randy, trying out his good behavior, calmly tells George: "It's milk only, for me, I'll pass up the drinks." Later, back at George's pad, we're all calling it a night, the time, about 10 P.M. As Randy repairs to George's bedroom, the latter confides that he's "hopeful." He says, "The dinner did Randy some good. But he's a wreck, he's got the blue meanies, the goddam withdrawal symptoms. I'll have to hold his hand, maybe he'll make it through the night." So it goes with the walking, boozing wounded! Needing the hand of someone like George—who himself was once the walking, boozing wounded!

Wednesday, up at 9 A.M. George and Randy have gone, you didn't hear them leave. Out on the sunny, flower-scented Venice streets. Looking for a breakfast spot. First you cross the railroad bed. Then you wander deeper into the maze. All the pastelly, bungalow-type houses. The dogs barking at your heels, the children romping in the streets. And still no eating spot, greasy spoon, or restaurant. Those, it finally hits you, are over toward the ocean, the opposite direction. So back to George's, scare up morsels from breadbasket and fridge, reheat last night's coffee. And you ring up Lawrence Lipton (got unlisted number from George). "The totem figure of Venice," one person tells you. "The man who wrote it all down," says another. "He's been off-putting, since his stroke couple of years ago," cautions a third.

Over the telephone, Lipton's voice is stop-and-go, his words broken

California Take Two

by a kind of wheezing pain. It puts you at something of a distance. But you hang in there, at least for a little while. You're passing through Venice, and want some of the early (mostly 60s) background of what was going down, you tell him. The wheezing gets heavier, the put-downs abound. First one's for you: *The good writer doesn't get his story just passing through!* (You respond, *Touché!*) And more rasping yet: *Where were they with their praise, when I was up and around, and getting Venice on the map.* Injustice collecting or not, the pain, the broken voice, gets to you. And you tell him thanks, understand what he's saying, try to ring off. But now *he's* hanging in. Ten-minutes, longer, longer. Tales of the washed-out glory, the used-up poetry/writing, the burned-out witness. Then at last, the trailing, broken *good-bye.* And you tell yourself: *Put that in your pipe, and smoke it, smartass of the world!*

On Wednesday afternoon, you move to Sandy's modest rancho, in the Santa Monica hills. She's on *Beyond Baroque*'s staff, and invites you to stay a couple of days, she'll show you the "whole Los Angeles shmeer." For starters—as we take off in her beige custom van—the Santa Monica drive-in supermarket. And what an eyepopper the cornucopia turns out to be! The fruit of the Cal' magic—baby, all that richness— spread out like no tomorrow! (And you thought New York's upper west side was supermarket country!) Sandy quick-marches past the bins and freezers. She half-fills a maxi shopping cart: "Just a few things for now . . ." The drive through the hills, and soon we're at the rancho. (Actually, Sandy's and Peter's.) It's modest, all right, 8-rooms-2-baths modest. And it has you smelling, drooling over, taking in, all the special treats. Like the velvety purple panoply of jacaranda, the blood-red bougainvillea, the ripening lemon and avocado, the twittering sound from treetops: *When the red red robin, comes a bob bob bobbin.* . . .

You meet Peter: He's granite tall, bluff talker, conservative dresser. Sandy's opposite: She's short and petite, always chatty, peacock colors wardrobe. *Vive le différence.* Maybe it's the secret, after some 25 years, of the good marriage. We have a round of drinks, and nonfussy din-din. During which, some verbal fencing, mostly about Venice. Peter badmouths the place. One might say, to the charms of Venice, he's permanently out to lunch. He puts it: So far from being avant-garde, or creative, or merely different, Venice is a "never was." A pretty good go, but you have to split for the *BB* poetry workshop. Sandy chooses the black Buick, from among their three cars, and rides you back to West

Washington. She says call if you don't get a lift back to Santa Monica, and she zips off again.

At the workshop, a crowd of about 25 sitting on metal chairs, tight for space in BB's whitewalled library. Most are under-30s, and most have brought their sheafs of poems, but not all will "nerve" the exposure. A big jug of wine is passed around the room. The poet in the "dock" (raised wooden podium, single chair for poet) is not distracted, for if anything the bubble-bubble, pour-pour sound of the passing wine jug adds a certain music to the readings. Nor can the poet see much of the audience through the hard glare of the spot. The evening's well along—it's about 9:30 when you get there—and you find a chair off to the side and wonder, if you're called on, as you expect you will be, what you should read. You soon notice John Harris—he's firing his pipe, tamping and firing it, as at the Davis reading—off to the opposite side of the room, his bearded face tilted now and then up toward the ceiling, his spare body slouched into a battered leather chair. He conducts the workshop like a coach, a friendly-tough pal. Sans the "this-that" or nuts and bolts prosody approach of the academic teach.

Soon he comes by, asks if you'll read "or say a few words, whatever you wish." Harris—after four or five "goes" with readers since your arrival—then introduces you with a line or two that you're from New York, and that you'll read, or rap, or whatever. You come forward, edge into the dock, dig out some material you brought with you. But first you talk about the trip, about "wanting to pin down the immensity and lushness of space out here. Not just the notion of a Fitzpatrick Travelogue; but the unique stretch-out for limbs and leisure; the horizontal way, whereas in the east it's all beehive vertical." And the 2d, and troubling, thought: That if the Cal' way is indeed stretch-out and leisure, it somehow doesn't stretch-out to *people*; what with concern over ranchos, multiple houses, multiple wheels. While the east, of course, is nothing if not a *grand mazurka* of people-mixing, taking them all ways. (The property-versus-people thing; and if only the twain would meet.)

After the rap, the read from your *Apocalypse* collection, a short essay—"The All-Time Be-In" (in Sheep Meadow)—that perhaps best illustrates, you tell them, the grand mazurka notion. And later, over drinks at the Brandywine, there's some good feedback. All the comings and goings, all things possible, in the whiskey-coffee euphoria. And a

California Take Two 207

heavy lit riff, you and Jim Krusoe, for a parting stroke. Both dropping the names, the "markers" on the pantheon highroad. Hemingway, Berryman, Thomas Wolfe, the perennial Fitzgerald. ("The downed ones," Jim calls them.) How the American split, the American "schiz," the buy-sell above all, does the writer in. (Krusoe, "Hemingway by fire; Berryman by ice." And you, "Remember in Hem's sea story, how the butchering sharks rob the old man of his magnificent catch?") Also, the backbreaker sectionalism, the US class-clash (of rich-poor), the disunity of these states. And maybe only the poets—poets like the gentle burner, John Harris—can be the unifiers, the give-a-damners, the push-and-shovers; surely, not the pols, the judges, the biggie wheeler-dealers. All the black-crepe, the roseate hopeful, dialogue, by turns. And a long way from a resolution, as Krusoe rides you back to the Santa Monica rancho.

Thursday morning. Sandy plans a doubleheader LA tour, sort of day and night games. Joining us, just before noon, is her longtime friend (they were UCLA classmates), a gynecologist named Mike, she's in from Zurich on short holiday. We pile into the van, and head for the LA maze. First stop is Papa Bachs Paperbacks, to LA as Gotham is to New York, or City Lights to 'Frisco. And funkier than both—posterwise, to begin with. On one wall, Mao, Lenin, Ché, Stalin (hmmmm, Stalin!); on the other, Keaton, the Marx Brothers, Bogie, Monroe. You case the customers: Who are the starlets, who the actor honchos, which the local literati? (Sales clerk, "The Hollywood trade? Not at Papa Bach, hardly. We sell books, not Tarzan comics.") Back outside, two points of interest, in odd juxtaposition. First the giant-sized alfresco mural—call it Disaster Kitsch (or San Andreas's Revenge)—that fills the wall of a 5-story loft with sickly-azure and fiery-sunset hues. It depicts the nightmare collapse of three or four intersecting elevated freeways in middle of the Cal' desert. And 2d the gleaming whitestone edifice—call that one Mormon Tabernacle Antiseptic—that's propped high-up and frozen like parody of missile (topped with statue of the Angel Moroni, who gave founder Joseph Smith the vision). It dominates the skyline in all its proud vacuity for miles around. Farther along, the UCLA campus: Can't tell school for country club lushness of grounds and plant. Sandy and Mike go nostalgic: "Remember when . . ." While you spot one building—lots of grillwork and open-spaces motifs—that's sort of Los Angeles avant-garde. And you guess: "It's the Arts and Leisure Center, right?" Sandy: "Wrong! Arts and Leisure, yet. It's the *carpark;* we just left the van in there; the sixth floor." And so back to Santa Monica rancho.

On spur of the moment, you join Mike for the beach. It's about 6 P.M., clear high-80s weather. Mostly a downhill stroll, of a mile or so, then the sand-slogged tunnel under freeway, at the other end of which, the fab' ocean vista. Mike, a true Cal' sea sprite, hits out directly for "the calm point," beyond the incoming rollers. You putter around, pants rolled to knees, in the beach shallows. Watch the winging jumbos in wide-arching takeoff from LA airport, the gradual climb over ocean and the swing past the sun as they head east. Later that evening—before the 2d LA tour—the four of us have drinks on rancho patio. Peter's in good form, his fencing is sharp. (He's an aerospace engineer, works a good ways south of Santa Monica, maybe 60-70 miles "portal to portal," he wheels it down and back like a subway ride.) You mention, in discussing some point or other, an item "from the *Times.*" The pregnant pause, then Peter's jugular hit: "Which *Times* are you talking about? We have one too, you know! *The Los Angeles Times!*" ("*Touché!* It's a very 'pro' newspaper, right?" you assure him.) The talk turns to "property ... houses," who's buying what, who's selling. It happens that Mike, though she lives and works in Zurich, owns a big sprawling house in Hollywood Hills. Several UCLA students are lodging there; and she wants to have a look-see. So it's off to Hollywood Hills, for the 2d LA tour. "Wait'll you see the splashing lights; you'll forget Manhattan," Sandy only half kids you. But first the question: Which car this time? And you say to her, why not the 3d car of the pool. Peter's yellow-and-gold-trim Volks, hand-painted and richly doodaded— including steel-weld bike rack like a Noguchi, highly patentable, at the least. Sandy dismisses it, "That's a no-no!" She adds, Peter's not joining us, and *only he* drives the Volks. And we take the van.

The long nighttime drive, the endless cityscape. Lights a plenty, marquees like giant winking pinballs of the skin game, and the home-product movie "premiere" game. And moving along Sunset Boulevard, up crops the famous mansion, kleig-lighted and deserted in the shadowy gloaming. Where brash Bill Holden got suckered into Gloria Swanson's bedroom; and later on, got hit with the bullet at poolside, fired by the monocled, cabbageheaded retainer Eric von Stroheim. (They shot the film in that very mansion, Sandy confirms.) And,

California Take Two 209

farther along, the Capitol Records Building, some 15-stories high; and shaped like its product, exactly saucer round; and, Sandy tells you, it's all lighted up—literally—like a Christmas tree, come the Yuletide season. And looking, in another way, like a mountain of Las Vegas gambling chips. (For sure, you can't tell the town, for the raunchy splash of symbols.) Pushing the rubber, and finally we're at Hollywood Hills. Up up and away, all the crazy turns, the every-which-way tilt of houses. Vertigo threatening gulp by gulp, as if out of a bottle, as the van keeps on climbing. (Bukowski, you're told, lives somewhere in these hills. Must be the *double* vertigo for the Buk; a little from one bottle, a little from the other.) At last we're there, Sandy bringing the van to a lurching stop at the curb. Mike goes off to look at the house. While Sandy nudges you out of the van, insisting the view from the HH cliffhanger is "diamond studded." All very impressive, you tell her, but where's the goatherd and flock?

Friday, last day of trip, a kind of scenario of push-pull moods. Up around 9, time enough to catch noon flight from LA airport. (Vibes tilting eastward: *Are the rats chewing up the garbage, on Manhattan's streets?*) Breakfast . . . just Sandy and you. Peter's gone hours earlier; and Mike, off in the van for *another* look-see, this time her mountain cabin east of LA. George Drury Smith phones: "Did you hear the news? Lawrence Lipton is dead! You got your story, after all!" You press him: How did it happen? When—? He doesn't have the details; it came over the radio minutes ago. Sandy riffles through LA *Times* home edition—dropped at rancho door—but can't find story on lipton. (Says next edition should have it; get it at the airport.) You finish your packing. You wonder: What if you were the last to talk with him? What if the *talk itself* did him in? (The apple fades out; Lipton's words come back strong.) The ride to the airport, Sandy chatting up a storm. How the girl from old-cracked-liberty-bell—Philly, Pa.—first met and wooed Peter. She a student at UCLA; he an aspiring Hollywood writer, and son of name movie scripter of 40s and 50s . . . Peter's "genius," but not for writing, rather for science . . . You're fading in, fading out, as Sandy breezes along. (*Lipton's last hurrah; the wheezing pain of that Wednesday phone talk!*) At the airport; huggings and partings. In rush to get on the plane, you miss getting the LA *Times*. But you find a copy on board—the later edition—and you flip through it even as the plane takes off . . . a zooming, climbing breakout with slate ocean below. Flipping page by page, then you find the story, top of 24: "Lipton, 77, died Wednesday at his home in Venice, after a long illness . . ." *Put that in your pipe.* . . .

The mythic *real* estate of these 50, jumbo striding the fleecy-cloud expanse, at 35,000 feet above the Lake Meads, the Salt Lake Cities, the Colorado Divides; and the mini ocean of the 5 Great Lakes sisters, the Ohios and Pennsylvanias of green and duncolored squares, the northern megalopolis of sky-scraper and cloverleaf. And the poets, the fictioners, the composers—doing the book, and the music. From Thomas Wolfe's homeward-gazing vistas, to Hart Crane's continent-spanning bridge; E. L. Masters' sleeping Spoon River acres, to Kerouac's Washington State timber forests; Faulkner's big bear foot tracks in the Mississippi pine country, to Langston Hughes's black-is-black poetry riffs. And Charles Ives's Yankee musical splurges, to Gershwin's smooth-as-velvet Gotham tunes, to Baez's-Guthrie's long-hair, tall tale hoedowns. The jumbo in the 5-hour curved flight, devouring the west-east polarities. And the ongoing saga of Robert Frost's . . . *The land was ours before we were the land's.*

New York City "bailout"

OPEN LETTER TO AN ARIZONA CONGRESSMAN New York City is worth saving. Not just a "bailout" for our budgetary sins. But the very environment that makes our town special. Its people, its energy, its openness, its scenes. Troubles we have—as what city doesn't?—but we have too the unique setting for 8-million that allows for constant play of imagination, challenge, expression of individuality. I'd like you to picture—from out there in the far spaces and non-crowded cities—one event of this fall season that would have given you some notion that our town has more to offer than just budgetary shakes and alarms.

A Sunday afternoon in October, the day before Columbus Day. You come out of the IRT station at Fulton Street, walk the three or four blocks east to the South Street Seaport Museum. This is an open pier hard by the Fulton Street Fish Market; and a focal point of the East River revival of last century when the riverfront was the watery

Open Letter To An Arizona Congressman 211

"garage" for all the big sailing ships whose handsomely carved bowsprits jutted out high above the street level. On this particular Sunday—warm and sunshiney with great cottony clouds riding over lower Manhattan—the crowds are moving into the pier with anticipation of the event labeled "Clearwater Day." The *Clearwater* is a Hudson River sloop—itself a "revival" in that it was built in recent years as model of the many similar craft that plied the Hudson River back in the '70s, 80s and 90s—and it's publicly funded and is actively engaged in the cause of cleaning up the Hudson as well as being used for up- and down-river tours to keep alive the "feel" of the lost sailing days.

As you walk the pier's wooden planks—walk the distance of some 300 feet at the end of which is tied the single-masted *Clearwater*—you are alerted to the folk singers strumming away at the mike and also to the five or six young ladies and men who are selling, among other items, the first fall crop of Hudson valley apples brought down to the pier by *Clearwater*. (Of course there's fresh apple cider too; priced at 25c the cup with "refill" at 20c if you use the same cup.) The strummers and the apple-sellers are all members of the Hudson River Sloop Restoration, as are the half-dozen young sailors of the *Clearwater* crew, and both groups are part of a growing membership—by no means all of which Manhattanites—that has helped spread the message of past Hudson River "glory." (They've won some battles too—against big-industry polluters up and down the river—won them to the point where Hudson shad, for one, has returned in goodly numbers in recent years.)

The Columbus weekend crowd is the typical mix: New Yorkers en famille, couples that like as not are visiting for the first time, out-of-towners with cameras making good use of the very special—call it "movielab"—Gotham scenery. (And if you have the right equipment—telescopic lenses, powerhouse boxes, etc.—you can shoot as far away as Verrazano's twin pylons rising in sun-blanched mist from the waters of the lower bay.) You move further along—after tarrying for a while to catch the "folkie" singing—to the pier's edge where others have positioned for a good look at the *Clearwater*. At the moment the sloop is tied up, the two huge sails lowered to the deck in accordian-like squeeze, and the long bottomed-out hull (vaguely like a Chinese junk) rising and lowering by inches with the swift East River current. On board the crew is readying for the 2 P.M. sail—one of two scheduled for the afternoon with admission scaled at $15 per family and down (the price includes one-year membership in the association) for the two and a half hour tour to Brooklyn Narrows and back. With limit of 35 passengers, the bearded young "captain," after checking his list, calls out a last, "Room for only two more, we're ready to push off."

The last two—in a whooshing rush—then tramp down the tiny gangplank with echo of friendly cheers going up from the crowd. As the crew gets busy—unhinging the lines from the pier stanchions and lowering the tire fenders to keep the sloop clear of the pilings—the watching crowd and the passengers exchange partings with two or three "bon voyages" heard among the former. One young pigtailed girl—no more than 6 or 7—is staring out at her mother from her seated spot on the deck housing and the thirtyish matronly woman (who's standing 10 feet away on the pier) offers a reassuring, "Have a good trip, darling!" to the girl, and as a parting caution the woman then shouts to the girl's older companion, "Hold her hand; I'll see you later when you return." With the all-clear moments later, the sloop then moves easily away from the pier on its motor power and heads out to midstream just this side—the south side—of the Brooklyn Bridge.

Picture, if you will, the setting. A setting that's at one and the same time, a single cameo out of New York' s considerable showcase of scenes, and "timeless" view of river, sloop and bridge—the three come alive in a dazzling, changing pattern of splashy sun and cloud-dappled shadow on an October afternoon. And picture the flurry of movement, the rapid positioning of camera-wielders, strung out along the pier's edge, as the sloop drifts along soundlessly, and as they (the shooters) keep snapping away to catch the endless variations of that one scene. To the key moment when—and here reality and conjury seem as one—there's the sudden rising, foot by slow-moving foot, of the 2 giant sails, at some 500-feet distance, both sails then burgeoning out to the full by turn, until they tower over the flat-bellied deck like enormous white garments—and later when the sails catch the brisk wind at the broadside and the sloop moves downstream, on its run to the Narrows, on sailpower alone.

You hold on to that one scene—the gentle yawing of sloop as it glides past Governor's Island at about 8 or 10 knots—for minutes on end, fix on it as if in a frame, for permanent hanging in the gallery of the inner-eye. Later you walk back to the folkies, who by now have drawn together hundreds of spectators, standing and sitting around on the knotty planks in a wide semicircle, several joining in as the strummers offer their varied repertoire—on ecology, on Hudson River lore, and more such tunes out of the *Clearwater* story. One belter, about 25 and redbearded, bright of eye, and with bravura talent for the improvised lyric, is introduced, and the name "Seeger" immediately alerts you: Is he, you wonder, related to Pete Seeger, folksinger's folksinger, and the very man who inspired—and rallied support for—the building of the *Clearwater*? "Pete Seeger is my uncle," he tells you, as you chat with him after he does his round. And the notion of connection, of a sort of generational bank of talent and commitment, strikes its own upbeat note: e.g., the human bank as opposed to, say, the garden variety (the Chase Manhattan) kind with *its* budgetary shakes and alarms.

On the walk back to Fulton Street, you stop for one last sweeping look from the pier. There's the squat-bottomed Hudson Dayliner *Robert Fulton* (you remember the summer vacation trips to West Point and beyond as a kid), the iron-hulled schooner *Wavertree* (its deck ghostly barren with the three masts sticking up like stilts), the red-nosed *Ambrose Lightship* (bucking at its hawsers as if in uneasy retirement). And dominating the whole scene, the high beauty of the Brooklyn Bridge span, with its lacework steel and gothic arches, lying now in deep undulating shadow on the running East River tide. Nor does one mean it snidely, good congressman, when one remarks: "It's the *real* bridge, not the assembled piece-by-piece London Bridge, that sits in ritual splendor out there on the Arizona desert."

So do pay us a visit, the scenes will keep, come what may.

Very truly yours,
SIDNEY BERNARD
November 8, 1975

1976

Literary society

THE PARTY-GO-ROUNDS NBCC BOOK AWARDS The great John Leonard, once litry prince of *Times Books*, now chief cultural correspondent, looking pale and krinkly, but handling booze with parlor room "suave" (in anteroom of Time-Life auditorium) of the Front Page pro. He's perhaps looser at the party give-take ("Don't have Leonard to kick around..."), now that he roams the bookscape sans the mine detector for all those explosives planted—now by big publishers, now by guerrila poets-writers of small press—under his floorboards when he edited *TBR*. He's cornered near the makeshift bar, by covey of talky, gesticulating book guys and gals. Leonard fields the chat-chats—his Cheshire smile a kind of Venice fly trap of the quick mot—with that cool, controlled artillery of the absurd. He knows the buried bodies (in closets of bookish pretensions) but he doesn't so much cry "Fire!" (in the smoking typewriter rooms), as croon a cool "Let em smolder in their own juices...."

Bill Cole of *Saturday Review*. Tall, high domed, and rivety eyed—wearing creaseless mix of sport jacket and contrasting slacks. Walks the room, stalks it on Cat's Paw heels, like your 18th century London blooded literary salon habitue. Has the stopwatch in his head, likely the *split-secondist* timepiece in the circuit, and he clocks the routers, the pacers, the front-runners, the also-rans in the book stakes. Clocks em with icewater disdain, couldn't care less what-who the other handicappers are touting. Norman or Truman; Allen (Ginsberg) or John (Ashbery); Susan (Brownmiller) or Germaine (Greer); Saul (Bellow) or Ed (Doctorow). (Latter copped NBCC's fiction award; never rains but it pours.) So don't place your bets till you get ol' Bill Cole's morning line.

Anchorman Wilfrid (Bill) Sheed. Wears at least 3 hats: Book of the Month selector, round-the-horn essayist, novelist on wry. And beware the Sheed style: elegant prose, roasted portraiture, in about equal parts. Everybody's anchorman, at P.E.N. klatches, Lion's Head boozer raps, National Book Award annuals. The everpresent cigar (puff puff puff), a kind of smoke signal, dips of Madison Square Garden, dabs of literary pow-wow. He's running it down, with former World Telly staffer Dick Walton, snifter of Scotch in one hand, curling-blue-smoke cigar in other. The two exchanging, in rapid-fire dots, dashes, and unfinished graphs, everything from Ali ringside poop, to Clay Felker folderol, to Marion Javits libber chutzpa, to ... The verbal strokes are to journalism as fiddler's practice bowing is to music.

Nona Balakian/Dick Lingeman. Two more from *Times Books* stable, the 7th floor (at 225 West 43rd) has emptied out in force. Linking the big apple critics, with all the others on the various national apples who showed. Like Ivan Sandrof (Worcester *Telegram*), Larry Swindell (Philadelphia *Inquirer*), Digby Diehl (Los Angeles *Times*), etc. And with this 1st NBCC round, the book journalists go mainstream, awards-wise. We've got the Oscars, got the Emmies, got the "Noneies." Now all we need is the book annual on network TV. Put across the superstar aura for the litry arts. To a point where millions will be saying, "Haven't seen the film, but I'm reading the book."

LION'S HEAD 10TH ANN' NIGHT   With tables cleared away (cold cuts and the like), the boozing can begin. Bill Sheed on line again, triangular rap with Mike Macdonald and roving. We're threading the CIA needle, recalling some "premature cousins," such as the *Encounter* editors who got the early swag (even before it was called "laundered"), for good marks in the cold war classroom. There was Lasky, Kristol, etc. Sheed: "Don't forget Stephen Spender..." Roving: "I dunno, he didn't traffic like the others. Just a poet, after all." But, says Bill (Mike agreeing), he knew the lyric. Sing a song of free enterprise supremacy/and send them (CIA) the print bill! Over to what's happening *now*. How many—20? 100? 200?—so-called journalists in the pay of CIA! They have the "beat," they cover the "story"; and all the while, they're chasin' around corners with the leather-coated NGB's; "our" spies versus "their" spies; and you see the kind of "journalism" comes outta that: the planted news, and the *unplanted* follow-up, for the computerheads up there in the agency. (So back to Orson Welles, already!)

The Party-Go-Rounds

PAUL KRASSNER AT ELGIN CINEMA They pour into the kicky movie house on Eighth, near-SRO, by time Paul ambles on stage—at 8 P.M.—and begins his free-form tour of the US map of conspiracy, political angst, assassination theories, Mae Brussell and Charlie Manson tidbits, and more of that menu. Paul—who's a kind of settled-down Mick Jagger of the pols-&-proles platform—strides the boards for nearly 4 hours (sideburns, and fancy boots, like a Mississippi-by-route-of-big-apple gambler), swiveling the hand mike round his neck, playing with it just short of the outre genitalia tickling of the rock vamper (or is it vampire?), and keeping the chatter going through the fire and ice of audience response. Mostly admiring, for his running anecdotes on Abbie, and the Chicago police-yippie chases (he made it sound like Keystone Komics), and the big bubble of the US boob tube (Dan Rather gives him "middle of night" screaming meemies), and the Hollywood "lifestyle," re Manson-Tate and others. ("Was Marilyn really a suicide; or somebody's hit victim?") And some audience downers, mostly from the east side shouters, the Yippie Times hawkers, the random angries cum crazies. One of whom—the shout cutting the dusty air like an invisible buzz saw—demands: "Goddam it, tell about the Yippies running a kangaroo for Pres in 76!" And the Mae Brussell flak: "Did she or didn't she call Izzy Stone 'a CIA agent' on WBAI?" (No, *he* didn't think Izzy was CIA.) For sure, he had his shit together, calling it—to some needling for political "substance"—the repertoire of "the comic, not the political sage." And he *is* the comic, uniquely his own style. None of your boyish whine of the Woody Allen "shlep" stick; rather a kind of kafkaesque fugal grope for the intestinal, the US mother (if mostly white) culture decline, the bicentennial detritus. Where he seems to tread water a little, seems indeed a bit too soapy in the warm bath of the familiar, is in the repetition of takes on the Kennedy deaths, the Sirhan Sirhans, the Mansons, the Chappaquiddicks; as if he—and all of us—are forever bounded by that waterline of "conspiracy"; which is of course our 60s and 70s baptismal ritual; we tread in those waters—a kind of nostalgia for that first and best dip of our rebellious youth?—as if fearing to lunge out into the deeper swim of *what's to be done now!*

NOTCHING THE YEARS Jerry Rubin out of the blue, promoting his new book (*Growing [Up] at 37*). (Growing up is fine, but you didn't have to shave the beard, inch up the sideburns, like a mere 17 growing up, did you Jer?) It's blowing a blizzard, but Rubin didn't wing in from San Francisco just to stay iced in friend's SoHo pad. What, he asks on phone, is happenin' on this bleak Monday? We tip him to "hot ticket" preview, 20th Century's *Next Stop, Greenwich Village*. Screening at 8th Street Playhouse, after-film bash at Village Gate. Hey, he shouts, the Paul Mazursky flick! I know the guy, gotta make that scene! (Pauline Kael, in *The New Yorker*, had already Kaeled the film, bandwagoned it, called it a very special art.) We tell Jerry, "Hot ticket or not, show up and we'll see." And several of us turn out; roving, Jerry and his friend Carol, Village-UK roamer John Wilcock, and some others. Non-ticketed, of course. (20th had this "very special Greenwich Village list.") We hunker by the box office, waiting for the main chance.

Sure enough, Jerry has the 20th flack hanging in, the high-voltage approach: "I was talking to Paul [Mazursky] only the other day, west coast, wished him all the best." Good for openers, the flack's buying it, guarantees Jer he'll give Mazursky the word. Meantime roving, and couple of others, do a flanker past the ticket taker. Jerry and Carol bringing up the rear. Once inside, past the three private fuzz, I nod to Jerry: "So that's how you did it at Chi, in '68 . . . first the soft-sell razzmatazz, then a little body English, and you're home!"

The flick—scripted, directed and produced by Mazursky. One of those gritted-teeth, perpetual motion, hyper-smartassed vehicles. The one-liners, sort of chicken soup ethnic, squirted out as if by water pistol. Veddy veddy Greenwich Village fifties. Actor's Studio jabber (viz, Marlon the magic namedrop!), cheapo quickie angst re the Rosenbergs, etc. As for mise-en-scène: One location shot, the Sheridan Square-Seventh Avenue triangle, flashed over & over again. The mob of 5 heros-heroines, bouncing by that on intersection, *with all traffic vanished*. (Authentic, see the Riker's and Village Cigars signs, it's the real turf!) Years of walking the scene, never did I see Seventh *that* empty of traffic. And the cardboard cutouts, doing their cardboard capers: Young comic bustin outta Brooklyn umbilical (gonna some day make it big in Hol!), his playmate-bedmate-nix-the-weddin-gal (see the big abortion scene!), the black feisty gay named Bernstein (doles out cement of humanity with trowel, it's an ooze!), the handsome Wasp nonproduced playwright (boudoir service to young and old at any hour!), the "I-don't-wanna-live" manic-depressive (she finally makes it, slashes wrists and out!) . . . and more of that gallery. Greenwich Village, circa the 50s? More like Anyplace-Anytime, the gang acting out the ineffable soap that can't utter its own name!

Out in the lobby, the crowd gathers for next stop, the Village Gate bash. Transport by way of NYC promo double-decker bus, 20th doing up the event in brown (and that satin finish green of bus). From 20th's very special Village list: Zero Mostel, Bucky Fuller, sculptor Noguchi, *New Yorker* arts crit Harold Rosenberg, and white-bearded Maurice (curbstone Village historian, prince of Bohemia, etc.). All pile into bus, it churns slowly through snow streets, finally pulls up to the Gate at Bleecker and La Guardia. All pile out, now the hairtrigger moment! Roving, this time, leads Jerry and Carol past ticket taker, the razzmatazz word: "We're here because we're here..." So to the grand entrance, on wave of biggies. The Redgrave acting sisters, the always-show Sylvia Miles, the *Village Voice* staffers (former and present): Newfield, Bell, Wilcock, Fancher, papparazz McDonough, and eh Clay Felker. Sweat out the chicken-&-salad line, edge the booze-beer off the slippery bar. And pockets of commotion among the visiting papparazzi: McDonough tips the camera boys and girls ... *Yeah, it's Jerry Rubin!* And they shoot up a flashbulb storm! (And there's a new Jer image. Sittin-standin cool, just observin the scene, takin in the new Karma, not hurtin at all, you know!) And not to forget Felker. He crosses over to greet Maurice: "Come back and handle the *Voice*/should never have happened/I say come back ..." (Maurice had been 86d, after hawking the *Voice* from the start, upon Felker's acquisition of the weekly.) Three times Felker makes the pitch; and three times Maurice says nada nada nada.

Jonathan Williams and James T. Farrell

MORE PARTY-GO-ROUNDS It was a kind of link-sausage holiday week. Starting with Lincoln's Birthday (Feb. 12), jumping to that jinxday (Friday, the thirteenth) for the voodoo minded, then to Valentines's Day (a Saturday) for lovers, and over to Monday the sixteenth Washington's Birthday (the latter change, made by federal fiat). A week of pushing the holidays, changed days, long-weekend-days. All that Roman calendar jockeying, not even natal days of heroes can hold off the profit motive! (There are profits, and *prophets*, and Exxon knows the difference.) They chip away at the Mount Vernon colonnades, phase out the Kentucky log cabins. Nothing sacred, not even the American heroes' pantheon, when they do surgery on calendar.

But hail to the new pantheon. Starting with Jonathan Williams, who looks the banker in 3-piece business suit, behind which lurks the small-press mover & shaker. He greets them at Gotham Book Mart party, Valentine's tribute to William's Jargon Society operation on its 25th year of publishing. The Black Mountain fraternity (Joel Oppenheimer and several others) are out on the floor, blowing on the coals of those early poems, those early encounters. All part of the special Carolina woodsy scene, where Williams and so many others got their starters. (And the ghost of Paul Blackburn, singing brother scribe of those good young days, is invoked with soft anecdote, with hearty reminiscence. Black Mountain days that were early-on, cutting edge of today's much wider littles and small-press network. And not to forget that other Williams, the Paterson medico/poet, and fine-tooled exemplar, of the Black Mountain line/shine/non-rhyme.) The party mood at Gotham was punchbowl staid, as befits *their* pantheon status. ("Where's Frances Steloff?" several ask. She didn't show, but she's in fine fettle, Andreas Brown assures them.) And Ted and Joan Wilentz, on trip down from Yale turf, running off a baker's dozen of the small-press breed, in a quick standup headcount: *Jargon*, *Geronimo* (Erje Ayden), Out of London Press (Luigi Ballenini), Something Else Press (Dick Higgins) *Mulch* (David Glotzer), *Parnassus* (Herb Liebowitz), Assembling Press (Dick Kostelanetz), *Broadway Boogie* (Mark Weiss), *Aperture* (Nyland Mortimer), *Chelsea* (Sonia Raiziss), and others, including: the Wilentz's *Corinth*. So hail to Jargon, going for 25 more years.

Flash to James T. Farrell's 72d, celebration at the American Irish Society digs, walloper 1880s manse directly across from Metropolitan Museum. Up the wide glistening stairs to 2d floor drawing room, JTF posted underneath glistening portrait of one Society founder, the *Studs Lonigan* crafter all good cheer (American beauty rose in lapel) as he greets the well-wishers. Spinning writing projects enough, for a good decade or more of books, autobiography, stories, polemics. And through the sheltered, big-mirrored, mahoganied, portrait-filled rooms, the party guests come and go, talking of James T. Farrell'o. ("He should get the Nobel, Farrell not Mailer, before he meets his whiskered maker with Irish harp," says one young poet, admirer.) . . . And night of Walt Lowenfels, doing a read at St. Marks in Bowery, bringing out sparse but mostly new-generation audience. ("Half the audience," he tells you in high glee, "is composed of my nephews, nieces, and godchildren. Nice going, don't you think?") Walt always the singer, beret over white curling hair, Mexican cape draped around shoulders, and sweet toned for all the nasal roughage of delivery. Singer of opened-out, orbiting, toughly personal poesy. Accompanied, on this Wednesday night round, by two young performers; bearded, sharp-tooting horn player; and neat-stepping mod dancer, her flowing chestnut hair the weaving baton to Walt's lines.

End & beginning

THE PRESIDENTIAL TIDINGS As the race for the presidency heats up, one has a sense of special destiny in '76. End of the Nixon era (Ford is an *end*, not a beginning!), succeeded by a sort of rush to meet new imperatives at a time of crisis in jobs, ecology, veracity in government, civilian-vs.-military priorities. The rush of new energy, release and commitment reminiscent of new deal days, these four decades later. One has the clutch feeling (like horse-player putting deuce on "overdue" longshot) of the very "climate" for great change in the air. The sense that if upward of 55 million stayed away from the polls in '72, the vast majority of that no-show number have—in 1976—nowhere to go but back to the voting place. Labor, just for starters, must opt back to the booths; return, as it were, from the boondocks of past "no-vote" policy; for good and sufficient reason of shrunken lunch pails, diminishing jobs, disenchantment with stagflation economy.

There's been an increase of other "injured" segments, since the hoopla day of Nixon landslide in '72. Teachers, college grads without jobs, professional and managerial people, Wall Street-Madison Avenue specialists (whose only specialty of late has been the unemployment office queue up), all the hardcore supernumeraries who've been forced out of the marketplace for jobs. And all of which groups may well pull together in movement for change (the eye of which, the Democratic Convention in New York City) that carries right into November and beyond, an upsurge on a higher level of challenge than even the pennypoors of the 30s decade.

And what of the candidates? The Carters, Wallaces, Udalls, Harrises, Jacksons, Churches, et al? One's sense is of a destiny spelled out by the issues; the gut needs of all those injured being a kind of conveyor upon which *the* candidate (if he has it in him to test fully the climate for change) can ride into office and in the process can outgrow the footling persona who wanted—who thought he *ought* to have—the win by mere declaration of his availability. The opening "Tie your shoe laces and get moving!" run of all the native-son sure shots is not more than a stumble; next to the great leaps needed for a prairie-fire sweep (heart and mind all the while ticking to the challenge) through the hamlets, and towns, and cities, and states; ending with the big prize at the great convention city itself; thus, the scenario of '76 for the candidate who can "hitch" the climate of now.

Who are they, and where are they going? There's the man from Georgia, disdained at first by city pols as some kind of peanut tycoon, but catching attention by route of a kind of southern populism with big-city accent. And the perennial Alabaman, who takes dabs at the populism now and then, but who is like a TV revival movie that somehow won't "revive." And the Arizona congressman, who looks-acts more like a New England agin-er, or loner looking for showdown with all the deadweighted bigness out there, and gathering (talk of your longshot!) legions of other loners to his-their cause. And the senator from Washington State (or "from the Pentagon," as the case may be), whose platform runs the gamut, from anti-détente to anti-Salt. And whatever later entries.

Dare the candidates intuit, not alone for themselves, but for the whole electorate, the tide that Brutus speaks of; which, taken at the flood, can lead to great and necessary change? Away from the dismal '70s rollcall, including the Chilean-style connections, the hemophilic waste of the Nams, the spidery spying of Americans on Americans (and the "us-them" spying, for that matter), the leakages and overruns of an economy of "free market," not people; in a word, the whole dismal rollcall, all motored by the great gray bird of turmoil, one beating wing of which cynicism, the other a "Me first!" pushiness and greed. Away from all that, and journeying toward the promise, the renewal, the uniqueness of true bicentennial.

Here in New York City, in these early rounds, there's been soundings of the tide; the place, the multi-columned and low-slung Great Hall of Cooper Union; where candidates (or their stand-ins) have been taking bows in a Monday night series, and speaking more directly to issues than the usual, "Hello, I'm Joe Candidate . . ." style of barnstorming. The very same hall from which Lincoln—that supreme rider of issues, and emancipator, in one—sallied forth with a key anti-slavery speech that won him the 1860 election. (Scheduled in the series were Harris, Udall, Carter, Gaylord Nelson; since all but Nelson had stand-ins, we could well ask: "If Lincoln made it, why not thou?") As for the convention city itself, it would seem to be the right place, at the right time. Crucible of a new era in the making, after coming off the floor of recent financial tremors.

Primary Day 1976

Park Avenue Specialist

THE BRONX KID'S MEDICAL DETENTE The Bronx kid has come a long way! He's just had an eye examination, at Park Avenue office of surgeon BK, and he levitates (with eye drops, you don't just walk, you *levitate*) past the two-way traffic, and he's thinking: "It's a stiff tab, but ain't going blind, anyway." The thirty-fiver in fact is a kind of mark of pride. He remembers back to the eye wound, the long-ago trauma of age 5 or 6, got it in a deadend junkyard caper, when shards of the flung Coke bottle all but shattered his eye. And now he's crossing Park, on his way to Fifth Avenue dentist. Looks like roundup day for the body, if not for the soul, but he's springing to it (those drops again!) with money-in-bank bounce: "I'm gettin the best diagnosis around. Good as Rockefeller's, almost."

Soon he's at Fifth office building of dentist HS, for "consultation" re some bridge work. He notices the lobby mosaic, arched ceiling of many-colored tile. It's the Dutch-and-Indian pow-wow, strings of beads and other trinkets, $24 worth, laid out before the chief-&-tribe. Somehow he carries the incised "24" of the mosaic in his head, as he scoots up elevator to dentist office.

Fifteen minutes in dentist's chair—he taps a couple of teeth here, scales with his delicately hooked instrument a gumline there—and the Bronx kid gets the word. The 4-part bridge—extraction of one shaky tooth up front included—goes for a nice roundhouse "one thousand dollars." This, to the Bronx habitue who remembers 5-dollar fillings, 50-dollar (maybe less) root canal jobs. Done by a steady *Bronx* pro, of course. He thinks: Boy, the price of new jawbite, even with TV-cosmetic-smile thrown in! And coolly—but how else?—he tells bridgeman: "Bill me for the consultation; I'll have to think it over." (That'll be a twenty-fiver, starchly dressed assistant tells him.)

He's still bouncy (the drops sure liquefy Fifth, like swimming in a tank), as he heads for another dentist just a few blocks away. Now—in the kid's mood for comparison shopping—he feels good for there's a possible "saver" of 400 in going to the 2d toother, the swifty pro JZ. (He'd gone there several weeks back, got an "off/cuff" quote of $600 for the bridge.) He arrives at East Sixty-fifth office, announces he's ready for "the works." He's then seated in chair under bullet of X-ray machine: "We'll need a full set before we can go ahead," he's told. Hygienist—sweet smelling and crisply uniformed—does the X-ray bit with smiles and wiggly despatch. He gets an appointment for one week hence. And the Bronx kid goes back out to Fifth. With more lickety-split motion. He's getting into the spirit, the rhythm of the body round-up. His medical detente at middleage.

Chalked up three, why not shoot for four. His longtime periodontist, the expert toother-scraper LH, is only couple blocks away (cater-corner to the Dutch-&-Indian building). Why not mosey by, get an opinion on the bridgework deal. As he rudders sort of wiggly-waggly south, the euphoria of the "mosey by" seizes him, becomes one with the off-cement bounce of eye drops. Nobody does a mosey by with LH, could be he's the hottest-ticket periodontist in town. Nobody but the Bronx kid, that is. (He's earned the nod. His jawbite impressions are "Number One" in LH's office showcase.) When he gets there—well, the man himself can't see him. LH is elbow-deep in instruments, busy with an emergency case. But no sweat, the kid is asked to wait around, the associate will give him a look. Finally he gets the word: the bridge deal is no big deal, periodontal-wise. (Associate didn't bat an eye, money-wise.)

Out on Fifth again, right at 57th Street golden triangle, for the select shopper: Henri Bendel's, Bergdorf Goodman, and Tiffany's. He observes the milling crowd, itself part of the New York gait, the special zig-zaggy motion, like clutch of gridiron stalwarts going for a loose football. He cages a look at Doubleday's windows, the book titles coming up as if writ on sand, through the prism of the still potent drops.

And a quick scan of Tiffany's windows, where the gems don't merely glitter, they bounce off his eyes in double and triple focus. (Dream parlay for the Bronx kid: TV smile and Tiffany's diamonds.)

Then he wavers toward the subway, the medical tour just about over. But wait a minute! It's two in the afternoon, still time to visit Vets Administration Hospital, catch a look at possibility of *VA* doing the big-bridge deal. "Service connected," of course. The Bronx kid seems to remember—it's a long shot, at that—an early (World War II) job of gum-scraping at West Twenty-fourth VA dental clinic. (And he thinks: Hell, they owned my body in wartime, ain't gonna *disown* it in peacetime!) But he hesitates: watch out for the shlock work! Besides, if Rockefeller gets the best, why not the Bronx kid! So he heads for his downtown office. He'll scare up the scratch, pay the body dues. 24 bucks for Manhattan Island; 600 (hopes it won't go higher) for the cosmetic bridge. You have to go with progress!

New game on Sheep Meadow

ULTIMATE FRISBEE Seen everything in Central Park's Sheep Meadow—you *thought*! So you walk the big open space, with circling bank of thick trees, and you're smack in the middle of the latest: ultimate Frisbee! It's a great fall day, leaves turning to russet and gold, and you move over to the sidelines. The field is a gridiron, about half the size of regular football field. The game's an odd combination of football pass, and one-on-one basketball, seven men to the side. You watch as the big white disk is thrown from man to man, swift bellybutton twirls, the offense and defense running downfield, and then a sudden long pass that's caught over the goal-line. Score one point for the Princetons, the seven in orange-black uniforms, similar to soccer garb, and they're patting up a storm (swatting each other's rump, etc.) as they line up for the next play. The long skyhigh throw, equivalent of the football kick after a score.

You talk to the umpire, guy in faded jeans, ponytail graying hair, whistle on leather string around his neck. He tells you the name-of-game, says it was invented on high school campus somewhere in Jersey, and that it's "spreading like prairie fire on campuses." The Princetons—behind at the moment by score of 20 to 17— are opposing a NYC pickup team, the latter decked in assorted shirts, soccer shorts, and cleated shoes. Not so elegant as the boys from Princeton, but not hurting either, so far as the score goes. Fact is that the city dudes—just at that moment—score still another goal. A long curving throw over the heads of team-mate and Princeton covering man, both running almost in tandem for the floating disk, the city player making a thrusting reach with right hand, grabbing the disk at the split second, *yanking* it out of the air as if he owned it! Great catch, cheers from the NYC sidelines. Mild dejection, kicking the turf, from the Princeton "bench" of 6 or 7. (The bench, as in basketball, can go in as replacements at any time.) And the dads and mums of the Princetons—active both as fans and analyzers of each play—talk up a small storm of encouragement to their orange-black charges.

Leaving the Meadow, and walking toward the Zoo, you stop and take a last look: Frisbee goes a'heaving (from the Princeton side) a good 30 feet past the goal-line, floats high against the azure sky, then comes gently down as two bodies leap for the disk. Broken pass, more cheers from the NYC sidelines. Two bodies leaping, on the playing fields of all our youthful times.

Block Fairs, Inc.

CRAZY TO LIVE IN NEW YORK You know the radio station WQXR blurb: "New York's a crazy town; and you gotta be a little crazy to live here . . ." It's a sleeper message, a reverse twist. Your first jolting thought is: Hell, even the *Times*'s radio voice joins the doomsayers' chorus. But then comes the switch: "Crazy about music, art museums, ethnic studies from Greek to Chinese . . ." The voice goes on and on, a minutes-long rhapsody of the bigcity's numero uno standing in the arts. Gotham, not so much big apple as hero sandwich of the cultural diet.

The show is always running, like the subways, sort of endless clatterings of self-expression. On backdrops of street corners, nabe block fairs, Central Park midway stages. May to September happenings, mini-carnivals to raise money for tree planting, cleanup drives, day-care centers, money-in-pocket for the young musician "working my way through Julliard." So it goes, in the "gotta be crazy" town.

Crazy To Live In New York

The West Side, a growth industry of nabe associations, practically invented the block fair. That, and its first-cousin, the rummage sale. In both cases, everything comes out of closets, the kitchen stoves, and off the home sewing machines. Families in highrises, singles out of brownstones, get together in the city version of all the Danbury fairs you can name. For the New Yorker who's originally from "somewhere else," it's mostly a case of "you can't take the country out of the native." The nabe fair is thus kin to all the country-cousin doings of a bright spring day. Overnight, the tables have been set, the streamers tacked in place. All for the cause: breaking the anonymity of thousands-packed to the block, by way of discovering your neighbor, where before you barely nodded in passing, day in and day out.

One such fair, on first weekend in May, with jumpy mix of light rain and dry splashes of sunshine. Two block associations have combined their efforts, part fair and part rummage sale, with dozens of tables laden with items not necessarily Bloomingdale's, but sort of cottage industry merchandise from apartment "workrooms." Business is brisk—from brooches to layettes to books to home cookery—with a good percentage of sales going into the nabe associations' coffers for their ongoing projects. The block is West 84th, Broadway to West End, and it turns up a surprise. Plaque on the corner apartment building which tells of Edgar Allan Poe's residence on that spot—in an earlier building called the Brennen Mansion—for a short period in the years 1844-1845. And where he composed, says the plaque, "The Raven."

Another May weekend, another part of town. Walking the SoHo area, in the Saturday parade of art openings, can be a long march with scant pickings. But all very democratic, so far as self-expression goes, or "What's 'in' in Soho." It seems that whatever comes off the easel, and onto the walls of the cubbyhole galleries, qualifies for a kind of open-ended genre: "South of Houston Latest." Be it acrylic-ugly, Sloane Furniture representational, mini-maxi-sideways pieces that inspire an occasional "Oh!" The good art, in this kind of assembly-line production, gets swallowed in the mass; and hence becomes anybody's discovery. Yet the SoHo Saturday ritual, pocketed crowds traipsing from one street gallery to another, is one of the steadiest games in town.

Off to another scene. The 2d Sunday in May, Central Park mall is alive, sort of opening rite of spring. This is the giant slalom of walk-arounds, the New York mix of ethnics with bongos, West Side (and East) marrieds pushing prams, bikers pumping wheels on the rolling macadam. Spectators and "actors" become one, as they all pour through the mall midway, do a kind of "theater" sans script or director. A sword-swallower has the crowd holding breath, as he devours flame like an orange cocktail. A group of kids breathing their own fire, as they go through the huff-puff motions of karate chops. With the group karate master, who could be a black-belter, keeping the cadence with a thin long baton. (And the coins roll on the green, making the show, if not a species of child labor, not exactly amateur time either.)

Same afternoon at Frick Museum on Fifth, no more than a loud holler's distance from the park mall, a performance of more private spheres and timbres. The Julliard Quartet in concert, flooding the courtyard sanctum with purling string music, a cameo scene with audience of mere hundreds. For the tuned-in ear—Haydn. For the roving eye—Franz Hals. In this most gemlike of picture palaces. Frick could well be (foot for foot) the most lavish cache of "greats" anywhere.

And more nabe doings. Poster on Fifth Avenue light pole, announcing the East Side twist. Girl Scouts sponsoring "A Day in May" street fair on 84th between Park and Madison, offerings from "Granny's attic: good junk cheap." Also, hay rides, sweets from the "Girl Scout Bake Shop." And a "rummage extravaganza" on 100th and West End Avenue, benefit for Purple Circle Co-op Daycare.

Crazy in New York; crazy for the nabe show.

1977

Ginsberg, Lowell & Anaïs Nin

CELEBRATIONS "You don't throw the kid out, no way!" The solo command, bursting from the St. Mark's audience, related to Gregory Corso's baby, who was acting up in mild baby talk, at an Ash Wednesday reading of Allen Ginsberg and Robert Lowell. The event was unusual, even for St. Mark's Church, that mini Roman Forum of the poetry readout. A crowd of about 500, with another hundred lined up outside the high-spired church on Second and Tenth Street, all with anticipation befitting the odd-couple casting.

People were squeezing, squatting down upon every inch of space. Added to the informality of seating, imbibing from Coke and beer cans, cross-shoulders raps and repartee was the dilapidated condition of the church itself, going through a stripped-down refurbishing of concave roof, narrow circular balcony, boarded up alter, and chipped walls readying for a paint job. Maybe a Sistine of East Side radical graffiti, melding with the Episcopal stained-glass religio.

Ginsberg, sans the harmonium, kicked off. Formal in suit and tie, crisp in delivery, he read some "short strokes" pieces. Travels, impressions, from Central Australia. Medicine-man lines, rolling thunder, aborigines. And an Einstein poem—witty, cosmic. And dialogues with his dying father, on the theme (voiced by the senior poet) "Don't grow old." Some of Allen's most personal, shading into elegiac, lines since "Kaddish."

Lowell sat in concentration, like a hunched ravaged version of Rodin's *Thinker*. Now his right hand, now his left, cradling the red-cheeked face, the straying gray hair. Physically, he seems a man of leashed power, moves with a kind of dog-worrying-bone tentativeness—a step back, a step forward—as he all but whispers into the mike. Now he stood up, applauded Allen vigorously, as did the crowd, and moments later, after a blue-ribbon intro by Maureen Owen of the Poetry Project (the Bollingen this, the Pulitzer that), Lowell responded with a kind of pained, totemesque shyness. He then started to read, but not before unlimbering—the step back, the step forward—with rambling ad-hoc comment, sort of private in jokes, the tone like as not self-mocking. And yet the crowd followed him with pindropping silence.

Mostly, short poems, from previously published works. Lowell then announced a long narrative poem: Circe and Penelope, the Trojan wars saga. He read from a looseleaf binder, five longish stanzas from a full manuscript. And now the *audience* went into a deep concentration, almost a ghostly scene of ritual intake, as Lowell droned out the long lines, only to be interrupted by uneasy growls from Corso, who sat with his party just 25 feet away. At one point Lowell came to a full stop, peered over his glasses toward Corso. Gregory: "I'm misbehavin', 'cause you're reading like we're in poetry class." Lowell: "It looks like we're about to have a happening."

By now Allen, and the crowd, were down on Gregory. Then came baby Corso's gurgles, suggestions that Corso and company leave, and the angry "the kid stays!" shout. All in line with St. Mark's etiquette. No matter the noise waves, you don't 86 anyone, they go *on their own*. Which Gregory, his black-curls baby (and cameo of the old man), his lanky, red-haired old lady and a few friends all did eventually.

The odd-couple reading. Bearded Paterson—East Side Hasid guru, tense ruddy history-ridden New England Brahmin. One playing Tolstoyan fox, the other Dostoyevskyan hedgehog. Lowell himself made the bridge: "Actually, we're from two ends of the William Carlos Williams spectrum." St. Mark's, the poetry temple, takes it all in.

Only a few blocks from St. Mark's, and 24 hours earlier, a more private kind of reading: Birthday Celebration for the late Anaïs Nin. (She would have been 74.) At the John Ben Snow Room, of the Elmer Holmes Bobst Research Library (we have names!), N.Y.U.'s gallery-like sanctum on Washington Square South. Seated in the mod designed room, with its low-ceiling maze of frosty electrical sculpture, a crowd of about 150, and a well-scrubbed constituency of Anaïs fans and intimates, publishing and librarian types, Women's movement writers and activists.

The mood was reverent and warmly anecdotal. It was "senior citizens" occasion of rare moment, far cry from the all-American merchandising of that label. Starting with Anaïs Nin herself, count all the years of seeding the inner landscape of the arts, the result of which all those bright flowers of self-expression; count the years, and you have a natural resource that renews itself, with each fresh reading of the text. And a most necessary resource, in a time of publisher bankrollers who shoot for the million-plus "property." Marguerite Young, Daisy Aldan, Glenway Westcott—were among those who paid tribute. With recollections, personal encounters, the retelling of which brought quick shafts of light on a richly complex personality. They spoke of her warming wit, her outgoingness, her rushes of self-revelation.

As Miss Young read from Nin's *Aphorisms*, one had the sense of Edgar Allan Poe revisited: mystery in the crystalline lines, built in imaginary layers, at the center of which, the sparkle trapped in the towers of all our Babels. Glenway Westcott, who strode forward like a 70s-plus sprite, announced "a surprise," after saying he didn't want to bore the audience "with personal chitchat." (Far from being bored, they lapped it up like kittens with bowl of milk.) He then read a short paper, composed before Nin's death, by Henry Miller; called "Venus Anadyomene," it was a luminous, loving appraisal, and personal memoir, of Anaïs Nin as archetype of femininity and Feminism. (The partisans held breath, then applauded loudly.)

Last was Joaquin Nin-Culmell, younger brother of Anaïs, who had to break out of a kind of envelope of grief, as he stood at the mike, faltering and going for his handkerchief, finally recovering, then giving his own birthday tribute: "Even when we were children, she would up-stage us all."

Ten years after

BE-IN OR NOT BE-IN The little green corner, southeast on Sheep Meadow, was crackling away. Like exposed wires in rain. With sounds of celebration, yippie and zippie war cries, half-hearted nostalgia greetings. On this Easter Sunday 1977, the Tenth Anniversary of Be-in. The crowd of about 250—little more than rivulet next to the sea of people back then—were all ten years older. All trying to relive the former excitement, the youthful freshness, the days of rage.

Are the times softer, the battles murkier? Certain veterans in the crowd—like WBAI's Bob Fass, street troubador David Peel, world traveller John Wilcock—would probably have called the question moot. They've clocked the years, made dents in the establishment marble. And they can't get out of the Red Shoes, the cement-city choreography, for all the political engagement. As for the newer breed "rebels," such as the trio of youths parading dope flags through the crowd (green-&-red marijuana leaf on black ground), it might be said that rebellion begins with innocence, grows (and grows up) in parallel with how it "reads the past," plugs into lessons and battles won.

Example: God knows it took long enough, yet how much longer, how many more lives, would it have taken to end Nam, were it not for the roars of protest, the crunch of bodies on Sheep Meadow's green—all through the 1960s and 70s! Measured thusly, the dope flags had the symbology of granny rags out of the attic. For we've traveled some distance beyond the marijuana crossroads, you know! And now there are other causes, other battles. The WBAI staff, those marathon runners of free radio, gathering signatures and bread. To keep open some space for people-rapping, or fail-safe of spirit and ideas, in the noisy tunnel of dollar broadcasting. And the graying cool Martin Sostre, jail-sprung man with worldly smarts, urging the crowd (through crackling mike) to own up to the swiss cheese of our State Department's pretensions toward the "other side's" repressions.

As they stepped off for the United Nations, for an "all nations" human rights sponsored by Amnesty International, they had to run the gamut of throngs crowding the smoking kebab stands, the chalk-faced clowns and rock folk singers, the sellers of craft leather and jewelry—all strung out on the cement mall in opening rite of spring. Had to run the gamut, too, of a trio of dudes who hawked, in a brazen chorus of "Check it out," some rolled leafy dope. "Nickel bags" that went for 2-bucks the hit.

Add to the marijuana flag, the free-enterprise flag.